MESSAGE OF THE FATHERS OF THE CHURCH
General Editor: Thomas Halton

Volume 1

MESSAGE OF THE FATHERS OF THE CHURCH

The World
of the
Early Christians

Joseph F. Kelly

A Michael Glazier Book
THE LITURGICAL PRESS
Collegeville, Minnesota

A Michael Glazier Book published by The Liturgical Press

Cover design by Lillian Brulc

2	3	4	5	6	7	8

Library of Congress Cataloging-in-Publication Data

Kelly, Joseph F. (Joseph Francis), 1945–
    The world of the early Christians / Joseph F. Kelly.
        p.   cm. — (Message of the fathers of the church ; v. 1)
    "A Michael Glazier book."
    Includes bibliographical references and index.
    ISBN 0-8146-5341-3 (case bound). — ISBN 0-8146-5313-8 (perfect bound)
    1. Church history—Primitive and early church, ca. 30–600 A.D.
  2. Sociology, Christian—History—Early church, ca. 30–600 A.D.
  3. Christianity and culture—History—Early church, ca. 30–600 A.D.
  I. Title. II. Series.
BR165.K44   1997
270.1—dc21   97-11070
                                                         CIP

Amy, filia mea dilecta:
Quasi flos rosarum in diebus veris (Ecclesiasticus 50:8)

Contents

Editor's Introduction

The *Message of the Fathers of the Church* is a companion series to the *Old Testament* and the *New Testament Message*. It was conceived and planned in the belief that Scripture and Tradition worked hand in hand in the formation of the thought, life and worship of the primitive Church. Such a series, it was felt, would be a most effective way of opening up what has become virtually a closed book to present-day readers and might serve to stimulate a revival in interest in patristic studies in step with the recent, gratifying resurgence in scriptural studies.

The term "Fathers" is usually reserved for Christian writers marked by orthodoxy of doctrine, holiness of life, ecclesiastical approval, and antiquity. "Antiquity" is generally understood to include writers down to Gregory the Great (+604) or Isidore of Seville (+636) in the West, and John Damascene (+749) in the East. In the present series, however, greater elasticity has been encouraged, and quotations from writers not noted for orthodoxy will sometimes be included in order to illustrate the evolution of the Message on particular doctrinal matters. Likewise, writers later than the mid-eighth century will sometimes be used to illustrate the continuity of tradition on matters like sacramental theology or liturgical practice.

An earnest attempt was made to select collaborators on a broad interdisciplinary and interconfessional basis, the chief consideration being to match scholars who could handle the Fathers in their original languages with subjects in which they had already demonstrated a special interest and competence. About the only editorial directive given to the selected contributors was that the Fathers, for the most part, should be allowed to speak for themselves and that they should speak in readable, reliable modern English. Volumes on individual themes were considered more suitable than volumes devoted to individual fathers, each theme, hopefully, contributing an important segment to the total mosaic of the early Church, one, holy, catholic and apostolic. Each volume has an introductory essay outlining the historical and theological development of the theme, with the body of the work mainly occupied with liberal citations from the Fathers in modern English translation and a minimum of linking commentary. Short lists of Suggested Further Readings are included, but dense, scholarly footnotes were actively discouraged on the pragmatic grounds that such scholarly shorthand has other outlets and tends to lose all but the most relentlessly esoteric reader in a semipopular series.

At the outset of his *Against Heresies* Irenaeus of Lyons warns his readers "not to expect from me any display of rhetoric, which I have never learned, or any excellence of composition, which I have never practiced, or any beauty or persuasiveness of style, to which I make no pretensions." Similarly, modest disclaimers can be found in many of the Greek and Latin Fathers, and all too often, unfortunately, they have been taken at their word by an uninterested world. In fact, however, they were often highly educated products of the best rhetorical schools of their day in the Roman Empire, and what they have to say is often as much a lesson in literary and cultural as well as in spiritual edification.

St. Augustine, in *City of God* (19.7), has interesting reflections on the need for a common language in an expanding world community; without a common language a person is more at home with his or her dog than with a foreigner as far as intercommunication goes, even in the Roman Empire, which imposes on the nations it conquers the yoke of both law and language with a resultant abundance of interpreters. It is hoped that in the present world of continuing language barriers the contributors to this series will prove opportune interpreters of the perennial Christian message.

Thomas Halton

Preface

There are many introductions to the world of the early Christians, and anyone writing another one has to justify it. That thought preoccupied me when the editors of The Liturgical Press first asked me to do this book. Every writer has an audience in mind, and I tried to structure this book for an audience that would use it as an introductory text. Some colleagues in my field teach advanced doctoral students who have access to research facilities, who are accustomed to working independently in religious studies, and who can read the original languages, but most of us teach students who plan to be computer programmers, accountants, and physicians, and who have virtually no knowledge of the ancient world. This situation can even apply to people who plan professional careers in religion; for instance, graduate students and seminarians who may be knowledgeable about medical ethics or pastoral ministry but who know little about the first Christians. My experience in adult education in local churches in the Greater Cleveland area has reinforced that impression.

It is obligatory for Early Christian scholars to lament this—and I do—but we must also consider what causes this gap. Although there may be general reasons, such as a declining interest in the past, the more likely reason is that we often do not meet the students where they are. The many questions of my students through the years, as well as those of various church adult education groups, have given me a sense of what may not be familiar to the non-specialist. Therefore, I have tried to focus on the basic questions necessary for historical background, for understanding the now lost world of Early Christianity, and to avoid assuming anything on the part of the reader. Parts of this book may appear too basic for some, but my hope is to make the book available to all, especially to those teaching introductory courses.

For instance, introductions to Early Christianity routinely deal with Greek and Roman philosophical influences on the Christians, such as Stoicism, Epicureanism, and Neo-Platonism, but few deal with the basic questions non-specialists ask: Why did the Christians use philosophy at all? Did it not make everything confusing? Why did they not just stick to the Bible? This book will not overlook questions like that; on the contrary, it will concentrate on them because the question of why Christians used philosophy is more fundamental than a list of which philosophies they used.

Many people often have erroneous views about the early Christians. Thanks to a centuries-old idealization of the first believers, many modern Christians think that their ancient spiritual ancestors were all impoverished, uneducated people from the lowest strata of Roman society. They also often think that the Romans persecuted the Christians from the death of Jesus until some unspecified later time when, for some reason, they stopped. Scholars know how erroneous these views are and how easily we can dismiss them, but we must recall that many people have heard these notions preached to them, have read about them in catechisms or other basic texts, and, worst of all, have seen them verified in films.

Often these misconceptions have a denominational base. One can still meet Roman Catholics who think that Jesus crowned Saint Peter the first pope, and he in turn promptly consecrated the rest of the apostles the first cardinals, and they all sailed around the Sea of Galilee like some miniature ecumenical council. Similarly, one can meet fundamentalists who think the only good thing the Church can do is to protect the Bible from the evil clutches of mainline Protestants, and that any doctrinal development subsequent to the completion of the Scriptures is actually the corruption of the biblical truth.

These misconceptions can run deep and often appear in strange places. A colleague of mine, a seasoned biblical archaeologist, appeared on a local Cleveland television talk-show to discuss discoveries in the Holy Land. When he asked the show's host if he had any questions, the host promptly inquired about the Shroud of Turin.

This book will address some of these misconceptions by considering the historical evidence and the complex nature of Early Christianity.

We must also consider how some ancient topics can be misleading to modern students. For example, scholars know that astrology presented a real challenge to ancient religions—pagan, Jewish, and Christian—but modern students see astrology as some minor diversion printed in the newspapers (next to the comic strips in American ones) or something believed by superstitious people. Naturally they will wonder how something so intellectually trivial could be a rival to major religions. The same is true for magic. This book will make a serious effort to explain terms and concepts whose modern connotations could mislead the reader.

So far I have spoken of topics or questions which may separate the modern non-specialist from the ancient Christians; now let me turn to an approach which I hope will unite them.

Like every "lost world," the world of the early Christians presents a combination of the foreign and the familiar, the unique and the commonplace. We can see the differences very easily. People on average lived shorter lives than we, they could not communicate quickly or easily with those at a distance, and comparatively few could read or write. On the other hand, they lived lives very similar to ours. They loved and hated, they strove for security, and most worked hard for what they had.

Today, as distances continually shrink and once foreign cultures now seem familiar to us, we are accustomed to the notion that all people on earth share a common humanity. This book will take the point of view that this applies not only to those with whom we now share the globe but also to those who went before us. We will approach the world of the early Christians by treating its inhabitants as people like us, not historical mannequins or museum pieces. We will consider their differences from us, but throughout we will keep to the idea that they were human beings, like us, trying to make their way in life. It is my hope in this book to explain the world of the early Christians, not just to describe it. That is why the book has the title *The World of the Early Christians* and not *The World of Early Christianity.*

An introduction, by definition, cannot go into much depth. Furthermore, there are many topics this book simply did not treat, such as sacramental theology. Many good books exist on early Christian topics, including several in The Liturgical Press' *Message of the*

Fathers of the Church series, which the reader can consult. I can only express my regret to readers whose favorite topic was not included.

Throughout, I have referred to original sources in translation, unless no translation is available. This is in keeping with the book's focus on the non-specialist who presumably does not read Latin or Greek but who yet may wish to follow up a particular reference. Modern translators generally adhere to high standards, and the reader can consult the translations with confidence. The scholar can always consult the original.

Finally, as a teacher I have often been frustrated with supposedly introductory books which tried to do everything and which I sometimes had to teach around. My hope for instructors is that this book will provide their students with a good introduction to the period but will not push any issue too far, allowing instructors the freedom to develop the topic as best suits their needs in a classroom setting. Since the book will probably be used for the historical background in most classes, I have deliberately avoided discussing topics like liturgy or theology, at least in any depth.

My thanks to my many colleagues in the North American Patristic Society, as well as to the many overseas scholars whose endless researches have helped me to understand the world of the early Christians. My thanks also to the administrators of John Carroll University, particularly Drs. Nick Baumgartner, Frederick Travis, and Sally Wertheim, who provided me with a reduced teaching load to work on this book. My thanks next to the university committee on research and service, chaired by Dr. Wertheim and later by Dr. Joseph Miller, who provided funds to support my work, and to my department chairperson, Thomas Schubeck, S.J., who supported my requests for reduced teaching loads so that I might pursue my research.

Special gratitude goes to Brian Daley, who recommended me to Thomas Halton, editor of the *Message of the Fathers of the Church* series, to whom I also owe a debt of gratitude. Thanks also to Don Molloy, who meticulously edited the text for The Liturgical Press and made many, many helpful suggestions.

My colleague at John Carroll University, Sheila McGinn, read early drafts of this manuscript; two of my graduate assistants, Christopher Merriman and Megan Bleil, proofread the whole text and offered helpful suggestions. I am glad to acknowledge my appreciation to them. Any defects in the text reside squarely on the shoulders of the author.

As always, my sincerest thanks go to my wife Ellen, a loving spouse and a generous partner, who took the time and energy from her own busy career and personal schedule to allow me time and energy to work on this book.

I dedicate this book to my daughter Amy, a delight to her parents for these twenty-three years.

Abbreviations

ca. from the Latin *circa* meaning "about" or "around"; scholars use this when they are uncertain of the exact dates, for example, Hilary of Poitiers (born ca. 315).

d. placed before a date to indicate that the person discussed died in that year.

fl. from the Latin *floruit,* meaning "flourished"; scholars use this when they do not know a person's dates of birth and death but do know when she or he was prominent, for example, Optatus of Milevis (fl. ca. 370–380) means that he wrote his most important works probably between 370 and 380.

Collections of original sources in translation and reference works cited frequently in the text*:

ACW   Ancient Christian Writers
ANF   The Ante-Nicene Fathers
EECh   Encyclopedia of the Early Church
EEXty   Encyclopedia of Early Christianity
FC   Fathers of the Church
MFC   Message of the Fathers of the Church
NPNF   The Nicene and Post-Nicene Fathers

*Full bibliographic references are provided in the bibliography.

Biblical citations are from the *New Revised Standard Version.*

Chapter One

Who Were the Early Christians?

1. What Does the Term "Early Christians" Mean?

Scholars use the term "Early Christians" to refer to the followers of Jesus who lived from the first century to approximately the sixth. The term derives from the three-fold division scholars make of Christian history into Early, Medieval, and Modern, that is, the period approximately coterminous with Christianity's life in the Roman Empire, the period extending from the end of that empire to the Reformation, and from the Reformation until today.

This designation, while chronologically convenient, has serious weaknesses and can be misleading. For instance, it clearly reflects a Western Christian view. In the fifth century, the Roman Empire had split into two halves, Eastern and Western, with two dominant languages—Greek in the East and Latin in the West—two emperors, and, increasingly, two cultures. (Even this view can be misleading, since fifth-century Romans still spoke of one empire.) The Western half consisted of Italy, Spain, Britain, Gaul (modern France), the Low Countries, some parts of Germany, and North African provinces, which would include modern Morocco, Algeria, Libya, and Tunisia. Although tribal dialects survived (Celtic in Britain, Punic in North Africa), the official language of this area was Latin. This part of the empire fell to invading Germanic barbarians in the fifth century; in 476 a barbarian named Odovacar deposed the last Western emperor, Romulus Augustulus, and, in the views of most scholars, this marked the end of the Roman Empire in the West.[1] By

---

1. This date was first suggested by the French scholar Ferdinand Lot, in *The End of the Ancient World and the Beginnings of the Middle Ages* (New York: Alfred A. Knopf, Inc., 1931).

the sixth century in the West, the medieval world was largely coming into being, and thus Early Christianity had come to an end.

The problem is that the Eastern part of the Roman Empire did not come to an end. The Eastern empire consisted of Greece, much of the Balkans, Asia Minor (modern Turkey), Syria, Palestine, Egypt, and Libya, areas for the most part untouched by barbarian invasions. Indeed, in the sixth century, the Roman emperor Justinian (527–565) invaded and reconquered some parts of the West ruled by the barbarians. Western scholars call Justinian a "Byzantine" emperor, but he considered himself a Roman, as would his subjects. Thus the designation of Early Christianity as being coterminous with the Western empire, or lasting until the Middle Ages began, overlooks the continued existence of Christianity in the Eastern Mediterranean in an imperial framework.

On the other hand, the Eastern empire lost large parts of its territory to the Muslim Arabs in the seventh and eighth centuries, so that even though the empire survived, it differed considerably from the earlier empire. Thus, many scholars would claim that the designation "Early Christianity" applies just as readily to the Eastern as well as to the Western branch of Christianity.

This discussion introduces us to an important concept in the study of history, that is, the role played by historical designations. These designations can impose artificial breaks in history or, contrarily, artificial unity where none existed. Furthermore, we must recognize that scholars apply these distinctions upon people who would not recognize them. For example, the early Christians certainly did not know that they were "early," just as the medieval Christians did not know they were "medieval." Historical designations provide helpful chronological divisions, but they occasionally leave the impression that at a certain time some voice from on high announced that the Early Christian period was over and the Medieval one had begun. Clearly some elements of life remained unchanged; farmers still got up with the sun and went to bed with the darkness. In their daily lives, many people would recognize no difference between Early and Medieval, thus the terms create an artificial distinction. On the other hand, if the farmers lived under barbarian kings but their grandparents had lived under Roman emperors, those farmers would recognize the distinction.

In this book we will use the common historical designations, but with the allowance that these must always be taken with the proverbial grain of salt. Having taken that grain of salt, let us use a common historical designation, pre-Constantinian and post-Constantinian, that is, before and after the reign of Constantine (306–337), the first Christian emperor. Before his reign, the Christians often found themselves subject to suspicion and occasionally to persecution; during and after his reign, the Christians were the dominant group in the empire.

2. Where Did They Live?

In general, the early Christians lived within the confines of the Roman Empire, and thus the study of them has emphasized the Greco-Roman nature of the Church. But there were Christians outside the empire—in Armenia, Ethiopia, Persia, and Ireland. One early Christian writer, the North African Tertullian (ca. 160–ca. 220) claimed that there were Christians in Britain beyond Roman territory.[2] Regrettably, we know little about most of these groups, certainly in comparison with what we know about the Christians in the empire. Furthermore, the vast majority of Christians were Romans, and studying them gives a far more reliable picture of Early Christianity than studying groups beyond the imperial frontiers; but it is important that we recognize that Early and Imperial Christianity are not equivalent terms.

[This discussion has led to another question: How do we know anything about the early Christians? We will treat this in chapter two.]

The Christians did not occupy the entire empire at once. The New Testament, particularly the epistles of Paul and the Acts of the Apostles, which deals largely with Paul, emphasizes the expansion into Syria, Asia Minor, and Greece. Most scholars believe at least two (Luke and Matthew) and possibly all of the gospels were written in Syria, and, in the Book of Acts, Luke makes Antioch a second center of Christianity after Jerusalem, and a missionary center as well. Paul also reached the city of Rome, although both Acts and the Epistle to the Romans make it clear that Italy had Christians before Paul got there. Ancient Roman tradition, accepted by almost all scholars, claims that Peter also came to Rome.

2. Tertullian, *Adversus Iudaeos* viii, cited in *Councils and Ecclesiastical Documents Relating to Great Britain and Ireland,* volume I, part i, A. W. Haddan and William Stubbs, eds. (Oxford: Clarendon Press, 1869; repr. 1964) 3.

Luke tells us (Acts 15:36-41) that after Paul and Barnabas argued about whether to take Mark (the traditional author of the second gospel) on another missionary journey (Paul felt that Mark had let him down on a previous journey), the two apostles split up, with Paul returning to Asia Minor and Barnabas taking Mark with him to Cyprus. We know nothing of their success there; we simply know that there were Christians on Cyprus in the first century.

Other evidence for the geographical spread of first-century Christianity is scattered and fragmentary. In Romans 15:24 Paul says he plans to go to Spain. Did he get there? A Roman Christian document, the *First Epistle of Clement to the Corinthians,* written *circa* 95, says that Paul "traveled as far as the Western boundary,"[3] but scholars are still doubtful that Paul did indeed get to Spain.

Although bibles list the Second Epistle to Timothy as Paul's, scholars have demonstrated that a disciple of his wrote it in his name, probably around the year 100. In 2 Timothy 4:10 "Paul" says that his co-worker Crescens has gone to Gaul (modern France), and although we cannot accept a Pauline commission for Crescens, this may reflect a historical reality, that Christians were in Gaul by the year 100. But the word "Gaul" does not appear in all manuscripts of 2 Timothy [see chapter five to learn how the early Christians wrote books]; many manuscripts read "Galatia," which is in Asia Minor and which Paul himself had evangelized and to whose community he had written a letter. Scholars are understandably reluctant to put the first Christians in Gaul.

Several New Testament books, especially the Acts of the Apostles, indicate extensive Jewish-Christian interaction, and it is clear that the first Christian missionaries followed the path of the Jewish Diaspora, that is, of the Jews who lived outside their traditional homeland. This has led scholars to argue that missionaries probably went to the great Egyptian port city of Alexandria, which had a sizeable Jewish community; they reason logically that if missionaries were going to the ancient equivalent of "dots on the map," that is, to small towns in Asia Minor, certainly some would have gone to the large Jewish community in Alexandria. Since the Alexandrian Jews practiced a form of biblical exegesis called allegory [see chapter five], which appears in the Epistle to the Hebrews (late first century), scholars believe that this epistle makes a case for Early Christianity at Alexandria.

3. Clement, *First Epistle to the Corinthians,* ch. 5, James Kleist, trans., ACW 1 (Washington: Newman Press, 1946) 12.

Finally, a variety of legends survive about the activities of early Christians. Some date from the Middle Ages and reflect the desire of the medieval Western Churches to give themselves a historical pedigree as old as the Mediterranean Churches. Thus we find the British claiming that Joseph of Arimathea, after he had buried Jesus (John 19:38), migrated to Britain to the site of Glastonbury Abbey. The French claimed that Lazarus, with his sisters Martha and Mary, settled in Gaul; Dionysius the Areopagite, after his conversion at Athens by Paul (Acts of the Apostles 17:34), traveled to Paris, where the pagan barbarians martyred him. The Spaniards believed that the apostle James had migrated to Spain and was buried at the appropriately named Santiago da Compostela. There is nothing inherently impossible about any of this: the Roman conquest of Britain began in earnest in 43, so Joseph could conceivably have gone there; Gaul and Spain had been Roman provinces well before Jesus' life, and Joseph, Lazarus, Martha, Mary, Dionysius, and James could easily have traveled to these places. But because something could have happened does not mean that it did happen, and it is best to treat these traditions as legends.

One legend sent Christianity east rather than west, the story that the apostle Thomas traveled to India. Christianity possibly reached India *circa* 200, and the so-called Thomas Christians of India claim descent from him. Another legend sent the faith north to Edessa (modern southeastern Turkey); the Church historian Eusebius of Caesarea (d. 339) preserves a letter supposedly sent by Abgar, king of Edessa, to Jesus, inviting him to come to his city. Jesus declines but sends the apostle Thaddeus to evangelize the area. Thaddeus (Addai in Syriac, the language spoken in Edessa) succeeded brilliantly and even evangelized in southern Armenia. Scholars do not accept the historicity of either of these accounts.[4]

The number of Christians grew considerably in the second century, and the evidence becomes fuller. The first-century bases remained secure and indeed were strengthened, but new areas were heard from, such as North Africa, Egypt south of Alexandria, and Gaul. Debatable evidence places Christianity in Spain in the second century, but the first solid evidence of Christianity there dates to the mid-third century. The great Anglo-Saxon historian, the Venerable Bede (d. 735), tells us that the British king Lucius wrote Pope

4. For the pertinent information on these topics, see the articles under Thomas and Abgar, in *EEXty,* Everett Ferguson, ed. (New York: Garland Publishers, 1997).

Eleutherius (ca. 174–189) to ask to be converted, but he is repeating a legend; most likely Christianity got to Britain in the early third century.[5] Finally, although scholars do not accept the legends of Thomas and Abgar, Christianity had reached Edessa *circa* 200 as well as Persia and probably Armenia; even India is a possibility.

By the third century the process of expansion had largely halted, except for Britain, where the first solid evidence of Christianity appears, along with the first conclusive evidence of the new religion in Arabia (the Roman province) and beyond Rome to the Persian Empire, although it may have been in those places before then. The real geographical change had become the growth of the Christians in areas such as North Africa, Syria, and Italy. The Christians had become a recognizable group within the Roman Empire; a sad testimony to this was the first empire-wide persecution of them by the emperor Decius (249–251).

The fourth century saw enormous changes in the geography of Early Christianity. When the emperor Constantine I (the Great) converted (ca. 319) and began to favor the Church, Christian missionaries evangelized at will and effected mass conversions. By the end of the century, some areas had become completely Christian (one town in Asia Minor requested that the emperor free them from all taxation because every person in the town was Christian). Some areas, like Italy, continued to be pagan strongholds, but Rome had by then become a Christian empire. Two more non-Roman areas received Christian missionaries, Georgia and Ethiopia, as did the barbarian Gothic tribes that had begun to occupy the northern Balkans.

Only two more areas remained to be Christianized in this period. The Irish received a bishop, Palladius, in 431, but he was sent by Pope Celestine I (422–432) to Christians already living there; how they got there no one knows. Finally, *circa* 540, two rival missions from Constantinople reached the African kingdom of Nubia, the area now known as southern Egypt and northern Sudan.[6]

This section started with the question "Where Did They Live?" The answer clearly depends upon the time at which we are looking, but in general Christianity continued to spread and to sink roots throughout the Roman Empire and sometimes beyond as it moved through the centuries.

5. For Lucius, see Joseph Kelly, *The Concise Dictionary of Early Christianity* (Collegeville, Minn.: The Liturgical Press, 1993) 99–100.

6. See articles on these people and places in *EEXty* for the particulars.

Although the Christians could be found all over the ancient Mediterranean world, they initially inhabited the cities.[7] This resulted largely from the natural desire of the early missionaries to reach as many people as possible and because the roads and sea routes went from city to city, just as today international flights go from Paris to London but not from a small Alpine village to a small Appalachian one. As an area became increasingly Christian, the faith spread to the rural regions.

The initial urban character of Christianity has inadvertently survived in several languages. The word "pagan" now means an ancient person who was neither a Jew nor a Christian, but originally it meant someone living in the countryside. From the Latin *paganus* come words like the French *paysan* and the Italian *paisano,* both meaning "peasant," that is, one who lives in the countryside. English has a parallel: the word "heathen" refers to one who lives on the heath, that is, in the country.

3. What Do We Know About Their Daily Lives?

We cannot accurately gauge the size of the earliest Christian communities; for that matter, scholars cannot accurately gauge the size of the general population of most Roman cities and provinces. In the middle of the third century, the Church of Rome had a staff of forty-six presbyters, seven deacons, and almost a hundred other staffers who served 1,500 widows and other needy persons. Some scholars have estimated that this could reflect a Christian population of approximately 30,000.[8] Helpful as this is for so important a Church as Rome, it still tells us little, because there were Christians in Rome before Paul and until the end of our period—what was that Church's population in the first or sixth centuries? And what about all the others? The science of demographics (studying peoples) depends upon numbers, and these are largely unavailable for the ancient world.

Although some Christians, like "Barnabas," author of a second-century epistle, considered themselves distinct from the Jews and Gentiles, most Christians lived lives like those of other Roman citizens. We can easily follow the cinematic version of Early Christianity

7. Wayne Meeks, *The First Urban Christians* (New Haven: Yale University Press, 1983).

8. Robert M. Grant, *Augustus to Constantine: The Emergence of Christianity into the Roman World* (New York: Harper & Row, 1970) 212.

and see nothing but persecutions, but this is simply wrong. As the brief history of Early Christianity in chapter seven will show, the persecutions were not ongoing affairs, but rather often broke out because of local factors. Until the empire-wide attack by Decius in 250, there were large provinces that were virtually untouched by persecution, such as Spain and probably Britain, while in other provinces where there had been persecutions, such as Gaul, the persecution was limited to a small area, such as the one at Lyons *circa* 177. In sum, many Christians lived and died in peace during an era widely believed to be one of constant persecution. And, of course, after the conversion of Constantine and his conquest of the entire empire (323), Roman persecution of Christians ceased.

We should correct another modern, idealizing misperception, that of Christians, confident in faith, singing psalms as they head off to face the lions. Not only were the Christians not persecuted constantly, they did not want to be. Thomas More made famous the saying "This is not the stuff of which martyrs are made"—although, ironically, he did die as one—but it could be applied to the early Christians. Although there are a few cases in North Africa when Christians forced themselves on the pagan authorities, Christians, in general, like any people, wanted to live in peace. The bishops, the leaders of the ancient Church, agreed and denounced the practice of intentional martyrdom. When Constantine offered the Church the hand of peace, the bishops grabbed for it and the people gladly went along. The Christians amply demonstrated their willingness to suffer and, if necessary, to die for their faith, but they wanted to be good citizens of Rome. To use a modern parallel, who would want to belong to a religion that would make him or her an enemy of the state? In some cases, such as the Stalinist Soviet Union, this was necessary, but people would have preferred to be both good Christians and good citizens.

In fact, they would have wanted to be more than just good citizens; they would have wanted to fit in. With the exception of out-and-out misanthropes, most people want to get along with others, to be included in parties and picnics and outings. We may safely assume that the early Christians wanted to get along with their pagan and Jewish neighbors; and even when there were no overt and legal persecutions, the Christians probably suffered discrimination or petty annoyances—quiet resentment, discreet silence when others learned they were Christians, suppressed giggles at their belief in a crucified carpenter who is the Son of God. One can imagine anxious Christian children asking their parents "Why are we different?" "Why aren't the other children allowed to play with me?"—the same type of discrimination visited upon Jews in later eras in Christian societies.[9] On the Palatine Hill in Rome there survives a wall-scratching of a crucified donkey and a man in front of it, with the inscription "Alexamenus worships his god."[10]

Thus we may safely assume that they shared many of the concerns of their pagan and Jewish fellow citizens; we can further assume that certain secular concerns brought them closer to non-Christians than to Christians. Modern sociological studies can demonstrate that middle-class Jews, Catholics, and Protestants have more in common with one another than with wealthy or impoverished co-religionists, and no doubt a Christian day laborer identified more with a Jewish or pagan co-worker—performing back-breaking tasks for little money—than with a wealthy Christian aristocrat secure on an estate. The Acts of the Apostles tells us that the apostle Paul and his co-workers Priscilla and Aquila (18:3) were tentmakers, and that his convert Lydia was "a dealer in purple cloth" (16:14). There was no Christian way to make tents or sell purple cloth; these Christians would have shared all the labor and reward of their tasks to the same degree as pagans and Jews.

In spite of a frenetic missionary career, Paul clearly took part in the life of the Mediterranean towns, and he almost certainly enjoyed it despite the challenge. Luke repeatedly showed him preaching in the marketplace, the center of the ancient social world. He constantly engaged in a give-and-take with his audience, which pleased them. As Luke observed of Paul's hearers in Athens, "Now all the Athenians and the foreigners who lived there spent their time in nothing except telling or hearing something new" (Acts 17:21).

Ancient people of all religions would have worried about their economic futures, taken pride in their children's accomplishments, been titillated at the scandals of the imperial court, and striven to be happy. Inevitably, the Christians were different in some ways, often in important ways, but we will seriously misunderstand them if we treat them solely as a race apart.

As for their social status, later generations of idealizing Christians have rhapsodized and romanticized the first Churches as communities

9. John H. Elliott, *A Home for the Homeless: A Sociological Exegesis of 1 Peter, Its Situation and Strategy* (Philadelphia: Fortress Press, 1981) 79–80.

10. For an illustration of this, see Everett Ferguson, *Backgrounds of Early Christianity,* 2nd ed. (Grand Rapids, Mich.: Wm. B. Eerdmans Co., 1993) 560.

of the poor, the enslaved, and the other marginalized groups, but this again is simply wrong. The gospels identify Jesus' father as Joseph, a carpenter (Matt 13:55), hardly a rich man but one with a marketable skill. Jesus' immediate followers included fishermen, that is, men with occupations similar in status to that of Joseph, and two of them, the sons of Zebedee, came from a family that owned its own boat and hired men to work it (Mark 1:20). Another, Matthew, was a tax collector (Matt 9:9). Several wealthy women followed Jesus' movement, including the wife of Chuza, steward of King Herod (Luke 8:3). Even allowing for the debatable historicity of some of the gospel material, we can see that Jesus' immediate disciples came from a variety of social classes, albeit mostly what we would today call the lower middle class.

The earliest converts likewise came from diverse social strata. The Acts of the Apostles speaks of mass conversions, such as 3,000 in one day (2:41). We need not accept the exact historicity of that account to see that social lines would be crossed by such a conversion. John Mark's mother owned a house in the city of Jerusalem and had a maid (12:12-13), while Paul was a tentmaker (18:3). Roman tradition identifies Domitilla, a cousin of the emperor Domitian (81–96), as a Christian who was exiled for her faith *circa* 95; if this tradition is accurate, Christianity had reached the highest social station within sixty years of Jesus' death.[11] Around 115, Ignatius, bishop of Antioch, who was being sent to Rome to be thrown to the beasts, so rejoiced in his coming martyrdom that he asked the Roman Christians not to prevent his death.[12] Safely assuming that they did not plan a commando raid to rescue him from his guards, we can say this implies that the Roman community had enough influence or money to mitigate his sentence.

In general, the ancient sources do not say much about people's status. The Christian sources tend to emphasize the achievements of bishops or theological matters, and the pagan sources often emanate from aristocratic circles, with little interest in non-aristocrats. Occasional hints about their work survive, for example, the ceiling mosaics in the fourth-century church of Santa Costanza in Rome show peasants leading an ox-cart filled with grapes while other peasants stomp the grapes in a large vat. Other hints appear in ser-

11. Original text translated in *A New Eusebius,* James Stevenson, ed., revised with additional documents by W.H.C. Frend (London: SPCK, 1987) 6.

12. Ignatius, *To the Romans* 1, 4, in ACW 1, 80–82.

mons, when preachers attempt to relate doctrinal matters to people's lives.

Further evidence that all the early Christians were not impoverished communitarians comes from the quality of the New Testament literature. Before the twentieth century, many scholars assumed the gospels to be historical accounts of Jesus' life and ministry, but modern scholarship has demonstrated clearly that these are sophisticated theological documents, reflecting considerable education and literary skill on the part of the evangelists. This does not mean that the evangelists were wealthy or noble, but it does mean that they had sufficient education to produce such works.

What did the early Christians do for a living? Literally, everything, although this depended upon where they lived and, to an extent, at what point in history we ask this question.

As we noted earlier, Christianity moved initially into the cities of the Greco-Roman world, and many of the occupations of the Christians reflected that urban environment; for example, we know of wine merchants and shoemakers. As Christianity penetrated into the countryside, the occupations naturally reflected the new geographical circumstances; for example, many Christians in North Africa grew olives and operated oil presses. When the Roman Empire became Christianized in the fourth century, many of the nobility converted, and the social status of the Christians rose considerably. Simultaneously, the conversion of the nobility often led to an increased conversion of their slaves. [On Christian attitudes toward slavery, see chapter six.]

There were some occupations that Christians in general avoided, such as acting, which moralists considered disreputable because actors supposedly led notoriously lewd lives. Despite the common belief that the early Christians were pacifists, there are accounts of Christian soldiers who found no conflict between their faith and their occupation; these included so famous a saint as Martin of Tours (d. 397). Many Christians who objected to military service did so not because of what soldiers did but because they often had to pledge themselves to the gods or perform some act of fealty that Christians considered idolatrous. Most Christians would have been grateful for the security that Roman arms provided, and they would have recognized the need for a strong military to defend the frontiers.[13]

13. On this topic, see Louis Swift, *The Early Fathers on War and Military Service,* MFC 19 (Collegeville, Minn.: The Liturgical Press—Michael Glazier,

After the conversion of Constantine, the Christians strongly supported the empire and its armies. St. Augustine of Hippo (354–430) greatly admired monastic life, but when a Roman military governor had decided to leave his calling and become a monk, Bishop Augustine, worried about barbarian attacks on North Africa, talked the governor out of his vocation.[14] By that time most of the Roman military officers were Christian, and the threat of idolatry had passed, but it is significant that Christians generally saw nothing inherently wrong with military service. There were, however, some Christians, such as the great Alexandrian theologian Origen (ca. 185–ca. 253), who held pacifist views.

4. Entertainment

Even the most driven person must relax occasionally, and we will now ask how the early Christians spent their leisure time. No one in the ancient world wrote specifically about this, and we must garner the information from a variety of sources, but a general picture can emerge. Since people choose their leisure activities, these can sometimes tell the historian quite a bit about them. Just as the question of immorality affected Christian views on the military, it impinged also on the lives of the Christians in the areas of socialization and entertainment.

The Romans enjoyed the public baths, and every city worth its name had such a structure; remains of these survive today, the most obvious being the English city of Bath, named after the Roman remains. These were often extensive, with a swimming pool, latrines, exercise rooms, and a sauna; some of the larger ones even had lecture halls and museums. They formed a focus of community life, and the public ones were open to all citizens, although men and women had separate bathing houses.

For many Romans, the baths served a social function, and the public nakedness of the baths did not concern them. But some Christian moralists, especially the North African Tertullian (ca. 160–ca. 220), considered the baths breeding places of immorality, especially homosexuality, which the Christians considered unsavory. This disap-

---

1983); John Helgeland, et al., eds., *Christians and the Military* (Philadelphia: Fortress Press, 1985).

14. Peter Brown, *Augustine of Hippo* (Los Angeles: University of California Press, 1967) 422.

proval caused some Christians to avoid the baths, although many apparently did not heed the moralists. Significantly, even when the empire became Christian, the baths continued to be popular; the great preacher John Chrysostom (ca. 350–407) railed against them to his congregations in Antioch, who listened politely and still went to the baths.

Maybe Christians could claim that the moralists treated the baths too strictly and that they were essentially harmless public gathering places, but no one could defend the morality of the gladiatorial games. These originated in the third century B.C.; the word "gladiator" comes from *gladius,* the Latin word for sword, because the initial combatants carried swords. As these games became popular, other weapons were introduced, such as the net and trident. The gladiators included prisoners of war, condemned criminals who obviously had nothing to lose, slaves specifically purchased to be gladiators, and even some men who did it for the money, a variation on the idea of a mercenary soldier.

Not surprisingly, the Christians considered the gladiatorial games a form of legalized murder, and Christian moralists condemned them roundly. When the Christians came to rule the empire in the fourth century, they put an end to the games. In fact, we do not know how many Christians actually went to such games; furthermore, it would be a mistake to think that all pagans enjoyed them.

The Roman populace could also see spectacles in which men fought against wild animals, such as lions or bears. While moderns would consider that cruelty to animals, there is no evidence that Christian moralists considered it immoral. People could also go to athletic contests.

Christian attitudes toward the theater were more ambivalent. Scholars have been able to find echoes of Greek and Roman plays in Christian writings, and there is no doubt that many Christians attended the theater. Some Christian moralists considered the plays immoral, not because the characters often included the pagan gods—indeed, possibly the reverse, since the playwright often reduced the gods to mere elements in the play and sometimes held them up to ridicule—but rather because of the play's values. Augustine tells us that the Roman playwright Terence "brought on to the stage a worthless young man citing Jupiter as a model for his own fornication."[15] It is unfortunate that our information derives largely from moralists

15. Augustine, *Confessions* I, xvi.26, Henry Chadwick, trans. (Oxford: Oxford Paperbacks, 1992) 19.

and not from the (probably) many Christians who were loyal to their faith and yet saw nothing particularly wrong with an evening at the theater.

The question of Christian attitudes toward the theater brings up the question of the attitude toward pagan literature in general. In an age before television, videocassette players, compact disc players, and interactive computers, literate people considered reading the prime form of entertainment. Romans had some marvelous works from which to choose—Homer, Sappho, Virgil, Martial, Catullus, and many others from what we now call classical literature because, in Western education, these books formed the basis of classroom instruction. There is no doubt that Christians read them; as with the dramas, scholars have had little difficulty finding many citations from pagan authors in Christian writers. According to the Acts of the Apostles, these writers include Paul the Apostle (Acts 17:28). Tolerant authors such as Clement of Alexandria (ca. 150–ca. 220) genuinely enjoyed pagan literature and quoted it comfortably in their religious works. But as the empire became more and more Christian, moralists again raised the question of pagan and/or immoral influence upon Christians. Two prominent figures of the late fourth and early fifth centuries illustrate this well.

Jerome (ca. 342–ca. 420) loved classical literature, especially the Latin orator Cicero. He clearly benefited from this love because he became a great Latin stylist. But Jerome had what the modern world would call a conversion experience, in his case a dream. He saw himself caught up before the heavenly throne, and he heard a voice asking him to identify himself. He said, "I am a Christian," but the voice angrily rebuked him, saying "You are a Ciceronian!"[16] Jerome then decided to reform his reading habits and to abandon his addiction, but, as his former friend and later enemy Rufinus of Aquileia (ca. 335–410) liked to point out, traces of classical literature continued to appear in Jerome's writings. But Jerome's condemnation of secular literature did have an impact on later generations of Christians.

Jerome's younger contemporary, Augustine, went through the same difficulties. In his *Confessions,*[17] he condemns much pagan literature as vanity, that is, emptiness, because it cannot lead to God;

16. Jerome, *Epistle* 22.30; cited in *Creeds, Councils, and Controversies,* James Stevenson, ed. (London: SPCK, 1978) 163–164.

17. *Confessions* I, xiii.20–22; pp. 19–20.

but he simultaneously admits that his reading of Virgil's *Aeneid* so moved him that he wept over the death of Dido. The attractiveness of this literature annoyed him; he wept for Dido but did not weep for himself when he sinned against God.

Augustine, however, had a more practical bent than Jerome. Rather than condemn pagan literature outright, he found a place for it in the lives of Christians. Although Christian intellectual life will be discussed in chapter five, we will note here that Augustine recommended the reading of pagan works if they would aid in the understanding of the Bible. While this most obviously applied to historical or philosophical works, Augustine, who read perhaps more carefully than anyone in history, recognized that a reading of pagan literature could give one a sense of written expression and meaning that would be valuable in understanding the Scriptures. Through that entrance, the Christian who wished to read classical literature could probably drive a truck, but Christians did heed Augustine's guidelines.[18]

The siren lure of pagan literature never quite died down, however, because at the end of the sixth century, Gregory I the Great, pope from 590 to 604, wrote an angry letter to an Italian bishop who was, in the pope's eyes, too fond of pagan literature for a bishop. But even Gregory had to admit that every educated person needed to know something of the classics.[19]

As for Christian literature, that which survives is largely ecclesiastical, that is, written by Christians for Christians. There remains little evidence of "popular" Christian writing, that is, writings intended primarily to entertain rather than to instruct or inspire religiously. There were exceptions. Falconia Proba (fl. ca. 350–360), one of few Christian women writers whose work has survived, composed a biblical cento, that is, a new poetic work made by taking complete or half lines from another poem. Strange as it sounds to the modern mind, this was a widely recognized literary device of the day. Proba's cento of 694 lines deals with the Creation story down to the Flood and then with Jesus' redemptive activity. Juvencus (fl. ca. 325–350) composed a biblical epic, a paraphrase of the gospel, in imitation of the great Latin poet Virgil.

18. This theory is outlined in *De Doctrina Christiana,* R.P.H. Green, trans. (New York: Oxford University Press, 1995).

19. See the discussion by G. R. Evans, *The Thought of Gregory the Great* (Cambridge: Cambridge UP, 1986) 9.

We should also note that many Christians enjoyed the genuine literary character of much inspirational writing, such as the poems of Prudentius (348–405) and Paulinus of Nola (351–431). Furthermore, Christian writers such as Ausonius (ca. 310–ca. 395) and Claudius Claudianus (d. ca. 404) wrote poetry with a distinctive non-Christian flavor, such as panegyrics for the emperor and even some mythological pieces. Two particularly exciting works were Athanasius' *Life of Saint Antony* and Sulpicius Severus' *Life of Martin of Tours,* vivid accounts of the monks' battles with the devil.

One entertainment the Christians absolutely favored was chariot racing, and nowhere was this truer than in the most Christian of cities, Constantinople. Constantine I built that city (literally, the *polis* [city] of Constantine) to be a Christian capital, with none of the pagan heritage of ancient Rome. The city contained famous churches, hordes of monks and clergy, a populace obsessed with theology (the city hosted ecumenical councils in 381 and 553), and the Hippodrome, where the best charioteers in the empire vied for the traditional fame and fortune. So identified were the citizens with chariot racing, that the different team supporters (what moderns call fans) considered their allegiance to the Blues or the Greens to be almost political. Emperors resident in Constantinople, especially in the fifth and sixth centuries, had to keep close watch on the activities of these factions, which could often become dangerous; but, tellingly, the imperial family had its own box at the Hippodrome. If the emperor were present, he presided over the races—much the way modern presidents and prime ministers take pride in the achievements of Olympic athletes from their countries—and he, too, would have enjoyed the excitement; and maybe, like the other fans, he would have made the occasional wager.

We may thus say that the early Christians relaxed the way most of their pagan fellow citizens did, except that Christian teachers warned about excessive participation in activities that might harm faith or morals. It is difficult to say how rigorously the vast body of Christians took these admonitions; that these admonitions appear generation after generation suggests that the majority of Christians took most entertainment less seriously than did their leaders. But these warnings at least caused the Christians to think twice about what they did.

The early Christians came from all parts of the Roman world and much of the non-Roman world; they worked in all fields except those considered morally harmful; they tried to relax after a hard day's work. They wanted to be good citizens, and they wanted their neighbors to like and respect them. They were sinners, but they hoped to do better. This could be said of most people in any period of history.

Chapter Two

How Do We Know
About the Early Christians?

The first chapter surveyed what we know about the early Christians as persons—when and where they lived, what they did for a living, how they spent what leisure time they had. This chapter will examine how scholars know anything about them.

1. The Problem of the Data

Every discipline depends on the data, a word taken from the Latin *datum,* or "that which is given." The plural form is *data,* or "things which are given." The data in any science are those chunks or bits of information with which scholars work. They compile data in a variety of ways; for example, in the physical sciences scholars can do experiments and gather data from observation; in the social sciences they can do surveys and compile statistics.

Note that in these cases the researchers can generate some of their data, but in history the researcher really does have "things which are given," that is, there is no way to generate data, and the historian must use whatever the past has given to the present. For example, if an economist wants to know how interest rates will affect people's spending, she or he can conduct a survey because the people exist today and so do the interest rates. It will be a difficult task, but it can be done. Historians, on the other hand, may discover more data, but they cannot generate new materials at will. In chapter one, we saw that Barnabas and Mark sailed to Cyprus, and that to date scholars know very little about Christianity there until the late fourth century. If the currently known fragments are never augmented by new discoveries, then the history of Christianity on that island in this period will always be obscure.

This concept can often present problems for modern people, who live in what is commonly called the Information Age, a time when we frequently have too much information to digest, and the amount keeps growing. Furthermore, in a rapidly changing society, people often think that a century was a long time ago, and two thousand years ago can seem like the Ice Age. While a century ago is indeed history, it is what scholars call modern history, partially because people then produced printed books with the time and place of publication, researchers footnoted sources, and even photographic records survive. In the world of the early Christians, all books were handwritten (manuscripts) and often without date or place of composition; writers routinely copied material from other writers without acknowledgment, and visual records (drawings, murals) did not record an instantaneous event the way a camera can. To understand the ancient world, we must begin by understanding how different the data are from what we now take for granted.

2. The Nature of the Written Data

In chapter one, we cited the chief source of our knowledge of the early Christians, that is, their own writings. Since the first Christians lived in small communities and had little influence, pagan writers say little of them. The first real information appears in the *Annales* of the Roman historian Tacitus (ca. 56–ca. 115), who recounts the Great Fire of Rome in 64, the people's suspicion that the emperor Nero (54–68) had ordered it set, and Nero's attempt to transfer the blame and thus the hostility to a little-known and therefore suspicious new religious group, the Christians. But Tacitus and the other Roman writers of the first and second century (Suetonius, Pliny) mention the Christians almost in passing, and they are not interested in them. They deal with the Christians only in the context of other, Roman matters.

This is not surprising. Ancient historians often limited themselves to political history (wars, treaties, legislative activities), and they concentrated on those who created such history, usually aristocratic men. They had little interest in social or economic history, for example, the role of women in Roman life or the situation of merchants— they simply took those groups for granted. For them, the Christians were insignificant and thus unworthy of serious notice. As the Christians grew in number and importance as the centuries passed, pagan historians noticed them more and more, but by then the Christians were writing their own histories.

This gap in knowledge is unfortunate because we always read history backwards, that is, as time passes we can recognize which events determined future developments and which did not. Often the people alive in a particular era do not recognize the importance of those who would wield enormous influence later. Clearly there is no doubt that prime ministers and presidents will make history, and so material about them always survives. But if one were to look at histories of nineteenth-century Europe written before 1917, one would find little mention of Karl Marx; yet his teachings influenced the way in which vast numbers—at one point almost forty percent of the people on earth—would be ruled. One would find even fewer references to Louis Pasteur because only recently have scholars investigated the history of science; yet Pasteur's discovery about the importance of cleanliness in keeping birthing mothers and newborn infants safe and healthy has contributed to the high survival rate of the human population in the modern world.

With the infallibility of hindsight, we can see what the ancient pagans could not—that their world would pass and that this despised, insignificant religion would long survive them. But the ancient historians lacked our infallibility, and so we must turn to the writings the Christians themselves left behind.

Christian writings come in all forms. Some are actual histories, and they provide the most valuable information, but scholars can glean material from almost any kind of writing. In fact, scholars can learn from books even before reading them. In an age when all books had to be written or copied by hand (think of copying the Bible by hand) naturally people copied only those books that held the most value to them. Therefore, the very existence of Christian books in a particular place indicates the existence of Christians who wanted to have copies of those books. To be sure, Christian books could have been stolen or lost and thus not have originated in the place where they were found, but the books still definitely prove some contact with Christianity. For instance, the thief who lived there had to have stolen the books from some Christians or a Christian had to be passing that way in order to have lost the book there.

The survival of Christian books can occasionally prove something stronger. Let us say that scholars find twenty manuscripts of a particular book, all dating from the fourth century and from the ancient city of Antioch. Let us further say that for the rest of the empire and for the rest of the early Christian period there are only ten other manuscripts of it. That tells us something about the Antiochene Christians in the fourth century, that is, that they considered the author of that book to be a major figure and this particular book to be the author's most significant work.

The real evidence lies in what the books say; yet what the books say is not the end of the quest—it is only the beginning. No book just came into existence. It had to be written by someone at some time in some place and to someone (even a diarist has an audience in mind). To understand what the book says, we must consider the circumstances under which it was written, such as whom the author was addressing, why she or he wrote at that moment, what the author presumed on the part of the audience, and similar matters. This can be applied to anything from an epic poem to a laundry list, and certainly to early Christian writings. Let us apply this to the earliest Christian literature, the epistles of the apostle Paul.[1]

The first thing we notice is that Paul does not usually identify himself at any length; he presumes that his readers know him—not just who he is, but they actually know him personally, although this is not the case for the Epistle to the Romans. Paul wrote to communities (Corinth, Thessalonica) that he had either founded or in which he had worked.[2] The importance of establishing this is that we cannot expect Paul to give us a lot of information; after all, his readers know both him and what he is talking about. Obviously, we can glean some information, but we have to look at the epistles very carefully, compare them to one another, and place them against the larger background of Early Christianity. Even after doing that, we find that some things still escape us. When Paul talks about Christians puffed up with knowledge (1 Cor 1–2) or about Christians who opposed his mission (Gal 3), he does not identify them individually or character-

1. There is a mountain of literature on Paul. For the most recent scholarly life, see Jerome Murphy-O'Connor, *Paul: A Critical Life* (New York: Oxford University Press, 1996).

2. Even the apparently personal letter to Philemon is actually to him, his wife Apphia, someone named Archippus, and the church that meets in their house (Phil 1–2).

ize them with a name. He left that to later generations of scholars, who have spilled much ink in trying to identify these groups; and a quick consultation of several commentaries on Paul will reveal how many theories scholars have advanced to solve these problems that remain unsolved.

Therefore, when we want to reconstruct the history of the first Pauline communities, we must recognize the nature of the source—its range and its limits. We certainly learn a lot about Paul and how he understood his mission and what values and teachings he passed along to his communities. We know something of what they thought, but we must be careful here because we do not have their communications to Paul, only his version of what they said. This does not mean that we must question Paul's veracity; rather it means that people rarely see the same matter in exactly the same way, and we would have a better picture of the Pauline communities if we knew the views of Paul's readers, for example, the letter the Corinthians wrote to him (1 Cor 7:1). [A common exercise in many New Testament courses is for the students to picture themselves as ancient Christians and to write a letter to Paul.]

We know even less about those whom Paul criticizes. Enemies are enemies, and we are rarely fair to them. Paul firmly believed that he had been "called to be an apostle of Christ Jesus by the will of God" (1 Cor 1:1). Those who opposed him therefore opposed the will of God. It would be unrealistic to expect him to be objective about people he thought were jeopardizing the eternal salvation of those in his communities. It would be like asking parents to be objective in describing someone who has tried to harm their children. This does not necessarily mean that what Paul says about them is untrue or even exaggerated; maybe he is being objective. But it does mean that we have to be careful when our only source is a negative, indeed hostile, one.

Paul's letters also show another element of ancient history, the accidental preservation of a document. In Philippians 2:6-11, Paul records a hymn that most scholars now agree is pre-Pauline, that is, the apostle has preserved a hymn known in the churches even before he began to write, a remarkably precious liturgical document and one of the few glimpses into the very earliest years of Christianity. Paul, of course, did not intend to preserve the hymn. On the contrary, he took it for granted that his readers knew what it was. It would never have occurred to him that this well-known piece would survive only because he decided to quote it. Similarly, the first-century Roman writer Clement preserved the doxology or prayer of praise of the Roman Church in a letter to the Church at Corinth.[3]

As noted earlier, Paul was not known personally to the community in Rome, but the Christians there knew him by reputation, and maybe that was not all good. Everyone writes for the reader. Paul might write personal epistles to communities he knew, but for the Romans he wrote a significant theological treatise. It is no accident that when biblical scholars write about Pauline theology, so many footnotes cite this epistle. Rome was the center of the empire, and possibly the community there had already (ca. 58) become important. Paul clearly wanted to impress them, and he very likely did. If, as most scholars believe, the final chapter is actually part of the letter, we can see that Paul was name-dropping to impress the Romans with how many of them were already known to him.

Thus we can see that the Epistle to the Romans presents a different situation, different readers, a different type of epistle from Paul's others. This is why the scholar must always approach the literature carefully.

But the scholar cannot evaluate merely what the letter says; she or he must also consider how it is said. For example, Paul wrote epistles. This was hardly the only form of early Christian literature although it was the most popular. The New Testament formally contains twenty-one epistles (all the books but the gospels, Acts, and Revelation), but there are also seven brief epistles in the Book of Revelation. Furthermore, scholars believe that 2 Corinthians is certainly an amalgam of three epistles, and Philippians very possibly of two, which would bring the total to thirty-one, an impressive case for the epistle format. But other early Christians wrote gospels, Luke wrote a theological history in the Book of Acts, and Revelation contains a collection of fantastic visions. In addition, Paul, as a practicing Jew, would have known that the Hebrew Bible (the Christian Old Testament) contained prophecies, sermons, laws, proverbs, psalms, and narratives. In sum, the apostle had a considerable range of literary types in which to express his ideas, and he chose the epistle.

Someone could readily respond to this by saying that since Paul was writing to communities he knew, a letter was the natural choice to make. But even if we concede that in Paul's circumstances the letter was perhaps the most natural form to use, it does not change the

3. *First Epistle to the Corinthians,* 59.4-61.3, ACW 1, 45–47.

fact that the form would still influence to some extent the content of the message.

What applies to Paul's epistles applies to all the other literature of the New Testament and to all the literature of Early Christianity in all its diversity: sermons, letters, narratives, monastic regulations, travel diaries, the lives of saints, court records of trials, decisions by regional and ecumenical councils of bishops, creeds both official and personal, theological treatises, spirituality, apologetics, and liturgy.

In chapter one, we noticed that as time progressed, the geographic spread of the Christians increased. That also applies to the literature. As they grew in numbers, and the distances between them grew, Christians had to write to keep in touch. Furthermore, as their teaching became more complex, they had to write more to explain it; a vast amount of literature survives from the fourth century, when theological controversy was at its height. Consequently, scholars know far more about Christianity in the fourth century than in the second.

The geographic spread of the Christians introduced another factor into the understanding of their literature—diverse languages. Jesus and his disciples would have spoken Aramaic, a Semitic dialect widely used in the Near East. Jews considered Hebrew to be a sacred language, so they used Aramaic for everyday affairs. The gospels portray Jesus as preaching to crowds in small Galilean towns, so it is likely that he used Aramaic. Greek was also in use in Palestine, and it quickly became the language of the Church that, thanks to Paul and other missionaries, spread to non-Jewish, Greek-speaking areas of the Eastern Mediterranean. All the books of the New Testament are in Greek.

The first extant Christian Latin dates to the late second century, and not to Rome but to North Africa. It recounts the martyrdoms of several Christians in the town of Scilli, still unidentified but thought to be close to Carthage, the capital of the Roman province of North Africa. The Scillitan martyrs were native Latin speakers and apparently not wealthy or sophisticated people. Therefore, when they tell the Roman governor who is interrogating them that they have the books of Paul, "a good man," with them, scholars conclude that the Pauline epistles, if not other parts of the New Testament, were available in Latin.[4] The Roman tongue joined Greek as one of the two great languages of Early Christianity.

4. Text translated in *A New Eusebius,* 44–45.

Many other languages soon joined them. Christianity reached Alexandria possibly in the first century, and in Alexandria people spoke Greek. But soon the faith penetrated to the countryside, where people spoke Coptic (in two dialects), a language derived ultimately from the ancient Egyptian demotic. By the third century Christianity had reached the Armenians, who translated the Bible and composed literature in their own tongue, as did the Georgians and Ethiopians later on.

In Syria, as Christianity moved its base out of Antioch and into the Syrian countryside, native speakers converted, and Christian books appeared in Syriac.

These non-Greco-Roman peoples did more than just translate the Bible and works of prominent Mediterranean writers. They often produced significant work of their own; for example, much early monastic literature survives in Coptic because that was the language of great monastic founders such as Antony (253–356) and Pachomius (ca. 290–346), while Ephraem the Syrian (ca. 306–373) composed beautiful poetry in his native tongue. On the other hand, these languages—and later Arabic—have also preserved the works of some great Greek writers, and occasionally a Latin one.

For some yet undetermined reason, the non-Greco-Roman peoples of the West did not leave a Christian literature even though they heard the faith taught in their own languages. North African priests gave sermons in Punic, the language of the inland people who did not know Latin,[5] while Irenaeus (fl. ca. 175–185) says that he preached to some Celtic-speaking Christians.[6] Saint Patrick (ca. 390–ca. 461) had been kidnaped by Irish pirates and was a slave in Ireland for six years, so when he returned to evangelize, he preached in the native tongue.

This wide-ranging literature obviously means that scholars of Early Christianity must learn some languages, although not all of them, but the problem goes further than that. For one thing, languages change, and sometimes quickly. In the United States in the 1940s, the word "drummer" could mean a salesperson who was supposed to "drum up" business, but now the word refers only to a musician. Sometimes a word can have different meanings, at least on the popular level, among two groups of people who ostensibly speak the same language. If a Briton has a flat, he or she has an apartment; if

5. Brown, *Augustine,* 192.
6. *Against Heresies,* I, Pref. 3; ANF 1, 316.

an American has a flat, he or she has an automobile tire with no air in it. (George Bernard Shaw is credited with the observation that England and America were two countries divided by a common language.) So scholars must not only learn the language but also how it was spoken at different points in history and in different places. This is not as difficult as it may sound at first, and it can often clinch an argument; for example, how a particular word is used or even spelled can indicate where or when a particular text was written.

The detailed study of language can often help to determine a work's authenticity. In the Middle Ages, when many of the manuscripts containing early Christian literature were copied, the scribes sometimes copied a book that they erroneously thought was written by a particular author, and thus wrongly attributed books survive under the names of Clement of Rome, Athanasius, Jerome, Augustine, and many others. By comparing the type of Latin or Greek in these books to unquestionably authentic works written by these authors, as well as the basic themes of the works, if that is possible, scholars can often discover an inauthentic work. They can then study the particular writer more accurately, since they are using only his or her authentic works.

That still leaves the inauthentic book, whose author is often labeled "Pseudo-Augustine" or "Pseudo-Jerome" to indicate that Augustine or Jerome did not write it but that it has come down under his name. In some cases, the pseudonymous (false name) work clearly dates well after the early Christian period and has little or no value to someone interested in the early period. Sometimes, however, the pseudonymous work is itself quite ancient and can be of great value.

For example, a man named Clement wrote a letter (ca. 95) on behalf of the Roman community to the community in Corinth. This letter is known now as the *First Epistle of Clement to the Corinthians* because for a long time people believed that he had written a second work called the *Second Epistle of Clement.* Commonly known as *2 Clement,* it is actually a homily that, as early as the fourth century, was mistakenly thought to have been written by Clement. Modern scholars analyzed the language of the two and easily concluded that one person had not written both, so now anyone wishing to study Clement of Rome relies only on the *First Epistle.* (Technically, of course, there is no first epistle without a second one, but scholars have kept the traditional name.)

But what about Second "Clement"? Scholarly analysis demonstrated the very early date of this homily, probably around 140, thus making it one of the earliest Christian homilies outside of the New Testament and a work of great value even though it is a pseudepigraphon (book written under a false name).[7]

There are also cases in which a work does not survive in its original language but in a translation. In the modern world people are accustomed to reading translations because such a wide variety of literature is available that it would be impossible to learn all of the original languages, and we do not want to deprive ourselves of reading a great work because we are purists who must read everything in the original. The modern standard of translating is very high, and, in general, people can be sure that they are reading a reliable version of what the original said. But as usual, things are not always that simple.

Reading a novel in which the language is not too technical is one thing, but reading a philosophical or theological treatise is altogether something else. Words often have nuances in their own language that cannot easily be transferred to other languages. This is why a translator will often put the original word or phrase into the text or into a footnote so that those familiar with the language can see what the original was. The word the translator chooses thus becomes the meaning of the original for the reader who does not have access to the original, and thus future translations present problems.

This happened with the Bible of English-speaking Christians, who were brought up on the King James Version if they were Protestants or the Douay-Rheims Version if they were Roman Catholics, and who have experienced both unfamiliarity and sometimes disappointment at the host of versions that have appeared in the last forty years. They know, of course, that the biblical languages are Greek and Hebrew, but translations become authoritative and people define their Bible in those terms. In the early fifth century, when an African church used a new Latin translation by Jerome, the congregation practically rioted, and Augustine cautioned Jerome about expecting people to give up a familiar version.[8]

Thus when a scholar of Early Christianity confronts a work written in Greek and surviving in Latin translation (much of the work of Irenaeus of Lyons, for example), she or he must wonder how accu-

---

7. For the information on Clement, real and pseudonymous, see *EEXty*, I. 264–265.

8. See Robert O'Connell, S.J., "When Saintly Fathers Feuded," in Thought 54 (1979), 344–364.

rate the translation is and how it might have been shaped by the Latin-speaking community that used it. Scholars working with such a text must always make allowances for that.

Although all the extant literature has value for scholars, some works stand out, sometimes because of their intrinsic value and sometimes because nothing else survives. It would take too long to list volumes in the second category, but in the first category we must mention the *Ecclesiastical History* of Eusebius, bishop of Caesarea in Palestine (ca. 260–339) and the first Church historian. Eusebius' work, marked by polemical concerns and the occasional fable, offers much to the historian not only because it presents the only general history of Christianity's first three centuries (other ancient histories covering this period have copied from it) but also because Eusebius included a large number of original sources. These, in fact, take up approximately twenty percent of the *History*. In some cases, his inclusion is not just the only original record of an event but even the only original record of a particular author, such as Serapion, bishop of the very important Church at Antioch in the late second century and an important figure in the Montanist controversy (see chapter seven). Eusebius presents many problems to the researcher, but he remains an invaluable source.[9] For the period after Eusebius, the historian has several histories, such as those of Socrates (ca. 380–450) or Sozomen (d. after 450), which also contain some material unknown elsewhere although not to Eusebius' extent.

3. The Nature of the Physical Data

The literary evidence deals largely with ideas, with how the ancient Christians expressed themselves about their world—personally, theoretically, historically. But much other data survives, data we can see and sometimes hold.

The first type of data we have already alluded to—books. We think of books as containers of thoughts. When we say a book is light or heavy, we mean that it was either easy to read or ponderous and difficult. But a book is also a physical object, and in an era

9. On Eusebius, see *EEXty,* 325–327; his *Ecclesiastical History* is available in several translations; a convenient one is by G. A. Williamson, *Eusebius: The History of the Church from Christ to Constantine* (Minneapolis: Augsburg Publishing House, 1975). The references to Serapion appear at v. 19 and vi. 11–12; Williamson, 226, 251–252.

when people had to copy all books by hand, they knew this better than we do. Although we will discuss bookmaking in chapter five, we will just note again what we said earlier. The physical survival of books tells us something about the life of the people who owned and read them; it can even tell us about their ability to produce books.

The second type is so large that we can often overlook it—the land. The nineteenth-century French scholar Ernst Renan called the Holy Land "the Fifth Gospel," and he was right. Seeing the places where Jesus and his disciples walked and talked, lived and died, gives one a sense of their world and thus a sense of them. Like most Americans, I can remember my first trip as a child to Washington, D.C., and visiting all the places I had seen in pictures and on television; it gave me a sense of the country's capital that all the pictures could not.

The difficulty here is that unless the site, that is, the land and the ancient structures on it, was preserved intact shortly after the events that made it famous, the modern person may have trouble recognizing it. There is little to see at some early Christian sites because the sites were largely destroyed, either by natural forces such as earthquakes or by human forces such as willful destruction by enemies, by simple wear and tear, or by later building.

In other cases, sites have been preserved, but not in their entirety, because they continued to be used by Christians in later centuries, who often wished to "update" these places to meet new tastes and new demands. The first-time visitor to Rome, for example, can be surprised to visit a famous ancient church like Santa Costanza and find a wedding going on. The visitor's reaction can be "What are all these people doing here?" The answer is that this is still a functioning church, and there are people for whom it is their parish church. Oddly enough, even though the visitors have a genuine and possibly scholarly or professional interest in the ancient church, the people using it for worship are the true descendants of the early Christians who used the church in the fourth and fifth centuries for their own worship services.

Although we can recognize that it is good for this church to continue in use, we can also see how this can destroy the early Christian character of a site. For example, one can go to several ancient Roman churches that now have almost completely baroque interiors. Visitors to Vienna have the same experience going into churches with medieval exteriors but baroque interiors.

But even with these difficulties, many early Christian sites have survived more or less intact, and visiting them helps us to understand a little better the people who inhabited them.

The third type of data deals with sites that have survived but have been covered up by the debris of subsequent history; this data derives from archaeology. Some would call viewing intact sites to be a form of archaeology called surface archaeology; we will use the term here for sites that have to be excavated.

Archaeology has been romanticized, and not just by novelists and film directors; in this discipline's early days, some archaeologists achieved public renown by making elaborate claims and mounting equally elaborate displays of what they had discovered. Magnificent finds such as the treasure of King Tut or the Dead Sea Scrolls capture the imagination, and the world is no doubt richer for them; but they can obscure the real work of the archaeologist.

Archaeology demands a great deal of time, money, and technical expertise, and even these cannot guarantee the success of a dig. Archaeologists usually dig for a season, that is, in a certain time of year, often the summer, since most archaeologists are university professors who must return to school. Thus a dig can stretch out over several years. Archaeologists must sometimes work in severe weather and, increasingly, in hostile or even dangerous political environments. Discovering a temple or beautiful gold object wins publicity, but archaeologists help the study of Early Christianity by discovering things that at first sight may seem pedestrian.

For example, when people plan buildings, they do so in terms of what they want to do in the buildings. If people plan to have large events with masses of participants, like a football game, they build an arena-like structure with little or no feeling of intimacy. If they plan to have small gatherings for something like chamber music or experimental theater, they build a smaller structure, perhaps with the central area or stage in the middle, and seats surrounding it. The building will always reflect the intent of the builders.

When archaeologists discover the remains of an ancient Christian church and are able to determine its outline and structure, scholars then learn not only about the structure of the church but also about the atmosphere its builders wished to create. Was it a place where people came together in intimate fellowship or was it a place where they came to be in awe of an awesome God? Was it a large, impressive building designed to make the worshiper feel insignificant in the divine presence, or was it a small, comfortable place designed to promote a communal feeling? More than one archaeologist has titled her or his book "The Stones Speak."[10]

Not just the stones speak. Digs often uncover smaller objects that can in turn uncover the life of an ancient community. Baptismal fonts can tell us something about baptismal practice; grave-goods can tell us something about belief in the afterlife. An excavated church with a large number of gold liturgical vessels suggests a wealthy community, while a second excavated church with no vessels, or perhaps only one, suggests a poorer community.

Phrases like "can tell us something" or "suggest" reveal something else about archaeology—its limitations. Archaeology deals with physical remains, and scholars must be careful in taking that evidence too far. For example, in the two churches just referred to, it is possible that the second church was actually the wealthy one but, in the face of an enemy invasion, the members of that church removed all the gold vessels and brought them to the first church to hide for safekeeping. When the enemy proved too strong and drove out the believers and captured both churches, the members of the second church were never able to recover their gold vessels, which were later discovered by the archaeologists in the first church, thus suggesting that the first church was the wealthy one. In no way could archaeological evidence alone have told us the story of the gold vessels. The scholar would have to find some ancient narrative that would fill in the details, if one even existed. There are many instances in which the archaeological evidence is the only kind, but scholars always supplement archaeological data with other kinds, if they are available, and vice-versa.

Although this discussion dealt with archaeology's contribution to our knowledge of the "Christian" character of early Christian life, archaeology can also tell us about the everyday life of the ancient believers—what kind of houses they lived in, what kind of stoves they cooked on, and the like. While this information does not reveal the religious character of their lives, it does tell us more about them and helps us to better estimate the character of their faith. For example, if the evidence shows they were poor and at the bottom of the social structure, the egalitarian belief of Christianity that all are equal before God would probably appeal to them.

10. For example, Paul MacKendrick, *The North African Stones Speak* (Chapel Hill, N.C.: University of North Carolina Press, 1980).

4. Iconography

The fourth kind of data is iconography. This is a combination of two Greek words, *eikon,* meaning "image," and *graphe,* meaning "writing." Technically, iconography means "writing with images," that is, conveying meaning visually. Iconography is hardly a familiar word, and at first glance it seems to be only something ancient; but it is as modern as a political campaign.

Although politicians issue position papers and stand by their party's platform or ideology, they also present themselves to the voters visually. Candidates for fiscal office want to appear businesslike and serious so that voters will trust them with money. Green candidates want to show dedication to a clean environment, and so they pose in front of a pristine waterfall (or, conversely, a waste dump, to emphasize the problem). In both examples the picture intends to tell the viewer something about the subject's character or values.

In one sense, the data from Christian art should be included under the second or third categories (Christian sites and archaeology), but it deserves a separate place because it was intended, right from the beginning, to send a deliberate message and not to be interpreted after an accidental survival. The Christians needed iconography because while many of them lived in cities and were often literate, there were many more who could not read; thus pictures became the books of the unlettered. Furthermore, as our brief look at modern political campaigns illustrates, even in a world of books, newspapers, magazines, online discussion groups, and e-mail, visual images still move people.

Although we will consider Christian art more fully in chapter five, let us note how scholars use iconography. Some uses are easily apparent. For example, in the ancient pagan world, when artists wanted to represent divinity, they portrayed light emanating from the head in the form of a circle; this is called a nimbus. The early Christians copied this device, so when the scholar sees some ancient Christian woman or man with a nimbus radiating from her or his head, the scholar knows this person is a saint. To demonstrate the uniqueness of Jesus, artists usually portrayed him with a special nimbus, one with a cross inside it.

Since ancient peoples believed that the realm of the gods lay above the earth, they often believed that divine or supernatural beings had wings to get them back and forth from heaven to earth. The Christians copied this device, too, and they usually portrayed an angel with wings for travel and a nimbus because the angel was also a holy being.

Sometimes the artist could convey the idea not by the outlines of the image but by some interior device, such as color. In Ravenna, in Italy, the Byzantine emperor Justinian (527–565) and his governors put up some magnificent churches with remarkable mosaics. They wanted to show Justinian's Italian subjects that the emperor was God's viceroy on earth. They did it in several ways. In the church of San Vitale, the mosaics portray both Justinian and the empress Theodora, who were still alive at the time, with nimbuses, to show that they were sacred persons because they ruled a Christian empire. The artists then reinforced the notion of imperial sanctity by dressing Jesus in purple robes, purple being the imperial color, thus representing the emperor and empress as Christian and representing Christ as imperial—not subtle, but effective.

5. Using the Evidence

We have demonstrated that a great deal of data about the early Christian world has survived in spite of some severe destruction, but is any of this data more valuable than others?

That question can be answered by both Yes and No, and whether the answer is Yes or No depends upon who is asking the question.

To treat only of the literature, let us look at the Christian writers John Chrysostom and Augustine of Hippo, both of whom left behind an enormous body of literature. Scholars thus know a great deal about these two bishops and about the churches in which they served (in Antioch and Constantinople for John, and in Hippo Regius, North Africa, for Augustine) and the controversies in which they engaged. This knowledge benefits everyone in the field, but especially people studying these two. But scholars can readily apply this evidence to other areas.

Both saints were great homilists, and we have hundreds of extant homilies from their pens, so someone who is not particularly interested in either Chrysostom or Augustine but who is interested in the history of homiletics or liturgy would still find much of value in their writings. Likewise, someone could investigate these to see how Christians appropriated pagan rhetorical techniques. Since preachers had to reach a large audience, linguists can get some grasp of what popular, spoken Greek and Latin were like, as distinct from the formal language used for theological treatises. As noted in the previous chapter, homilists often used familiar images drawn from life, and scholars can get a glimpse of everyday life. Since the homilists frequently addressed matters of concern to their congregations, we can see what elements of Christian life and teaching most mattered to people, at least in a particular place and time.

The list of side benefits to scholars can be lengthened considerably, and what can be said of John Chrysostom and Augustine can be said of almost any Christian writer who left behind a considerable body of work.

On the other hand, someone interested in Early Christianity on Cyprus before the year 300 would not find the sparse literary remains of great value compared to those from Rome or Constantinople, although, consequently, the few items that have survived would therefore be of great value. Scholars in that field would have to rely more upon archaeology.

Inevitably, there are some people or topics that are virtually unknown regardless of the type of source; for example, the popes have traditionally traced their line to Peter the Apostle via a long list of Roman bishops, but for several of the earliest there literally survives only the names—Anacletus, Alexander I, Evaristus—and these survive not in a Roman source but in the writings of a Gallic bishop, Irenaeus of Lyons.[11] Other ancient figures are known from literally only a paragraph or two, such as Polycrates of Ephesus (d. ca. 156), bishop of the most important church in Syria and a major figure in the Quartodeciman Controversy (see chapter three), known only in a fragmentary reference in Eusebius' *Ecclesiastical History*.[12] Finally, there are cases in which the evidence actually raises more questions than it answers. The life and career of Saint Patrick of Ireland provide a classic example of a historical figure hidden behind scant evidence and buried under a welter of theories.

A. Technology

In spite of the historian's inability to generate new data, there is no shortage of it for the early Christian period; just the reverse is true. The written material alone runs to tens of thousands of pages. Indeed, many historians consider dealing with the data to be a problem, and

11. Irenaeus, *Against the Heresies,* III.3.3; ANF 1.416.
12. Eusebius's excerpt in *Eccl. Hist.,* v. 24.2-8; Williamson, 230–232.

one that is only magnified by the ever-growing mountain of secondary material, the books and journal articles composed about Early Christianity (like this one!). Modern computer technology has considerably advanced scholars' ability to work with and through the data.

Technology has always aided scholarship. By the middle of this century microfilming made it possible for scholars to examine on film valuable manuscripts that could not be lent from libraries. Microfiche cards enabled scholars to purchase miniature reproductions of books at a greatly reduced price and, of course, at a size that made it possible to store far more titles than if they had come in book form. More effective communication techniques made interlibrary loans possible so that scholars could get access to needed books at libraries other than their own and often from considerable distance. Fax machines have made it possible to send reproductions immediately to any office with a similar machine.

Computer technology has increased this accessibility by now allowing scholars to access library catalogues to see which libraries have the necessary book or journal. Computerized bibliographies enable scholars to review recently published books and articles in their field; they can even access reviews of books. Thanks to the Internet, some journals are completely online so that students can stay in their rooms and read a journal on the computer screen.

But modern technology has done more than make accessibility to books possible. It has made access to people possible as well.

That may sound a bit silly. After all, people can always communicate by telephone or letter or even by personal contact at a meeting of a learned society. That is so, but it presumes that one scholar knows the other or at least knows about the other. What about new scholars who are not well known yet? What about graduate students and doctoral candidates who are working in new areas? For that matter, what about the more established scholars who are simply hard to reach? Enter e-mail and the Internet.

These make it possible to contact people just as quickly as by telephone but without the cost, and at first sight it seems that this is a cheaper way to do what always had to be done, that is, to know who the scholars are and to contact them. But there is more. Virtually every scholarly discipline has an online discussion group, that is, a group of individuals devoted to the study of a particular field or even a subfield. When the scholar goes online with the group, she or he sends a message to all those in the group, potentially hundreds or even thousands of others. This enables scholars to extend their range considerably.

For example, suppose someone wishes to study Egeria, an important Christian woman writer of the late fourth and early fifth centuries. This person would go online with the group and announce that she or he would like to know about any recent publications on Egeria. Usually within the hour others will send return messages, suggesting titles. Since the whole group sees the messages, often others will get online to say that this title is all right but that this one is even better. Remarks like that inevitably invite more, and often the person who asked the question is treated to an extensive bibliography with a discussion of its value.

Oftentimes someone will go online just to get a question answered, as this author did several times in the writing of this book.

Where the online discussion groups are most helpful is when a group of scholars sets out deliberately to study a topic. In the spring of 1995, one group of scholars tried to determine the date and theology of the Didache, an important second-century text (although some online people argued for a first-century date). Another scholar offered a seminar on Augustine, and he invited his graduate students to put their seminar papers online and to invite responses. In both of these cases, scholars, ranging from established leaders in the field to first-year graduate students to others who were not specialists but were curious about the topic, became involved, and knowledge and criticism that otherwise would have taken years to disseminate via books, journals, and meetings were available immediately to all in the discussion group. It is virtually impossible to estimate the value and importance of this approach to scholarship.

Computer technology has also enabled scholars to deal with the perennial problem of trying to find out what a particular writer or school of writers thought about a particular topic, but to learn this without having to wade knee-deep through thousands of pages of print. Enter the CD-ROM.

Suppose, for example, a scholar wished to know what Augustine taught about the devil. She or he could start at the obvious places, commentaries on Genesis[13] and on the gospels, but since the early Christians believed that the devil played an enormous role in their

13. The third chapter of Genesis does not identify the serpent with the devil, but the Book of Wisdom (2:24) and Revelation (12:9) made the identification, which was accepted by all early Christians.

daily lives, clearly Augustine's references to the devil would far out-strip his biblical commentaries. The scholar could then consult a CD-ROM edition of Augustine's works and institute a search for the word "devil" to see where it appears in Augustine's works. The scholar would also look for related words, such as "demon," "Satan," "Lucifer," "Beelzebub," as well as phrases like "father of lies" or "ancient enemy." Since Augustine wrote in Latin, and since transla-tors do not always agree on vernacular equivalent, the scholar would use the Latin edition of Augustine's works and would look up *dia-bolus* instead of "devil"; the same would apply to the other terms.

Let us further suppose that the scholar has a more focused inter-est, that is, not just Augustine's teaching on the devil but on how the devil tempts human beings. In that case, she or he could enter a re-quest for all entries in which the words "devil" and "temptation" ap-pear close to each other. Often the program may demand that the words appear within a set number of words, such as seven. But since Augustine could have used the phrase "diabolic temptation," the scholar would also consult adjectival forms as well. To this can be added "demonic temptation" as well as the verb form of temptation, such as "the devil tempted," and so forth. This would all be done with Augustine's original language, Latin, and, since Latin is an inflected language, that is, its nouns and adjectives take different forms in dif-ferent cases,[14] the scholar would have to allow for changes in the Latin words.

Hunting for individual words will never substitute for a solid knowledge of the ancient writer, and someone who knows Augustine only via word searches will never know Augustine. On the other hand, this method saves scholars considerable amounts of time and gives them instant access to enormous amounts of material, access that in the past could require months of work.

This outline of how technology affects the understanding of the world of the early Christians can be only provisional because com-puter technology changes constantly. We may safely presume that new generations of scholars will use even more advanced equipment to access and exchange information, and this is all to the good. Modern technology, so evident in things like space programs, the

14. In English, one could say "the bread is on the table" and "the child ate the bread," and the form of "bread" would not change, even though it is the subject in the first form and the direct object in the second. In Latin, bread would be *panis* as a subject and *panem* as a direct object.

military, and entertainment, has significantly advanced our knowledge of a world whose members could never have dreamed of such technology.

B. How Do We Understand the Evidence?

Whenever we have a new present, we have a new past. What happened remains the same, but we understand it differently. Any study of the past involves the ever-changing relationship between the data and the historian.

Everyone has heard of the famous theoretical question physicists cite about whether a tree on a deserted island falls soundlessly if there is no one there to hear it. In a similar way, we can ask whether a past event exists if no one knows about it; it is meaningless because it is unknown. There must be the event and those who know of it.

The study of the past is not passive, that is, we simply do not learn about what happened. We actively involve ourselves in searching for and deciphering the data. In some cases, this is almost visibly obvious: an archaeologist surveys five sites to excavate and chooses, for good professional, personal, and financial reasons, to excavate one of them. No matter how good the reasons, that decision guarantees that we will know what remains in the one chosen site and not in the four unchosen sites. The other sites might be excavated at a future date, but that is irrelevant to us now and may indeed never happen.

Yet rarely does the historian impact the data in that way. Far more frequently the historian influences our knowledge of the past by how she or he understands the data, an understanding of the past determined largely by the present. But we need not go to history to show how we can experience different understandings of the past.

Let us consider an example on the individual level. Suppose a crowd of people sees an automobile accident in which the driver is injured. Paramedics arrive to help the victim. Among the witnesses is a ten-year-old girl, who is so moved by the work of the paramedics that she starts thinking about a career in medicine. Probably all of the people who saw the accident will remember it, but someday a fifty-year-old physician will look back at an incident that determined her career. She will view the accident differently than the other witnesses because it had a formative and lasting effect on her life. Her present determines her view of the past.

We can see this procedure at work on a larger scale in the treatment of women's history, especially in Church history. Until the

1960s, most Christian denominations treated women as second-class citizens (some still do), barring them from many ministries and offices and restricting them to "acceptable" (to the male leaders) tasks. When women began to attain their rightful, equal place in society—the first woman astronaut, the first woman prime minister—it was inevitable that women and many men would re-evaluate women's role(s) in Christian history, that their present would determine their view of the past.

Much emphasis fell upon what women are doing today, but this re-evaluation also included how women were understood historically. At first glance, this seems like a fruitless task. Women played a small role in the Church of the past, so why bother to look?

In one way, this skeptical approach has some value. Those denominations that wanted to keep women in low status often claimed that women never played a role in the Church and therefore should not today. Advocates of equal rights logically feared that if they based their arguments on the role women played in the past, they could be shut out of the present. Therefore they argued that women indeed did not play a prominent role in the early Church, but that is irrelevant because people in the ancient world viewed women as the weaker sex, dependent upon men, and the like, and therefore we need not be bound by what ancient Christians thought. To use an easy analogy, these same ancient Christians thought that the earth was in the center of the universe, but, since we know they were wrong, we do not feel obliged to hold their views. We also know that their views of women were wrong, so who cares what they thought? Women in the contemporary Church should not be bound by history.

However valid and effective that approach might be, there were still scholars who took a different approach, that is, they argued that there is indeed evidence for the role women played in the early Church if only we know how to search it out.

The first step was simple awareness, the awareness that the old ways of looking have gone as far as they can and that new ways are needed.

One of the delightful elements about looking at evidence with different eyes is that familiar passages tell us something new. For example, in Acts 18:26 we read that Priscilla and Aquila taught the faith to Apollos. Too many Christians know only 1 Timothy 2:12, in which someone claiming to be Paul says "I permit no woman to teach," and thus conclude that women did not teach in the first church. Yet Luke, in Acts, preserves evidence suggesting the contrary, and he lists

Priscilla before Aquila. But if both pieces of evidence have always been there, why did Christians notice one and not the other? Because 2 Timothy 2:12 fit the prejudices of later generations, whereas Acts 18:26 did not.

In Romans 16:1 Paul speaks of Phoebe, in the original Greek, as a *diakonos* or "one who serves," the same word used elsewhere of men who serve. Many bibles translated the word "deacon" for men but for Phoebe they had "deaconess," a feminine form, to be sure, but also one implying that men and women *diakonoi* (the plural form of the Greek word) had different functions. Furthermore, in other and later Christian literature, it is clear that deaconesses performed functions of lesser importance than did deacons. Translators put "deaconess" because they assumed that Phoebe functioned like the later deaconesses. Yet, when we look past the translation to the original Greek, we realize that Paul did not distinguish between male and female *diakonoi*. There is absolutely no justification for thinking that women *diakonoi* performed less important functions or even different functions from the men in the Pauline communities.

But even a new look at old texts would take matters only so far. Is there not other evidence? As we saw earlier, historians cannot generate evidence, but they can cast an ever-widening net in a search for what has survived, and sometimes the results are surprising. The Church historian Elizabeth Clark studied church dedications, and she discovered that in the fourth century women played a significant role in the Latin churches in dedicating and supporting local churches. This stood in the common Roman tradition. It was taken for granted—it was the custom—for the local nobility and for wealthy citizens to be benefactors, to build a bath or forum or some other public facility for the community. This demanded considerable resources, and the local citizens showed their gratitude, usually by putting up an inscription which acknowledged the benefactor. Professor Clark demonstrated that Romanized Christians followed in this tradition, that is, wealthy benefactors now endowed churches and the grateful local Christians recorded their generosity with inscriptions.[15] The Church could bar women from hierarchical offices, but they could still play important roles in Church life.

Women do not constitute the only group previously overlooked because ancient authors did not say much about them. The ancient

15. "Patrons, Not Priests: Gender and Power in Late Ancient Christianity," *Gender & History* 2 (1990) 253–273.

Romans considered slaves to be property, and few writers would "waste" space on slaves in their books. In the modern world, we view all people as equal, and we are interested in the status of slaves. For that matter, even free people with money—merchants—were also ignored by Roman writers, who usually came from the landed aristocracy and who considered commerce vulgar (basically, it was your fault if you were not born wealthy and had to earn money), so even the study of middle-class life is something new. The list could include children and non-Romans, who were routinely dismissed as barbarians.

Looking anew at the old evidence includes not only an openness to what might be found but also an aggressive, proactive approach of using new methods. In the ancient world the social sciences, such as psychology and sociology, did not exist. Ancient people were aware that forces they could not identify sometimes moved them; even Paul admitted, "For I do not do the good I want, but the evil I do not want is what I do" (Rom 7:16). They also knew that social classes differentiated people, but they could not study psychological or social forces in any systematic way. Modern scholars have searched the available evidence for psychological and social clues, and they have achieved some impressive results that have not just illuminated these aspects of Christian life but others previously thought to have been explained. For example, we know now that some heresies, traditionally thought to be doctrinal issues, often reflected the aspirations of social, economic, and ethnic groups. The British scholar W.H.C. Frend demonstrated that the North African Donatists, routinely treated as schismatics and heretics, represented a genuinely patriotic African Christianity, often at odds with that of the churches elsewhere in the empire.[16] Psychological studies have often uncovered sexual strains and concerns in Early Christianity.[17] Patricia Cox Miller has emphasized the importance of studying dreams for understanding ancient people, including Christians.[18]

16. W.H.C. Frend, *The Donatist Church: A Movement of Protest in Roman North Africa* (Oxford: Clarendon Press, 1952); see also A.H.M. Jones, "Were the Ancient Heresies National or Social Movements in Disguise?," in Journal of Theological Studies, new series 10 (1959), 280–298; Frend, "Heresy and Schism as Social and National Movements," in *Schism, Heresy and Religious Protest*, Derek Baker, ed. (Cambridge: Cambridge University Press, 1972) 37–56.

17. Steve Young, "Being a Man: The Pursuit of Happiness in *The Shepherd of Hermas*," in Journal of Early Christian Studies 2 (1994), 237–255.

18. *Dreams in Late Antiquity* (Princeton, N.J.: Princeton University Press, 1994).

Occasionally, new approaches have revivified older disciplines. For example, scholars have always used literary analysis to understand Christian literature; in the classic ancient work on interpreting the Bible, Augustine stressed the importance of understanding the function of words to reach God's revelation contained in literature.[19] Today, literary scholarship has gone beyond the standard analysis of a written work as the product of an author and has tried to understand what the work meant to the community in which it was read, a community of understanding, in which the work took on a life of its own; this scholarship also notes the relationship between texts and their users.[20] Inevitably, with new methods, some of the investigations have come up barren, but others have produced remarkable, even exciting, results, such as using the contemporary philosopher Jacques Derrida to interpret Augustine's notion of the self.[21]

Perhaps the most revolutionary change of view has been a religious one, the rise of ecumenism and religious tolerance.

For generations before the ecumenical era, Church historians viewed this period as the formative one for Christian doctrine, when the great Fathers of the Church established the basic tenets of the faith, distinguishing Christianity from Judaism and preserving the truth of the apostolic faith from the wily intrigues of heretics. The Fathers really did not teach anything new; they merely drew out the logical conclusions of the Bible's teaching. Their version of Christianity was the pure one, and the heretics, arriving late to the feast, tried to change what had always been true. The Fathers accomplished all this while fending off persecutions by the bloodthirsty Romans; the Church rewarded their achievements by recognizing their sanctity, for example, *Saint* Cyprian, *Saint* Athanasius.

The Fathers were the Fathers of "the Church," and to understand them correctly, one had to have a correct understanding of the Church. For Catholics, the Church was a hierarchical institution dominated by the papacy, and the Fathers taught the truth as long as their teaching conformed to what Rome believed. For Protestants,

---

19. *On Christian Doctrine.*

20. For an example of the new literary approach, see Mark Vessey, "Conference and Confession: Literary Pragmatics in Augustine's *Apologia contra Hieronymum,*" in Journal of Early Christian Studies 1 (1993), 175–213.

21. See Susan Mennel, "Augustine's 'I': The 'Knowing Subject' and the Self," in Journal of Early Christian Studies 2 (1994), 291–324.

the Church consisted of only the predestined elect who adhered to the plain truth of the Bible, and the Fathers taught the truth if they adhered to the plain truth of the Bible, even if that "plain truth" differed from denomination to denomination. Catholics and Protestants might have disagreed with one another on what the Fathers taught, but they did agree to disagree with the Orthodox churches.

Happily, little of the foregoing applies today. The ecumenical movement has emphasized what the different Christian communities have in common, and few scholars study Early Christianity to prove denominational points. Confessional concerns have given way to historical ones as scholars try to understand what early Christian writers meant when they wrote their texts and what roles those texts played in the community. Clearly, scholars of different communions will draw upon their own religious background in understanding a text—how could they not?—but they no longer approach the text with the assumption that it must teach exactly what their denominations believe. For example, Catholics now recognize that the emergence of Rome as the leading bishopric of the Church occurred over centuries, that it was not recognized immediately by all other Western Christians (and not at all by the Eastern Christians), and was somewhat augmented by the popes' efforts to extend their authority. Protestants now recognize the formative and creative role played by the community in determining the canon or list of books in the Bible—Christians did not recognize the New Testament as we have today until the late fourth century—and they no longer hold the Fathers to a standard developed only in the Reformation.

The ecumenical movement also changed the role of Judaism in Early Christianity. The two faiths did go their own ways, but scholars now recognize the enormous debt the early Christians owed to Judaism (such as the notion of an inspired Scripture), and they also recognize the continued influence of Judaism on Christianity into the third and even the fourth century of the Christian era. Scholars further show a refreshing openness in discussing those points which separated Jews and Christians in these centuries.

Earlier views of the development of doctrine depended upon a simple view of Christian history, that is, that everyone alive then knew what the truths of the faith were and only by ingenious and devious casuistry could the heretics try to undermine the faith by their novel ideas.

Giving one-time "heretics" the benefit of the doubt results from more than a sense of fair play; scholars now recognize that the "truths of the faith" were hardly obvious at the beginnings of Christianity. Paul's letters refer repeatedly to Christians whose teaching differed from his; in Galatians 2 he accuses no less than Peter of failing to understand the role of Gentiles in Christianity. The gospels of Matthew and Luke routinely alter passages in Mark, while the Gospel of John presents a unique view of Jesus. To their credit, the early Christians accepted many different views into their New Testament, and modern scholars, in a sense, have followed their lead, acknowledging the validity of these independent views that existed in Early Christianity even if later generations rejected them.

Scholars have also re-evaluated the contributions of churches often relegated to the periphery of Christian history. The traditional dichotomy of Early Christianity falls into Latin West and Greek East; from those two traditions all of importance emerges. This is a classic example of reading history backwards, that is, since Latins and Greeks dominated later Christian history and became the Churches from which modern Christians are descended, they therefore must have been the only significant groups even in the early period. To be sure, most of the great names did write in Latin or Greek, but scholars now recognize the enormous importance of the "lesser" Churches of the East. Foremost among these are the Syriac and Coptic Churches, the former referring to the Syriac-speaking communities that dominated so much of Christianity's eastern region and the latter to the extensive Egyptian communities outside the Greek-speaking regions around Alexandria. Scholars now evaluate the authors and traditions of these Churches with strict objectivity and not as pale comparisons to Greek and Latin ones. Other Churches in Georgia, Ethiopia, and Armenia have not left as much material as the Syriac and Coptic Churches, and consequently we know less about them; but they, too, have benefited from the new openness.

Strange as it sounds, other beneficiaries of religious tolerance include the Romans, hitherto the merciless pagan persecutors of innocent, saintly Christians. No one denies the reality or the horror of the persecutions, but scholars now realize that, in general, the Romans respected diverse religious traditions, including the Christian, and persecuted only when they thought these believers or traditions threatened the empire. We now recognize that the Christian-Roman interaction involved more than the desire of bloodthirsty pagans to kill Christians.

Finally, and perhaps most importantly, we recognize that we, the modern readers, have views that differ considerably from those of the

Fathers. For example, Saint Augustine believed that sexual activity in marriage, except for purposes of procreation, was at least a venial sin. Saint Jerome, a contemporary of Augustine, believed that in heaven monks and virgins would occupy a higher place than married people. These unfortunate views have cast a pall over Christian views of sexuality for centuries, yet virtually no one would accept them today. Interestingly, their contemporaries who held opposing views, Julian and Jovinian, were condemned as heretics, yet most modern Christians would agree with them on this point more than with Augustine and Jerome.

Although the data will always be finite, our approach to the history of Early Christianity will always be changing. We cannot know what questions future generations will ask or what methods they will develop to answer those questions, but we can know that they will build upon the work of previous generations and that the picture of Early Christianity, probably never to be completed, will always become clearer.[22]

22. For a survey and evaluation of some newer approaches, see Frederick Norris, "Black Marks on the Communities' Manuscripts," in Journal of Early Christian Studies 2 (1994), 443–466.

Chapter Three

The Physical World

A discussion of the physical world in which the early Christians lived echoes our discussion of history, that is, the physical world may be the same—the sun rises in the east and sets in the west—but how people understand their world can differ significantly.

The Christians did little in the area of the physical sciences before the Middle Ages, but their religion did in fact determine how they viewed the world, for example, their belief that the one God of the Bible created it. It also determined how they learned about that world, for example, they mastered astronomy to determine the date of Easter, which then set the schedule for the rest of the liturgical year; they also learned astronomy to determine the locations of heaven and hell.

1. The Cosmos[1]

Today we view the cosmos as limitless, certainly indefinite, possibly infinite. We know that the earth is the third planet from the sun (after Mercury and Venus) and that six more planets are farther away. We further know that all these planets revolve around the sun, which is a star called Sol (the Latin word for Sun), and that we live in the solar

---

1. A good text, accessible to the general reader, is *The Beginnings of Western Science: The European Scientific Tradition in Philosophical, Religious, and Institutional Context, 600 B.C. to A.D. 1450* by David C. Lindberg (Chicago: University of Chicago Press, 1992); as the subtitle indicates, Lindberg relates scientific developments to religious and other developments.

system, that is, the star Sol and all within its gravitational pull. Within this system there are occasional random bodies, such as asteroids and meteors, and several more bodies that move with considerable regularity, the natural satellites or moons that revolve around some of the planets. We also know that our solar system is part of a large system called a galaxy, and the one in which we live is called the Milky Way. Our solar system lies away from the center of the Milky Way, and the sun is one of the lesser stars in the system. Huge as this galaxy is, it is but one of countless galaxies in the universe, which, by current scientific consensus, began with the Big Bang—an inconceivably powerful explosion that sent matter expanding endlessly in all directions sixteen billion years ago. We cannot really speak of a center to this universe, and scientists continually debate the rationality of its structure—is it an orderly whole or are there random elements at work, or does chaos ultimately prevail?

The early Christians shared almost none of these views.

They derived their view of the cosmos largely from the Bible and ancient Greek thinkers such as the philosopher Aristotle (384–322 B.C.) and an Alexandrian astronomer named Claudius Ptolemy (fl. A.D.127–148), who created a cosmology that drew from a variety of earlier Greek thinkers. The ancient universe was minuscule compared to ours, and it was orderly. We call it geocentric because the earth (*gaia* in Greek) occupied the center, and around the earth the planets moved in concentric circles. The planets included the moon and the sun, although not Neptune, Uranus, or Pluto, which had not yet been discovered. Beyond the spheres of the planets were the fixed stars, and, for believers in God, beyond the fixed stars lived God in heaven.

Let us consider some of the particulars, such as the fixed stars. When the ancients looked at the heavens, they could see the sun and moon very clearly and they reasoned that these were very close to earth—correct, of course, in the case of the moon. Everything else in the sky, except for the occasional meteor or asteroid, looked like a star. With a half-dozen exceptions, these stars always appeared in the sky in the same place in relation to the other stars; this was especially noticeable in the formations called constellations. Thus the ancients believed that the stars were fixed, immovable, in some vast space beyond the last circle.

But where did the notion of circles come from? From the half-dozen exceptions to the fixed stars. When we look at planets with the naked eye, which all people did before the invention of the telescope, they look like stars, bright white dots in the sky. But what distinguishes the planets from the other "stars" is that they move. Modern people do not usually realize this because most of us live in heavily populated areas with many sources of artificial light, and ground lights make it difficult to see many stars. Anyone who lives in a city and goes to a deserted area on a clear night can understand this—the sky seems filled with stars in comparison to what one sees in an urban area. Furthermore, modern people do not count on the sky to provide a calendar; we merely look at the one on the wall or on the desk. Nor do we depend upon it for travel; we just consult maps. But ancient people lived in a world without any artificial lighting, and they depended upon the sky and its occupants "for signs and for seasons and for days and years" (Gen 1:14) as well as for a reliable guide in traveling. Not surprisingly, they noticed that not all of the stars were fixed.

The ancients applied the Greek word *planeo,* "to wander," to these stars, recognizing that they were something different. Since they wandered against the background of the fixed stars, they had to be between those stars and the earth. But they were not just out there.

The ancients believed that the earth, as the center of the universe, represented the heaviest part of the cosmos, the most material part. Beyond the immediate atmosphere was an area free of the change that so characterized terrestrial experience. (Some speculate that this may be why the ancients gave names of the gods to some of these planets, such as Mars, Venus, and Saturn.) The planets moved around the earth, but they did so in circles, not necessarily because the ancients could prove that they did, but partially because they considered the circular to be a perfect movement, always at the same distance from the center, moving at the same rate eternally and thus appropriate for extraterrestrial bodies, free of earthly materiality. Since the fixed stars never moved but the planets did, the ancients saw the latter moving constantly in front of the former.

Since we know that the planets, including earth, revolve around the sun and that the moon revolves around the earth and that the planets' orbits are elliptical rather than circular, it is not difficult to realize that a system which assumed that all planets moved in perfect circles around the earth had to cause some problems for observers. Ancient astronomers dealt with this by a variety of hypotheses that historians of science can explain. But it is important to realize that this cosmology had a natural appeal to the early Christians, first because it worked (recall that no one seriously challenged this cosmology until Copernicus in 1543),[2] and second because it fit well with their view of creation.

The Christians took their view of creation from the opening chapters of Genesis. Although that biblical book did not mention anything about spheres, it did make it clear that the created world had a rational origin, that is, in the mind of God. As we shall see later, many Christians, although believing God to be the creator, knew that the Genesis story was not to be taken literally, and so they understood God's creation of light as a symbol of reason, traditionally symbolized by light. In fact, even those who took the account literally could also give it a symbolic value. Genesis presented a picture of primal chaos, symbolized by darkness, and thus when God created light, he banished the chaos by bringing order to chaos (*cosmos* is the Greek word for order).

The acceptance of Genesis also meant that the Christians had to reject some pagan views. For example, Aristotle believed that the cosmos was eternal and had always existed,[3] but the Christians insisted that this could not be so because Scripture said that God had created the heavens and the earth at the beginning of time.

Since Genesis immediately moves from God's creation of the cosmos to the specifics of his creation of the earth, Christians could only speculate about how God established what we call outer space; furthermore, most Christians felt that they could believe what did not contradict the Bible, even if the Bible did not teach that particular point, so Ptolemy's spheres presented no threat to Christian belief.

More importantly, the prevailing Greco-Roman cosmology showed an ordered world, running smoothly day to day. Philosophers called Stoics emphasized this character of the cosmos, but by the end of the first century, the Christian writer Clement of Rome cited this, too, as proof of God's power.[4] Philosophers might be willing to let the world run smoothly on its own, but the Christians always saw the divine hand in it.

In the second century, a group of Christians whom scholars call Gnostics claimed to have a special kind of knowledge (in Greek *gnosis*) about the cosmos, and they built their theories around Greco-

2. A Greek named Aristarchus of Samos (ca. 310–230 B.C.) suggested that the earth revolved around the sun and not vice versa (heliocentrism), but his notion did not catch on. See Lindberg, *Beginnings,* 97–98.

3. Ibid., 54.

4. *First Epistle to the Corinthians* 20, ACW 1, 22–23.

Roman ideas. For example, some of them believed that each of the planetary spheres had an angelic guardian; others believed that after death the individual soul had to pass through a series of spheres and had to know the correct password to give to the angel guardian in order to ascend to heaven. An anti-Gnostic writer named Irenaeus of Lyons recorded that a Gnostic named Basilides believed that emanations from a primal being he called the Unborn Father kept pushing down toward earth, which resulted in 365 heavens between the earth and the Unborn Father, and that angels created the earth.[5] Another second-century writer, Justin Martyr (d. 165) believed that God appointed angels to govern the world on his behalf. For many Christians, the cosmos was organic, alive, and populated by higher beings. This spiritualizing interpretation of the cosmos matched, to an extent, the view of the great pagan philosopher Plotinus, who spoke of the souls of the stars.[6] This all has a distinctly modern ring, although more for New Age spirituality than for science.

2. The Earth

The Christians saw the earth as a creation of God. This at first seems like an obvious point, but it is actually quite important. There are religions for which this world has little or no value: it is a poor reflection of a spiritual world or it is a place from which we must somehow escape. Often these negative views extended from the world as a whole to individual creatures, such as humans. Some Christians considered the body to be corrupt; one of them, Marcion (fl. ca. 140–160), claimed that he never even looked at his body, he found it so offensive. Other Christians, whom scholars call Docetists, accepted their own corruptible bodies as unavoidable. They tried to save Jesus from this horrible fate by claiming that he did not have a real but rather a phantom body. Yet no antimaterialist world-view ever won over the majority of Christians.

The reason for this was the Old Testament, specifically the Book of Genesis. Some Gnostics wished to reject the Old Testament because, they claimed, it contained foolish myths (a talking serpent, a talking donkey), petty legalisms, and a violent god. The majority of Christians, however, recognized that this was the Bible of Jesus and

5. *Against Heresies,* I,24,3–4; ANF 1, 349.

6. Plotinus, *Enneads* IV 8; English trans. Elmer O'Brien, S.J., *The Essential Plotinus* (New York: New American Library, 1964) 64.

Paul, and so they accepted the Hebrew Bible and thus Genesis. Since God created the world and saw that it was good, the Christians could not consider it evil. Nor could they consider any individual creatures to be evil either. Many early Christians, especially monks, considered the body a threat to the soul, and they tried strenuously to control it; furthermore, many Christians used the word "world" to refer to materialism. Yet few Christians could ever go so far as to consider the body or the world as inherently evil. Some Christians had trouble reconciling how a good God could create harmful creatures such as vipers or scorpions, but ultimately they saw a good God reflected in his creation.

Ancient pagans routinely saw the gods manifested in this world; the great scholar of comparative religion, Mircea Eliade, called this phenomenon a hierophany, the manifestation of a higher being in nature. Thus mountains, awesome in height and bulk, represented the strength and permanence of the gods; any plant represented the power of life. Furthermore, pagans could see the human body as a representation of the cosmos, comparing the two eyes that received light to the two lights in the heavens, the sun and moon.[7]

In general, Christians avoided such interpretations of the earth, although they naturally believed that God would provide for their material needs as had the pagan gods. For example, farmers had for generations prayed to the gods for the fertility of their crops and animals. They expected the Christian God to do no less for them. Since the Christians believed him to be active in the world, this was a reasonable expectation.

People routinely thanked God for the good things of this world; they did not see him in it but at work in it. When the third-century Roman emperor Aurelian (270–275) elevated the cult of the Unconquered Sun to his personal religion, the Christians could cite Genesis 1:14-18 to the effect that the emperor's god was merely a creation of the true god. The created world was not God but could point to him. Paul went so far as to contend that knowledge of the creation led to knowledge of God (Rom 1:19-21); those who claimed not to know God were "without excuse."

Clement of Rome used a somewhat different tack. He knew that pagans doubted the resurrection, thinking it was simply ridiculous to believe that someone could rise physically after death. To refute

7. The theories appear in many of Eliade's works; the most convenient source is chapter 4 of *The Sacred and the Profane* (New York: Harper & Row, 1961).

them, he cited the well-known story of the phoenix, a fabled Arabian bird, the only one of its kind, that lived for 500 years, returned to its nest, and was consumed in fire; but from its ashes emerged a worm that eventually grew into a new phoenix.[8] This hardly sounds like a convincing proof to the modern mind, but Clement placed great confidence in it, although he used other "proofs" as well.

He was not alone in looking to the natural world for a theological proof. At the end of the second century, the Christians were moving toward accepting specifically Christian writings as inspired, that is, they were shaping the New Testament. Many gospels circulated then, and the Christians struggled to determine which and how many could be authentic. Irenaeus argued that there must be only four gospels, partly from Scriptural proof (the four winged creatures of Ezekiel 1:5-14 and Revelation 4:6-8) and partly from the nature of the physical world:

> For it is impossible that the Gospels should be in number either more or fewer than these. For since there are four regions of the world wherein they are, and four principal winds, and the Church is a seed sown in the whole earth, and the Gospel is the Church's pillar and ground, and the breath of life: it is natural that it should have four pillars. . . .[9]

For Irenaeus, numbers possessed a symbolic value, an old idea going back to the Greek philosopher Pythagoras (fl. ca. 530 B.C.), and thus the numerical structure of the physical world had a value into which he could tap to prove an important theological point, that is, which gospels authentically contained Christ's revelation.

The notion that Francis of Assisi was the first Christian to appreciate the natural world is simply mistaken. The ancient believers thought of the earth as a good place, corrupted by the evil of sin, but still a good place. The author of the Book of Revelation and many Christians after him believed that Jesus would come to this planet again to establish an earthly paradise. While most Christians eventually abandoned that idea, they continued to see the earth as a theater of divine activity. They saw God in the beauty and order of his creation; Clement and Irenaeus and others could not have written as they

8. The *First Epistle to the Corinthians* 25, ACW 1, 25; Clement could have taken the well-known story from any of several Roman writers; see note 79, ACW 1, 109.

9. *Against Heresies* II,11,8; ANF 1; 428–429.

did without that vision. Besides, in caring for the world they followed a divine exemplar:

> For God so loved the world that he gave his only Son, so that everyone who believes in him may not perish but may have eternal life. Indeed, God did not send the Son into the world to condemn the world, but in order that the world might be saved through him (John 3:16-17).

The ancient cosmos was a limited one, and some scholars would even call it a comfortable one, that is, humans were in the middle of an ordered world, the center of God's universe. The same could be said of the earth, which for most people was quite small. Thanks to Aristotle, the ancients knew that the world was round, but no one had any idea of its extent. People accepted the idea that huge sections were simply *terra incognita,* unknown land, to them, and they lived in their own corner of the globe. Inevitably some people wanted to explore those unknown areas; as early as the sixth century B.C., a Greek named Pytheas of Marseilles sailed into the North Atlantic far enough to see the aurora borealis. In the second century A.D., Greek merchants representing the Roman emperor Marcus Aurelius paid a call on the Chinese emperor in Beijing. Roman commercial fleets regularly sailed to India, and sailors from Alexandria navigated south on the Nile into Ethiopia.

But these people were few and far between. Few people traveled outside the Roman Empire. The empire's borders were often hostile ones, such as the Rhine, across which the Romans faced barbarian German tribes, or the Sahara, a desert region where Roman farmers and Bedouin nomads shared an often uneasy peace. Only in the East did Rome confront another empire, Persia, and the two great states vacillated between war and peace. The Christians generally shared the views of other Roman citizens: that they lived in the greatest and most civilized state of the day, that the Romans should keep the barbarians at bay, and that the Persians represented a constant threat. Some Christians evangelized among the barbarians and Persians, but scholars know little about contacts between the Roman Christians and these others.

The Romans considered some countries, such as Armenia, client states, that is, they kept their independence, but they did nothing to threaten Rome. Occasionally, a client state could prove to be a problem, as the Near Eastern kingdom of Palmyra did in the third century, but for the most part there was peace. Christians in these countries had regular relations with their Roman counterparts; for example, bishops from the client states attended ecumenical councils held in the empire.

If few people traveled outside the empire, not many traveled even within it. Most people lived and died close to where they were born, especially if they lived in rural areas. When we read about the travels of Paul, we get the impression of a Church on the move; this is reinforced by the travels of Lydia, Priscilla, Aquila, Apollos, and other Christians passing through the Acts of the Apostles. But we should also realize that Jesus apparently spent almost his entire life in Galilee, except for a few trips to Jerusalem; his life was far more typical than Paul's.

But even if few Christians traveled, they still considered themselves citizens of the world. They recognized no barriers to the spread of their faith, and they saw their faith as something that might unite all peoples, even barbarians and Persians, and, in that sense, they believed in the oneness of humanity.

3. The Other Worlds

Creation included the earth and the surrounding spheres, but it also included heaven and hell, which could be physically understood, and possibly another spiritual world as well.

Modern believers in an afterlife envision it as a spiritual reality or a state of being, but the ancients believed that both heaven and hell could be located physically.

A. Heaven[10]

Heaven had two meanings for the early Christians. The first meant the sky, as we use the phrase "the heavens opened" to mean a severe rainstorm. As such, this heaven formed part of the cosmos, of the physical world.

The other heaven was the realm of God and the blessed angels who lived beyond the cosmos, beyond the fixed stars. As such, it became the goal of the Christians to win a place there; those whom the Church believed to have succeeded in that quest were called saints.

10. "Heaven," in *EEXty,* I. 512–514.

The New Testament does not provide an extensive vision of heaven. In Luke 16:19-31, the parable of the rich man and the beggar Lazarus, heaven is a place in which the inequities of earth are made good. The rich man who abused the beggar at his gate wakes up in fiery torment after his death, suffering bitter thirst; looking up, he sees Lazarus in the bosom of Abraham. Between heaven and hell, "a great chasm has been fixed."

Several gospel passages portray the blessed afterlife as a great dinner (Matt 8:11-12, Luke 13:29), and this motif repeats itself in the earliest art of the catacombs. John's gospel speaks of heavenly mansions (14:1-3), while Paul in Philippians refers to a heavenly citizenship (3:20). He believed that the body would rise in a spiritual form (1 Cor 15:35-58, Phil 3:21), and he apparently believed in a series of heavens, at least three (2 Cor 12:2).

Much of this speculation about a blessed afterlife derives from Greek thought. For centuries the Jews believed only in a place called Sheol, a post-mortem netherworld of continued existence but not a place of rewards and punishments. The Greeks, who arrived in the Near East with Alexander the Great, brought with them strong notions of immortality and of reward and punishment in the life to come. Some Jewish groups, especially apocalyptic ones, picked up these ideas; the Christians took them from these Jewish groups but found them expanded in the Greco-Roman world.

Clearly no one could explain such a reality as heaven, and early Christian writers recognized this. But that did not stop them from contemplating it. The blatant physicality of the first notions repelled the more intellectual believers; by the end of the second century, Clement of Alexandria (fl. ca. 190–205) suggested that in heaven the saved receive the vision of God, a theme picked up by later theologians, especially as Christians stressed heaven as a place for the immortal souls of the saved and placed less emphasis upon the resurrected body. Some Christians, especially in the East, believed that humans would be deified, that is, made like gods in heaven, although the Westerners settled for simple beatification, that is, a state of eternal blessedness. It is likely, however, that many less educated believers preferred the more graphic image of an idealized earth in the world to come.

Significantly for Christians, heaven was not closed; that is, they believed in the organic unity of the believers on earth and those in heaven. Angels, the winged divine messengers (*angelos* is Greek for messenger), traditionally made the trip back and forth between heaven and earth, but by the late fourth century and very much in the fifth, Christians developed a belief that the saints, and especially Jesus' mother, Mary, still played an active role in their lives as intercessors. They could intercede with us before God, carrying our prayers and petitions to the divine throne. This represented a departure from the Bible; 1 Timothy 2:5 names Christ Jesus as the only mediator between God and humanity. Several theories exist to explain this, such as the Arian Controversy, which had the effect of pushing Christ into heaven and thus making him impossible as a mediator,[11] or that the saints acted like late Roman petty nobility, who interceded with the imperial government on behalf of merchants and small landholders.[12] Whichever may be correct, it is clear that heaven, no matter how distant physically and spiritually, was somehow always present.

B. Hell[13]

Hell, often expressed as Hades, from the Greek concept of the underworld, or as Gehenna, from Matthew 13:42 (in Greek), represented the physical and spiritual opposite of heaven. The Christians believed it was an actual physical place and that its threatening fires really burned human bodies, but hell also represented a frightening spiritual reality, an eternity of despair, an eternity of separation from God.

The New Testament does not provide many details about hell. The Gospel of Matthew says that God prepared it for the devil and his angels (25:41) but that it also received sinners after death; all the gospels warn people lest they sin their way into hell. The Book of Revelation provides the most vivid descriptions—a bottomless pit (9:1, 20:3), a lake of fire (20:14). It portrays the punishments of hell in very physical terms, and this notion persisted. The two terms Hades and Gehenna became confusing; eventually most Christians concluded that Hades represented a temporary state of punishment

11. Joseph Jungmann, *The Place of Christ in Liturgical Prayer* (New York: Alba House, 1965) 264–278; idem, *Pastoral Liturgy* (New York: Herder and Herder, 1962) 1–63.

12. Peter Brown, *The Cult of the Saints* (Chicago: University of Chicago Press, 1980) 56–68.

13. See Alan Bernstein, *The Formation of Hell* (Ithaca, N.Y.: Cornell University Press, 1993).

between the death of the individual and the Last Judgment, when Christ would come to judge all humans, and that Gehenna represented a place of eternal punishment.

Although the seventeenth-century poet John Milton in his epic poem *Paradise Lost* placed hell nowhere, for early Christians hell had location. By the second century they had confidently placed it in the center of the earth, a place of total darkness and at the opposite end of the cosmos from God. In general, the Christians did not elaborate upon the kinds of punishment suffered there by the damned. The Greek notion of the punishment fitting the crime (Tantalus, Sisyphus) appears in some apocalyptic works, but medieval literature, especially Dante, produced the most striking images of infernal punishment. Satan and the lesser evil angels, usually called demons, inhabited hell along with the damned, functioning as both jailers and inmates.

This mobility that characterized some of heaven's citizens also characterized some of hell's. Just as angels could leave heaven for earth to carry divine messages, so demons could come up to earth to tempt people and occasionally to possess them. To counteract this, angels or saints came to earth to aid humans against temptation. How the angels and devils made it back and forth from their homes to earth was uncertain; artists solved the problem by giving them wings.

Just as the boundaries between earth and these other regions could be crossed, even the boundary between heaven and hell was occasionally uncertain. An African writer, Tertullian (ca. 210), suggested that saints in heaven would be able to see the damned in hell (in fact, he actually said that would be one of the "joys" of heaven).[14]

All Christians believed that heaven was eternal, but some, like Origen, suggested that God could redeem all his creatures, including the devil, and thus hell would not exist eternally. Most Christians considered this view unbiblical (Revelation 20:10 speaks of the devil's being tormented in the lake of fire "forever and ever"), and they accepted the eternity of hell.

Hell, like heaven, lay beyond the abilities of anyone to explain clearly, but it did form part of the Christian world-view. Indeed, the inhabitants of both heaven and hell regularly intervened in the world of humans, and most ancients just took it for granted that spiritual beings were a part of this world.

14. Tertullian, *On the Shows* 30; ANF 3, 91.

C. Another World?

Several Christian thinkers shared a belief held by pagan philosophers that before our birth in human bodies, our souls lived in a spiritual, disembodied world. At first sight, this world sounds like heaven, but there were important distinctions. The apostle Paul had said that we would have spiritual bodies after the resurrection, but this theory allowed for no bodies at all. It also included another important concept, that is, that these souls sinned while in this spiritual world, and God punished them by encasing them in bodies until such time as the humans could escape from them. Some thinkers thought that they would return to the spiritual world, but this varied from the Pauline notion of a risen body. Besides, if this spiritual world were heaven, how could the souls have sinned in the first place, and could they not sin again?

This notion did not present the difficulties for pagan philosophers that it did for Christians. The incarnation, the taking of a human body by the Son of God, not only made up for the sin of Adam and Eve but also elevated human nature; the Garden of Eden could have been a perfect earthly location, but heaven represented a different, unique, and higher form of life. Since pagan philosophers did not accept the notion of original sin and did not believe in the incarnation, they could see this spiritual world as a place to which the soul could return after its sojourn or exile in the body.

The pre-existence of souls, definitely believed by Origen and probably by Augustine at some point in his life, never became a point of Christian doctrine. Debates raged about the origin of the soul, but, as best as scholars can tell, few Christians believed in a spiritual world of pre-existent souls.

4. Time

We live not only in space but also in time. The two relate inextricably because the measure of time depends upon space. Although we define a day as twenty-four hours, we know that this is not exact, and we actually define a day as the time the earth takes to make one revolution on its (imaginary) axis. The same is true but even more obviously so for a year. We define a year as 365 days, but our need to add an extra day every fourth or leap year proves the inaccuracy of this form of measurement. The true definition of a year is the time the earth takes to orbit the sun.

The mysterious nature of time puzzled Christians; Augustine admitted that if no one asked him about time, he knew what it was, but if someone did ask him, he did not know.[15] To be sure, most Christians took it for granted, accepting the division of time into days, months, and years, but clearly they had their own unique view of it.

Surprising to most moderns, that view did not include the notion of B.C. and A.D., which, on the surface, seems to be the most obvious Christian contribution to time. This calendar reckoning is indeed an early Christian one, but it appears only in the sixth century, and even then it did not meet with immediate acceptance. A Syrian monk, Dionysius Exiguus (d. ca. 545) lived in Rome in the first half of the sixth century. A great scholar, he edited the decrees of Church councils as well as the decrees of the popes; this work made possible the medieval development of canon law. Dionysius also translated several important Greek Christian works into Latin, and he worked on computing the date of Easter, a crucial question for the Church, since that date determined most of the liturgical year.

His computative interest led Dionysius to revise the calendar, suggesting that Christians center the measurement of time on the birth of Christ, which, to him, represented the dawn of a new age. He concluded that Jesus was born 753 years after the founding of Rome, but, unfortunately, that turned out to be wrong. Under his system, Herod the Great, who, the evangelist Matthew says, reigned when Jesus was born, died in 4 B.C., so the date of Jesus' birth is off by at least four years. But Dionysius' general concept caught on, and since then Christians have measured time "Before Christ" (B.C.) and *Anno Domini* (A.D.), Latin for "in the year of the Lord." Because the Western nations that use this calendar have become so politically and economically dominant in the modern world, other nations have begun to use this calendar but without the religious reference, for example, Jews use B.C.E. and C.E., that is, "Before the Common Era" and the "Common Era." Scholarly publications in religion often use that system.

Yet important as Dionysius' work has been, it came at the end of the early Christian period, and thus the most influential Christian contribution to the concept of time had little influence on most ancient Christians, who were happy to use Roman dating, the so-called Julian calendar. Most ancient Christian calendars concern themselves not with the computation of a particular year but rather with the Christian events, such as feast days, within that year.

15. *Confessions* XI, xiv.17; 230.

But the Christians had notions of time far beyond determining feast days. For example, Christians wanted to know what God was doing before the creation. Augustine quotes a snide question of the Manichees as to what God was doing before he created the world; in response he cited an old joke that God was busy creating hell for people who asked questions like that.[16] The great African did not just dismiss the question humorously; he suggested that we cannot properly speak of time before the creation. God lives eternally; we live in time, and thus there is no time without creation. Other Christian thinkers would have agreed with that view.

Their view of time was linear, that is, it moved in a line from the creation until the end. This may seem obvious, but many ancient pagans viewed time cyclically, that is, they believed that the physical world moved through cycles, constantly returning to the beginning.[17] They derived this notion from a constant observation—the sun rose and set every day, the moon went through a monthly cycle, the sun returned every year to the point where it had been the year before. Primitive peoples do not see themselves as masters of nature but as part of it; they thus logically concluded that if space moved in cycles, why not time as well? And these were not just the views of simple people. The Stoics believed that all creation moved in a great cycle, eventually returning to its starting point, only to repeat itself again. This repetition differed from the purely physical one in which the sun moves through the same path every year; the Stoics believed that history would literally repeat itself. An early Stoic named Chrysippus (ca. 280–205 B.C.) wrote:

> . . . the cosmos is restored anew in a precisely similar arrangement as before. The stars again move in their orbits, each performing its revolution in the former period, without any variation. Socrates and Plato and each individual person will live again, with the same friends and fellow citizens. They will go through the same experiences and the same activities. Every city and village will be restored just as it was. And this restoration of the universe takes place, not once, but over and over again—indeed to all eternity without end.[18]

16. Ibid., XI.xii.14; 229.

17. The classic account remains *The Myth of the Eternal Return: Cosmos and History* by Mircea Eliade (Princeton, N.J.: Princeton University Press, 1971).

18. Cited in C.K. Barrett, *The New Testament Background: Selected Documents* (New York: Harper & Row, 1961) 63–64.

But Genesis and the incarnation would not let Christians believe that. God had created the world once and had interceded in history in a unique and decisive way in the person of Jesus; time would have an end, the Second Coming of Christ.

Time may not have been endless, but the very first Christians and many in succeeding generations saw it as extremely limited. In 1 Thessalonians 4:17, Paul says that he expects to be alive when Jesus returns to earth; he repeats this notion in 1 Corinthians 15:51. In the Book of Revelation the seer John offers a series of visions of "what must soon take place" (1:1). But both Paul and John were wrong; the world did not end. The Second Letter of Peter, written *circa* 125, shows that the continued delay of Christ's return had made some Christians skeptical of the very idea, so the pseudonymous author dismisses them as "scoffers" (3:3), and rather speciously tries to rationalize the matter by saying that "with the Lord one day is like a thousand years, and a thousand years are like one day" (3:8). Jesus may be gone now for almost a century, but it only seems like a few hours to him!

But the author of 2 Peter had nothing to worry about; people continued to believe in an imminent end of the world. In the middle of the early Christian period, the African writer Cyprian (ca. 250) suggested that only the presence of Christians in the empire kept Rome from the day of judgment; at the end of the period, Pope Gregory I (the Great), appalled at the sufferings of the Italians at the hands of the Lombards, mused about an imminent end.[19] In every century of Christian history, people have believed that the time is short, that the day of wrath approaches; undeterred by two thousand years of Church history, they continue to read into the Bible and find the signs.

As with so many other areas of Early Christianity, scholars cannot accurately determine how widespread these views were. Certainly many first-century Christians held them, but it is difficult to picture people in the fourth century, for example, believing strongly in an imminent end that had now been three centuries in coming. Yet all Christians believed that God could intervene to end history at any moment, and, in that sense at least, they differed from their pagan contemporaries. The same God who created the world kept it in existence and could destroy it at will.

19. Robert E. McNally, "Gregory the Great on His Declining World," in *Archivum Historiae Pontificiae* 16 (1978) 7–26.

Although they could not know when God would end the world, the early Christians knew that he would definitely do so. They firmly believed that he would precede the destruction with signs. In Mark 13:4 the disciples ask Jesus, "Tell us, when will this be, and what will be the sign that all these things are about to be accomplished?" The Lord gives them the signs and then warns them about "false messiahs and false prophets" who will "produce signs and omens, to lead astray" (13:22).

After the signs came the end. The Book of Revelation presents a vivid picture of the Last Judgment, with all the evil ones being sent to perdition, those who had died rising from the grave (earthly or watery), the present heaven (i.e., the sky) and earth passing away, and a new heaven and a new earth coming into being (chs. 20–21). The seer John saves his best imagery for the New Jerusalem (21:1-22:5), coming down from heaven with pearly gates and streets of gold (21:21). [This verse is the source of those two famous images.]

At the Last Judgment, the Lamb (Christ) will look in the book of life for those to be saved. Revelation implied that there would be a new era on earth, thus the heavenly Jerusalem descending to earth. This view caught on; for example, in the second century, an Asian bishop named Papias said "Days will come when vines will grow each with ten thousand shoots, and on each shoot ten thousand branches, and on each branch ten thousand clusters, and on each cluster ten thousand grapes. Each grape, when pressed, will yield twenty-five thousand measures of wine."[20] But as Christian theology became more sophisticated, these notions seemed coarse, and in the fourth century, the great Church historian Eusebius of Caesarea could dismiss Papias' ideas as foolish.[21] The later Christians continued to believe in an end to time at the Last Judgment, but they also believed that there would be no more time after that; the current heaven and earth would both pass away, and with them time. A new era, an eternal one, would begin, and time would be no more.

Every society divides history into times, usually based upon historical changes. For example, Western peoples often refer to the nineteenth century as the time of the Industrial Revolution because their societies changed significantly as a result of industrialization. This designation has no qualitative value and is obviously inapplicable

20. Fragment preserved by Irenaeus of Lyons; Francis X. Glimm, trans., in *The Apostolic Fathers,* FC 1, 384–385.

21. *Ecclesiastical History* iii.39; cited in FC 1, 376.

to those societies that did not industrialize. The title merely reflects the historical situation for the West. Views of historical periods and even names may change as historians rethink the events of the past.

Yet in the ancient world people could delimit time on more than just historical grounds. Many Christians believed that the Hexameron, the six-day creation of the world, contained both history and symbol.[22] Moderns can readily understand the history but not the symbol. In the modern world the word "symbol" has connotations of irrelevance, as in the notion that something has only symbolic value. Although psychology has demonstrated that symbols indeed have great value in every age, for the most part we see facts as true, and symbols as marginal. But in the ancient world symbols carried great weight. For example, the emperor Gaius Caligula (37–41) insisted that a statue of him be put up in the Temple at Jerusalem. The Jews refused and objected strongly that Gentiles were not permitted in the Temple. The emperor, of course, would not have been there personally, but, to the ancient mind, if he was there symbolically, he was there in reality. Caligula would not back down on this point and the Jews prepared to resist by force if necessary, but the emperor's death obviated the problem.[23]

Augustine studied the opening chapters of Genesis almost endlessly, and he concluded that the six days of creation symbolized the six ages of history.[24] For Augustine, history meant biblical history, which he divided into the periods 1) from Adam to Noah, 2) from Noah to Abraham, 3) from Abraham to David, 4) from David to the Babylonian Captivity, 5) from the Babylonian Captivity to the career of Jesus, and 6) from the career of Jesus to the end of the world. Augustine went beyond history in his interpretation. Since God rested on the seventh day, that symbolized the eternal rest of the blessed in heaven.

For us moderns these can be just convenient divisions, reflecting clear distinctions in biblical history, but not for Augustine. These divisions were forecast by the biblical text. He believed that he did not

22. The seventh-century Greek writer Anastasius of Sinai claimed that as early as the sub-apostolic age Christians agreed that "the work of six days" referred to Christ and the Church; cited in FC 1, 383.

23. Josephus, *The Antiquities of the Jews,* book xviii, ch. 8, in *The Works of Josephus,* William Whiston, trans. (Lynn, Mass.: Hendrickson Publishers, 1980) 389–392.

24. This notion is found in many texts, such as *Eighty-Three Different Questions,* No. 58, David Mosher, trans., FC 70 (1982) 105–106.

impose these ages on the text but rather drew them from the text. He did not have a choice in the matter; the text demanded this conclusion from him.

Some Christians disagreed with Augustine, but that does not detract from the central point that history could have meaning for Christians, reflecting the intent of God in the Scriptures. In fact, the idea that Scripture could tell believers about the nature of time is a scriptural idea. The Book of Daniel initiates Jewish apocalypticism, that is, the belief that history tends toward a final point, now about to be revealed. In a pioneering book, the German biblical scholar Hans Conzelmann argued that, for the evangelist Luke, time fell into three periods—that of the Father before the coming of Christ, the career of Jesus, and the age of the spirit after the ascension.[25]

Liturgical time reflected the Christian celebration of certain days. The most important day was the Lord's Day, celebrated on Sunday, the day on which Jesus rose from the dead. Because Sunday came after Saturday, the Sabbath, the seventh day, it was sometimes called the eighth day, indicative of a new creation, but it still reflected the resurrection. The first Christians honored Sunday by reserving the Lord's Supper for that day. When the emperor Constantine converted to Christianity, he made Sunday an official holiday (321), and then it began to take on the characteristics of a day of rest, a notion still preserved today, although often without religious overtones.

Not all Christians observed Sunday, nor did they observe it as the only Lord's Day. Some Christians of Jewish descent (Jewish-Christians is the common designation) and people who thought like them continued to observe the Sabbath as a holy day, and they also kept Sunday. The Sabbath retained its biblical character of a day of rest, whereas Sunday became the day when Christians assembled in fellowship. Eventually the Church abandoned this practice, and Sunday became the only weekly Christian feast day.

But there were other feast days, those that occurred only once a year. This followed a longstanding practice among the Jews, who observed Passover and Hannukah. The pagan Romans had similar customs. Saturnalia, the feast of the god Saturn, they considered the merriest day of the year, a day on which gifts were exchanged and slaves received a temporary liberty. The Romans also observed the Lupercalia, a day of fertility rites, and New Year's Day. It was only

---

25. *The Theology of Saint Luke,* Geoffrey Buswell, trans. (London: Faber & Faber, 1960).

natural that Roman Christians would want to have their own festivals, and these generally fell into two categories.

The first category included those days observed by all in the Church, the most obvious and the most troublesome being Easter, the anniversary of Christ's resurrection. The Greek term for Easter is *pascha,* from the Hebrew *pasah* or Passover. The origin in Passover shows one of the chief characteristics of Easter, that is, it always remained part of the entire Holy Week observance, starting with Holy Thursday, the day on which many Christians believed Jesus had celebrated his last Passover meal with his immediate disciples. In fact, in the earliest Church, emphasis fell upon Christ himself as the Paschal Lamb (1 Cor 5:6-8), a Pauline symbol repeated constantly in the Book of Revelation. The growth of Sunday as a Christian replacement for the Sabbath inevitably increased the importance of Easter.

But Easter brought a great problem with it. When should it be celebrated? Some Christians, such as Melito of Sardis (d. ca. 190), an Asian bishop, wanted to celebrate it on the Jewish Passover. The Jews started their celebration of Passover on sunset of the fourteenth day after the full moon at the spring equinox; this was 14 Nisan, the first month of the Jewish religious year. Possibly the link of spring and the resurrection, both symbols of new life, made this dating attractive to many Christians in Syria and Asia Minor. The Latin word for fourteen is *quartodecimus,* and thus the Christians who opted for this form of dating were called Quartodecimans.

This meant, however, that unlike Christmas, Easter did not fall annually on the same day or even on the same day of the week. Since it commemorated Christ's resurrection, the Christians increasingly wanted to celebrate it on Sunday, the Lord's Day. Furthermore, by the late second century, most Christians were Gentiles who followed the Julian calendar, a solar calendar, and they rejected the lunar calendar used by the Jews. The Asians and Syrians soon found themselves in opposition to many of their fellow Christians; scholars call this the Quartodeciman Controversy.

Basically, it centered on the value of ecclesiastical traditions. The Quartodecimans argued that their tradition went back to the time of the apostles, which it probably did, but their opponents claimed that their own traditions were just as valuable. Probably behind the opponents' views lay not only the difference in solar and lunar calendars but also a reluctance to have a Jewish feast determine the date for the most important Christian feast. In the mid-second century, two opponents, the Quartodeciman Polycarp of Smyrna (d. ca. 156) and Anicetus of Rome (ca. 155–ca. 166), agreed to disagree on this issue; but by the end of the century, Victor I of Rome (189–198) had decided to excommunicate those bishops who disagreed with the Roman dating. The matter was not settled until the first ecumenical council at Nicaea in 325, which rejected Quartodecimanism.[26]

The winners in this debate did not enjoy complete fruits of victory, since the Julian calendar contained many inaccuracies and needed occasional fixing. Determining the date of Easter remained a problem for some centuries to come.

When the Christians found a way of determining the date of Easter, they could determine the rest of the liturgical year. The Holy Thursday/Good Friday/Holy Saturday/Easter sequence became the most sacred period of the Christian year, and, in some sense, marked the beginning of a new year. For example, converts received their baptism during Holy Week, often at Easter, a symbol of their new life as the new liturgical year began. (Some churches also baptized at Pentecost and, in the Eastern Mediterranean, at Epiphany.) So significant had Easter become that by the end of the fourth century it had acquired a forty-day preparatory period called Lent, originally observed by candidates preparing for baptism and then extended to all Christians.

Christmas was another universal feast, but one that took much longer than Easter to be established. The early Christians may not have been sure how to calculate the liturgical feast of Easter, but at least they knew it had followed after the Passover. No one had any idea on what day Jesus had been born because the gospels give no clue.

Scholars are uncertain as to the origins of Christmas, which has no biblical foundation. Two gospels, Matthew and Luke, speak of Jesus' birth, but no New Testament book mentions a celebration in connection with it. Some scholars believe that when the Docetists and some Gnostics questioned Jesus' genuine physicality, other Christians reacted by recalling liturgically his birth. In the third century some Christians suggested that since the new year began on the vernal equinox, March 25, then that would be an appropriate date for Christ's birth. An African, Sextus Julius Africanus (ca. 160–ca. 240), took this in a different direction, saying that since this day commemorated the creation, it was a better date for Christ's creation, that

26. For a clear and brief account of this controversy, see "Pasch, Paschal Controversy," in *EEXty,* II. 876–878.

is, his formation in Mary's womb. This meant that he would have been born nine months later on December 25.

But that reasoning never achieved much popularity, and many scholars believe that the Christians adopted the now familiar date to oppose the cult of the Sun, whose birthday fell on December 25 (in association with the winter solstice). By 336, that date had established itself in Rome and was spreading. Not until the sixth century, however, did Christmas become important enough to get its own preparatory time, Advent (from the Latin *advenire,* to come toward).[27]

For Christians, the Holy Week sequence and Christmas were sacred days, literally qualitatively different from other days of the year and to be marked by prayer and pious gestures such as fasting. There was the sense that Jesus was somehow among the community again, but this time ritually. The "Happy Easter" and "Merry Christmas" so familiar today took centuries to develop. Inevitably, other universally observed feasts appeared; for example, by the late fourth century Christians celebrated the feast of Christ's ascension, always on a Thursday, since it occurred forty days (Acts 1:3) after Easter.[28]

The second type of feast day was that of the local saint or martyr. This possibly grew out of the Roman practice of having a memorial meal on the anniversary of someone's death. There was no good reason for Christian converts to abandon such a practice, although they quickly changed its character. Since they considered death an entrance to heavenly life, they celebrated the person's date of death. Obviously, those closely related to the deceased would have had the normal pain and grief, but within the community, this date recalled the making of a saint. The more important the deceased, the more important the date, especially if she or he had died a martyr's death. As the number of saints and martyrs increased, so did the number of feasts. Many observances continued to be local ones, but some saints achieved such stature that their feasts became universal ones. For example, by the fourth century, both Eastern and Western churches honored John the Baptist with two feasts, one for his death, August 29, and one for his nativity, June 24, six months before Christmas Eve, because of Luke's gospel that said John's mother Elizabeth was six months pregnant when the angel Gabriel appeared to Mary (1:36).

27. See Susan K. Roll, *Toward the Origins of Christmas* (Grand Rapids, Mich.: Wm. B. Eerdmans Pub. Co., 1995).

28. For the references to its observance, see "Ascension," in *EECh,* I, 83.

The Christians always considered the feasts of saints and martyrs to be memorial ones and not like Christmas and Easter, times when Christ came especially close to his people.

In viewing the physical world, as in other matters, the early Christians combined the existing ideas of the pagans and Jews and added interpretations of their own—sometimes important, sometimes trivial—but always intended to make sense out of God's creation.

Chapter Four
Others

Because the Christians emerged as the largest and most significant group from the ancient world, it would be easy to concentrate too much on them, on their internal development and concerns, and to forget that others shared the world with them. In this chapter we will examine who the others were and how the Christians understood them. Significantly, some of the "others" were Christians too.

1. The Jews[1]

Judaism and Christianity have gone their separate ways since the first century. Too often this separation has led to misunderstanding, mis-

---

1. Because of the importance of this topic, an enormous body of literature deals with it; the reader is advised to consult the standard scholarly journals, especially those dealing with the Bible and Early Christianity, for the literature. Some standard titles include: E. P. Sanders has edited two books entitled *Jewish and Christian Self-Definition* (Philadelphia: Fortress Press, 1980 and 1981) that survey the field; Alan Segal's *Rebecca's Children: Judaism and Christianity in the Roman World* (Cambridge: Harvard University Press, 1986) offers a sociological perspective; James D. G. Dunn has edited *Jews and Christians: The Parting of the Ways* (Tübingen: Mohr, 1992), and Judith Lieu has edited *The Jews Among Pagans and Christians in the Roman Empire* (London: Routledge, 1992); for a picture of the later period, see Jacob Neusner, *Judaism and Christianity in the Age of Constantine* (Chicago: University of Chicago Press, 1987). A standard work is *Verus Israel* by M. Simon, originally published in French in 1948, now available in English (Oxford: Oxford University Press, 1986). A new work, *Related Strangers: Jews and Christians, 70–170 C.E.*, by Stephen Wilson

trust, suspicion, and outright hostility, the last of these being a particular problem for Christians who only in the twentieth century have, for the most part, recognized the immorality and horror of anti-Semitism.

But this history of division can mislead us about the enormous influence that Judaism had on nascent Christianity.[2]

From the Jews the Christians acquired a belief in one God, something that seems obvious today (even atheists reject belief in one god, not in many), but it was hardly obvious in the first century. If a Christian preacher told a crowd of pagans that Jesus was the son of God, the pagans would legitimately wonder "Which one?" The Jews also gave the Christians a higher ethical code than that of the pagan world. Even pagan writers who did not care for the Jews had to acknowledge that.

That Christianity spread to the West rather than to Asia can be attributed to a variety of factors, such as the conquests of Alexander the Great, which made Greek a universal language, the language of Paul and the gospel writers. It could also be attributed to Rome, since Judea (the name for the Roman province) formed the empire's eastern frontier; thus the early missionaries, all citizens of the empire, took the familiar route to the West.

But there was also the Jewish Diaspora, that is, the scattering of Jews into settlements outside of their homeland, a situation that exists even today. In the Acts of the Apostles, Luke portrays Paul as following the route of the Diaspora on his missionary journeys. Scholars legitimately question the historicity of much of Acts,[3] but they concede that the general movement to the West followed the line of Acts. Furthermore, virtually every location scholars advance for the writing of a biblical book had a sizeable Diasporan community, such as Antioch, Rome, and Alexandria.

Judaism had a number of sects, ranging from the apocalyptic group at Qumran, which produced the Dead Sea Scrolls, to the Pharisees, who were active in people's daily lives, to the Sad-

(Minneapolis: Augsburg Fortress, 1996) deals with a formative period for both religions.

2. This book deals with the development of Christianity; there was also Christian influence on the development of Judaism. See some of the titles listed in note 1.

3. See Ben Witherington, ed., *History, Literature and Society in the Book of Acts* (New York: Cambridge University Press, 1996).

ducean guardians of tradition. Similar groups emerged in the history of Christianity, possibly even as descendants of these Jewish groups.[4] Like the Jews, the Christians had sacred meals, liturgical washing, and simplified places of worship; for example, synagogues functioned primarily as meeting places, and early Christians met in the homes of prominent members. At no point, however, did the Christians have anything comparable to the Temple at Jerusalem.

Perhaps the most distinctive gift that Judaism gave Christianity was the Bible, that is to say, the notion of written revelation. Pagan religions had meals and washings, and some educated people believed in one god, but Scripture was altogether something different. To be sure, the pagans had sacred writings, the most famous of which were the Sibylline books, a collection of prophecies by several pagan female seers. Yet, in the Christian era, the Roman senate had to approve any consultation of those books, a far cry from the routine and even daily reading of Scripture by Christians and Jews. Since so much of Christian history, both intellectual and institutional, has depended upon how the Bible has been interpreted, one can say without exaggeration that Jewish influence on the younger religion continues to be enormous.

But the two religions did separate, which was not the initial intention of the Christians. The apostle Paul hoped to reconcile the Christian message with the Jews. His own writings show a continued respect for, and devotion to, the Law of the Hebrew Scriptures, and the Acts of the Apostles pictures him constantly preaching in synagogues before turning to the Gentiles. In Paul's day, that is, approximately 35 to 64, the Christians were reaching out, unsuccessfully, to the Jews.

The Christians obviously thought that their message was compatible with Judaism, indeed fulfilled it, but the majority of Jews did not. This is understandable. The Jewish religion had worked a miracle. A small, politically insignificant people had survived, with the help of its god, while the Egyptians, Assyrians, Babylonians, and other great Near Eastern peoples had passed into history. (The Jews also outlasted the Roman Empire.) The Jews could see the harm Rome had wrought in the Near East, they were appalled at the moral laxity of the Romans, and they were saddened by the empire's

4. See W.H.C. Frend, *The Rise of Christianity* (Philadelphia: Fortress Press, 1984) ch. 1.

treatment of the downtrodden.[5] Their faith, their loyalty to the Law, had preserved them; why should they give that up for some new teaching? Judaism had experienced tension, and the Jewish historian Josephus could enumerate distinct groups among the Jews.[6] But all Jews were concerned with how to live the authentic Jewish life as prescribed in the Scriptures, and few found sympathy with the notion that a crucified carpenter's son from Galilee had fulfilled the Hebrew Scriptures' prophecies.

Some Jews resented the Christians and resisted them strongly. We say "some" because the vast majority of Jews probably had little contact with Christians in these early years. These problems occasionally broke into public disputes and riots, and inevitably both sides found more and more to resent in the other. Ironically, both paid the price with the pagans.

Many Roman pagans did not like the Jews because they were a people apart, a unique people who insisted on their own laws and on their chosenness—the last a ludicrous notion to the all-conquering Romans. This dislike magnified significantly during the Romano-Jewish War of 66–70. On the other hand, the Romans respected the Jews as an ancient people with well-authenticated historical traditions and a strong moral code.

At first the Romans could not tell Jews from Christians. Acts 18:12-17 portrays the Roman proconsul of Achaia, Gallio, dismissing a Christian-Jewish dispute as a purely Jewish matter. In 49 the emperor Claudius expelled the Jews from Rome because of rioting started by someone named Chrestus, which most scholars interpret to mean Christus (Christ in Latin), which means that Christian Jews had arrived in Rome and were preaching and causing an upheaval in the Roman Jewish community. The first time we can be sure the Romans knew the difference occurs with Nero's persecution of the Christians in 64.[7]

5. In the fourth century the anti-Christian emperor Julian (361–363) complained about the pagan lack of charity toward others, and contrasted this with the concern shown by Christians and Jews. See *Creeds, Councils, and Controversies,* James Stevenson, ed. (London: SPCK, 1966) 66–67.

6. *The Jewish War,* ii.viii.2; Whiston, 476. Josephus here describes what he calls "philosophical" sects; there were also political groups, such as the Zealots.

7. Chrestus is found in Suetonius' *Lives of the Caesars,* Claudius, xxv. 4; the account of the fire and the persecution in Tacitus' *Annales,* xv.44.2–8; both texts are translated in *A New Eusebius,* 1–3.

Although Roman revolutionaries drove Nero from the throne and to suicide in 68, the Christians had acquired a stigma; for the Jews, any connection with the Christians could only be negative. When the Jewish War broke out in 66, the Christians were no longer anxious to be associated with the Jews. Both sides were moving irrevocably apart.

The separation derived from more than both communities' relations with the Romans or from the tensions of two communities living side by side in some cities. It derived from religion. Judaism of that day, as noted above, contained more than one sect; even John the Baptist's sect survived his death. (Acts 19:1-7 portrays followers of John active in Asia Minor twenty years after his death.) But Christianity, thanks largely to Paul, did not view itself as another Jewish sect but rather as a faith to be preached to the world and open to Gentiles. The Jews did proselytize (Matt 23:15), but Christianity tried to convert all persons and, after Paul, did not require them to observe the Jewish laws, a direct, frontal rejection of what most Jews held sacred.

The Christians had to justify what they had done, and they claimed that Jesus had come to fulfill the Law (Matt 5:17), which said, in effect, that the Law had largely served its purpose. Furthermore, by not following Jesus, the fulfillment of the Law, the Jews had failed to be good Jews. Christianity, not Judaism, was the *verus Israel,*[8] the true Israel, called by God.

For the Christians, the Romano-Jewish War proved that this attitude was correct. To the surprise of the Romans, the Jews held them at bay and prolonged the war for four years, with some resistance groups holding out until 73 at Masada. When the Romans captured Jerusalem, they destroyed it utterly. The Gospel of Mark, written soon after the event, portrays (13:1) the disciples earlier praising the size and beauty of the (now demolished) Temple of Jerusalem. These rather natural remarks of rustic disciples seeing the wonders of the big city provoke Jesus into a fierce prediction of the destruction that will befall Jerusalem and the sufferings of his disciples in synagogues as well before kings and governors, an allusion Mark put in about Christian suffering at the hands of Jews and pagans. The early Christians saw the destruction of Jerusalem and its Temple as the fulfillment of Jesus' prophecy and a divine judgment on a sinful people. What better proof that the religion of the Jews no longer carried God's Word?

8. Phrase taken from M. Simon's book of that title; see note 1.

But this view did not really work. The Jews survived and regenerated themselves both politically and religiously. Politically, Judea remained a Roman province, but in 132 the Jews revolted for a second time. This time the war lasted three years and again ended in defeat for the Jews, who were forbidden to go anywhere near Jerusalem. Yet again the people survived. The rabbis revived Judaism with study, a sense of community, and an emphasis upon the interpretation of the Law. The Temple and Jewish freedom may have disappeared, but the Jews had not, despite what the Christians had expected.

Many Jews considered the Christians apostates, who had given up the faith of their ancestors and created an increasingly Gentile religion. Many Christians believed that the Jews as a people (and not just a Jerusalem mob) had rejected Jesus and that God had in turn rejected them. The continued existence of the Jews puzzled many Christians.

Not all Jewish-Christian contacts were hostile. No doubt in many parts of the empire members of the two faiths lived in harmony—farmers united by the struggle against drought or flood, merchants brought together by the vagaries of the sea and the roads. We can also assume that Jews and Christians, face to face with pagan idolatry, must have recognized what they had in common. The second-century Christian intellectual Justin Martyr (d. 165) debated with a learned Jew named Trypho, while the great scholars Origen and Jerome both consulted and studied with Jewish scholars. Clearly some Christians found Judaism attractive religiously as well. Even in circumstances in which there was little respect between the two, Roman law kept the peace between them. An officially pagan state favored neither, although the continued growth of the Christians frightened the pagans (see the next section).

But the tensions were there, largely caused by the Christians' need to justify their role as the True Israel and the various elements associated with that role, such as the appropriation of the Hebrew Scriptures, which they began to call the Old Testament. That name is important. It derived from growing belief in a unique, inspired, and fixed collection of Christian Scriptures that were to be called the New Testament, but the word "old" suggested that this revelation had seen its day. That the Jews continued to use it only proved to the Christians that they had failed to recognize the new situation Jesus had brought to humanity.

[Some modern, ecumenically minded Christians now use the phrases Hebrew Bible for the Old Testament, and Christian Scriptures for the New Testament. The problem with this designation is that Christians believe that the Old Testament is indeed part of their Scriptures, and to limit the phrase "Christian Scriptures" to the New Testament is theologically incorrect. Some scholars are experimenting with the title Second Testament for the New Testament; this would make it possible for Christians to maintain their complete Bible without using offensive titles.]

Let us briefly consider some elements of the early Christian approach to Jews and Judaism. In the second century a Christian writer named Barnabas, from either Egypt or Syria, wrote a letter to a now unknown correspondent, in which he argued that the Jewish people had rejected the Lord's covenant, not just at the time of Jesus but actually back at the incident of the golden calf (Exod 32), and that the covenant now belonged to the Christians. Barnabas accused the Jews of interpreting the Scriptures and especially the Law literally, but now the Christians fulfilled those injunctions spiritually, for example, circumcision is of the heart, not of the flesh; the eighth day (Sunday) had replaced the seventh day (Sabbath).

In the early third century, the African theologian Tertullian wrote a book entitled *Adversus Judaeos (Against the Jews),* in which he argued that the Jews had rejected the grace of the Lord and so the Old Testament interpreted literally has no more validity. Christians are now the only true expositors of the Law, which must be taken spiritually, for example, the law of love has replaced the notion of an eye for an eye.

Both of these works date before the conversion of Constantine and the establishment of a Christian empire, that is, from a time when the Christians lived in fear of persecution and might have been expected to see enemies on several sides. Might not the situation have changed for the better after the conversion?

The situation did not change, partially because anti-Semitism had become ingrained in the Christian world-view and partially because, in Christian eyes, the Jews stubbornly refused to recognize the truth of the new religion, presumably manifested by the triumph of the Church over its pagan persecutors. Thus the fourth-century Church historian Eusebius of Caesarea still interpreted the fall of Jerusalem this way:

> . . . and as if holy men had utterly abandoned the royal metropolis of the Jews and the entire Jewish land, the judgment of God at last overtook them for their abominable crimes against Christ and

His apostles, completely blotting that wicked generation from among men.[9]

If anything, the triumph of Christianity spurred some Christians to even stronger measures. John Chrysostom (ca. 350–407), bishop of Antioch and later of Constantinople, led a genuinely heroic resistance to imperial influence in the affairs of the Church, opposed the unscrupulous and politically minded patriarch of Alexandria, Theophilus, and suffered exile and an early death for his moral preaching. But all of his struggle and suffering did not make him sympathetic to the Jews, whom he denounced in a series of homilies, citing the worn theme of the Jewish rejection of the true Messiah and their deserved punishment for that rejection. Interestingly, these homilies also reveal that the Jews of Antioch continued to be a significant social force in the city and, furthermore, that some Antiochene Christians found Judaism attractive, which no doubt added fuel to the bishop's fire.

A Western bishop, Ambrose of Milan (ca. 339–397), revealed anti-Semitism at its pettiest. When a group of Christians in Callinicum, in Syria, burned down a synagogue, the Christian Roman emperor Theodosius I rightly ordered them to pay for its rebuilding. Ambrose considered it outrageous that the emperor would force Christians to build a house of worship for Jews, and he severely censured the emperor for this order, which Theodosius subsequently revoked. Unfortunately, the bishop's anti-Semitism carried more weight than the emperor's sense of justice.

Few people in the ancient world believed in religious freedom, and it was probably inevitable that once the Christians came to power they would restrict the legal rights of others. In the fourth century the Roman state forbade Jews to make converts, forbade Jewish-Christian marriages, and excluded Jews from some public offices. These restrictions increased in the next century. When the civil authority, believed to be headed by an emperor chosen by God, treated the Jews as second-class citizens, one can understand why ordinary Christians felt that anti-Jewish acts were permissible.

There is no way to end this section on a positive note. Anti-Semitism has been a sad and repulsive feature of Christian life from the ancient world until today. Maybe the present generation will learn from history.

9. *Hist. Eccl.,* iii.5; Williamson, 111.

2. *The Pagans*[10]

Because we read history backwards, the Christians' relationship with the Jews, still a problem, looms as very important; but, in fact, Christian-pagan relations concerned the ancients far more. As with virtually everything else considered in this book, we must break this discussion into two chronological segments, the pagan Roman Empire and the Christian Roman Empire.

Who were the pagans? They can best be defined negatively as those who were neither Christians nor Jews. In general, paganism meant belief in many gods (polytheism), which differentiated it from the monotheism (belief in one god) of the biblical peoples. Some philosophic "pagans" believed in one god, but the number of gods in which one believed distinguished Jews and Christians from pagans most obviously.

Although the common image of the pagans of that era is of blood-thirsty Romans cheering on the lions in the arena, the term covered very diverse peoples, such as the barbarians (another negative term, this one meaning non-Greeks and non-Romans) who lived outside of the empire: the Germanic and Celtic tribes east of the Rhine, north of the Danube, and in the non-Roman parts of the British Isles, and the various North African tribes normally separated from the Romans by the desert but occasionally irrupting into Roman space, as well as the tribes of Arabia, destined some day to influence mightily the Roman world. Like many Romans, the Christians had occasional contact with them but actually knew little about what gods, if any, these people worshiped; but, as barbarians, they were pagans.

Different from the barbarians were the empires to the east, primarily the Persians, who were Zoroastrians, and then the Indians and even the distant Chinese. What the Christians knew about their religions

---

10. There is also a sizeable literature on this topic, albeit not as much as on Christians and Jews. The articles on "Paganism and Christianity" in *EEXty* and "Pagan-Paganism" in *EECh* are good places to start. Some accessible titles are: Robin Lane Fox, *Pagans and Christians* (New York: Knopf, 1987); Robert Wilken, *The Christians as the Pagans Saw Them* (New Haven: Yale University Press, 1987); the volumes by E. P. Sanders cited in note 1 of this chapter; a classic work, E. R. Dodds' *Pagan and Christian in an Age of Anxiety* (Cambridge: Cambridge University Press, 1965) should also be consulted.

depended upon Greek and Roman visitors' accounts.[11] The same was true for the kingdoms to the south, the African kingdoms of Ethiopia and Nubia, destined some day for evangelization, but initially as unknown as the rest.

Thus, for most ancient Christians, pagan meant the Greco-Roman pagans, but even that designation had varied meanings. For instance, most moderns learn about the Greco-Roman gods via mythology, the great tales of the Golden Fleece and the Trojan War, of the wanderings of Odysseus and Aeneas, and of many lesser tales, such as the weaving contest between Athena and Arachne. Names like Zeus and Hera, Diana and Apollo are familiar, and while there were pagans in the Christian era who worshiped those gods, paganism meant far more than that.

This resulted largely from Roman political practice. Although the Roman persecution of the Christians leads most people to think that the empire enforced intolerance, in fact just the reverse was true. When the Romans conquered or absorbed a new area, they set their sights on two absolutes: peace and taxes. On everything else, they were willing to compromise. For example, they frequently governed areas through client kings, that is, a native ruler who pledged allegiance to Rome and who was thus allowed to continue ruling and even to pass along the kingship to descendants. If the king turned against the Romans, they might then depose him and make his kingdom a Roman province, but they might just as easily find a local replacement for him. The Judean dynasty of the Herods provides a good example of this. Basically, the Romans strove to find what would work.

The Romans had a religion of their own, but they saw no need to impose it on others. They tolerated other religions as long as these posed no threat to the empire. One religion they did persecute was Druidism in Britain, because they believed that the Druids promoted British nationalism and thus threatened Rome. As noted earlier, they persecuted the Christians occasionally but not on a regular basis; the first persecution, Nero's, resulted from the emperor's need for a scapegoat for the Great Fire of 64, and he probably chose the Christians because theirs was a new and foreign cult and thus suspicious to many people. It is very significant that when this was going

11. See Max Cary and E. H. Warmington, *The Ancient Explorers* (Baltimore: Penguin Books, 1963) for a readable survey of the Western knowledge of Asian lands.

on in the capital, the Roman governors in the provinces did not persecute the Christians.

Religious tolerance made political sense. The Romans ruled lands which had been independent for centuries and which had often been great states—Macedonia, Judea, Egypt, Greece. They ruled peoples far different from one another, physically and culturally—Britons and Syrians and North Africans. They ruled an empire which stretched from the Atlantic to the Near Eastern desert, from the North Sea to the northern Sahara, and which required months to traverse, and then only if traveling conditions were favorable. In sum, the Romans faced so many problems governing that they had no need to multiply those problems by religious intolerance.

This meant that large numbers of cults could be found within one political entity, and when Christianity encountered "paganism," it encountered national and local cults, virility and fertility gods, peaceful and bloody rites, ancient and new religions. In some cases, Christianity advanced rapidly but in others very slowly, depending to an extent on the strength of the local religion. As we saw earlier in this chapter, Christianity made little headway among the Jews, whose ancient, vibrant religion combined with the historical nationalism ("the God of our Fathers") to maintain itself. On the other hand, Christianity apparently had considerable early success in North Africa, which had become heavily Christian by the end of the third century, while the empire as a whole remained pagan.

But why did the pagans not convert in large numbers as soon as they encountered Christianity? The Christians believed that one reason they did not was because their gods had power and thus were often able to answer people's prayers. At first glance, this seems ridiculous. How could Christians believe pagan gods had power? Because the Christians believed the gods were actually demons, using their power to delude the pagans into false worship.

This was not the biblical view. The anonymous prophet whom scholars call Second Isaiah provided the classic biblical attitude toward the pagan gods. He described a pagan craftsman making an idol:

> The carpenter stretches a line, marks it out with a stylus, fashions it with planes, and marks it with a compass; he makes it in human form, with human beauty, to be set up in a shrine. He cuts down cedars and chooses a holm tree or an oak and lets it grow strong among the trees of the forest. He plants a cedar and the rain nourishes it. Then it can be used as fuel. Part of it he takes and warms

himself; he kindles a fire and warms himself; he kindles a fire and bakes bread. Then he makes a god and worships it, makes a carved image and bows down before it. Half of it he burns in the fire; over this half he roasts meat, eats it and is satisfied. He also warms himself and says, "Ah, I am warm, I can feel the fire." The rest of it he makes into a god, his idol, bows down to it and worships it; he prays to it and says, "Save me, for you are my god" (Isa 44:13-17).

The prophet made it clear that the carpenter got more from the meal and the heat than he ever would from the god, which is simply nothing.

This notion of the pagan gods as literally fantasies of their worshipers appears again in narrative form in the story of Bel and the Dragon, accepted by some Christians as part of the biblical Book of Daniel (ch. 14). The king of Babylon told the prophet Daniel that the god Bel must exist because every evening the god consumed the food and drink left in front of his statue. That evening Daniel secretly spread ashes in front of the statue, and in the morning he showed the king the footprints of the pagan priests who had collected the god's food and eaten it themselves. Once again the Jews showed that the pagan god did not exist.

This attitude initially appealed to the Christians, but it waned quickly. The Christians had a very strong belief in the devil who, they believed, waged constant war against the human race. They considered him to be in league with their enemies, especially the Romans, whom the seer John pilloried in the Book of Revelation.

Significantly, in Revelation 9:20, John linked demons with idols, writing of those who "did not repent of the works of their hands or give up worshiping demons and idols of gold and silver and bronze and stone and wood, which cannot see or hear or walk. . . ."

Second-century Christians quickly took up this clue and identified the gods of the pagans as demons. This fit well into their world-view, that the demons were urging the Romans to persecute Christians as part of evil's overall assault on the forces of good.[12] Once the identification had been made, it persisted throughout the entire early Christian period. Now the Christians had an explanation for the power of the pagan gods. The power was not apparent; it was indeed

12. Two good surveys of the Early Christian view of demons are: Jeffrey Burton Russell, *Satan: The Early Christian Tradition* (Ithaca: Cornell University Press, 1981), and Everett Ferguson, *The Demonology of the Early Christian World* (Lewiston, N.Y.: Edwin Mellen Press, 1984).

real. But it derived not from gods who did not exist, but from demons, who most certainly did exist.

Although this answer might suffice for then, how do modern scholars explain paganism's enduring popularity?

Religions exist because they meet human needs; when people stop believing that their religion can help them, they abandon it. Although Jews and Christians reviled paganism as idolatry or devil-worship, its adherents usually saw it as a positive force in their lives. Clearly, the nature of that positive force varied from sect to sect, but it was always there. What forms did it take?

A. The Popular Cults

Probably the most important characteristic of ancient paganism was its personalism. Alexander the Great had created, however briefly, an empire encompassing the eastern ancient Mediterranean world and much of the Near East; and the Romans did likewise with the whole of the Mediterranean, which they called *mare nostrum* or "our sea." The older gods of the Greeks had supported the *polis* or city-state, but under the Romans the individual had little or nothing to say about government. Many scholars believe that as people turned away from civic involvement, they favored religions that offered personal achievement and satisfaction. Although the ancient Jews and Christians found many of these cults coarse and vulgar, modern scholars, armed with the findings of the psychology of religion, can recognize the cults' values.[13]

For example, many pagan cults dealt with virility and fertility. They had a strongly sexual nature, but they also had rites of initiation—a secret oath, a sacred meal, a ritual washing. Today we understand the importance of sexuality in people's self-image and self-esteem. Thus we can understand why many people venerated the Great Mother, who not only brought fertility to the land and the herds but also to humans. The best-known Great Mother resided at Eleusis in Greece, but variants of her could be found throughout the empire, such as Isis

13. For a helpful survey of these, see the contributions of various scholars to *Religions of Antiquity,* Robert Seltzer, ed. (New York: Macmillan Publishing Company, 1989) esp. 237–304; for handy texts in translation, see Luther Martin, *Hellenistic Religions: An Introduction* (Oxford: Oxford University Press, 1987). Two older collections by Frederick C. Grant, *Hellenistic Religions* (Indianapolis: Bobbs-Merrill, 1953) and *Ancient Roman Religion* (Indianapolis: Bobbs-Merrill, 1957) remain very valuable.

in Egypt. Although moderns reject the notion of a woman as a "baby machine" (the phrase is Napoleon's), in the ancient world, to be a "real woman" was to have many children. Thus a fertility goddess provided not only children to help on the farm or to care for parents who would eventually age, but she also gave a woman personal self-esteem and a place in her community because she gave her husband heirs. Even today this ancient standard continues to be a determinant for women in many societies.

The Great Mother at Eleusis, however, admitted men to her mysteries. For many people, then and now, the world can be a frightening place, and the image of a nourishing, nurturing mother has great appeal. The rites of Demeter, the ritual name of the Great Mother, included her reunion with her daughter Persephone, who had been kidnaped by the forces of darkness and taken underworld, and with Zeus, the father of Persephone. Thus, the rites re-establish harmony among the gods and, by extension, among humans. Those initiated into the rites could enjoy this maternally organized harmony. "No longer was the initiate homeless in the midst of a chaotic, labyrinthian world: through initiation, the rule of that world was revealed as that of divine providence."[14]

The definition of "real man" unfortunately had many of the same connotations then as now—sexual prowess, physical strength, occasional violence. For real men, Mithra became a favorite god. He was originally a Persian virility god whose cult spread to the West; Roman soldiers considered him a special favorite. Wherever the Roman armies went, Mithra went along. Almost astonishingly, one can find a *mithraeum* or Mithraic cultic site at Hadrian's Wall in northern England, about as far as one could get from Persia in the ancient world.

Mithra performed the great act of slaying the cosmic bull, and, although scholars are uncertain, the bull may symbolize the constellation Taurus. Some Romans venerated him as *Sol Invictus Mithras,* that is, Mithras the Unconquered Sun, and his birthday fell on December 25. Sun gods usually symbolized resurrection, a victory over the forces of darkness; artists portrayed Mithra as a warrior or a hunter, reinforcing this notion of victory. Only men could partake of his cult, which involved seven grades of initiation, associated with the seven planetary spheres.

14. Martin, *Hellenistic Religions,* 62.

This discussion of the rites of the Great Mother and of Mithra included several mentions of rites and initiations. This aspect of their worship provides the name for these religions in general, that is, mystery religions. The word mystery in English suggests the detective story, a puzzle that can be solved, but the Greek word *musterion* meant something far different—a reality, usually divine, that lay beyond our capacity to understand. We could never "solve" the mystery. The gods' actions might always be beyond us, but we could still partake of their benevolence.

The gods, like royalty, could not be approached informally. A certain protocol had to be followed—titles to be known, acts to be performed—before one could enter the presence of the divine. And just as one did not approach royalty unaccompanied, so the gods had priests and priestesses and attendants to show the devotee how to approach the deity, what to say and how to act. When the believer had gone through this process, that is, had been initiated, she or he then shared the benefits of the mysteries.

This approach has a strong psychological attraction. Everyone wants to belong somewhere; even political radicals who reject society seek out others who reject it too. The mysteries offered people who may have been poor or uneducated or physically unimposing or social outcasts a chance to transcend all these perceived deficiencies. By partaking of the sacred meal, by repeating the hallowed words (sometimes in an archaic language),[15] by viewing the hidden rite, by washing in the sacred spring or fountain, the ordinary mortal could become one with the god or at least share in the god's bounty. That these rites were often carried out at night or in darkened locations only added to their mysterious nature. Those outside the group could know little about it, which reinforced the initiate's feeling of being special.

More than that, initiation into the mysteries made people feel reborn, younger, stronger, more secure, and better able to face the world. They had passed through the darknesses, overcome the evil forces, and now had the god(s) on their side.

The appeal of this type of cult to the socially marginalized is obvious, but wealthy, aristocratic people, and even the Roman emperors Hadrian and Marcus Aurelius also took part in the mysteries. Few aspects of Roman life had such a democratic element.

15. Recall that down to the 1960s, the Roman Catholic Church offered Mass in Latin, an archaic language unfamiliar to most of the worshipers.

Something equally obvious is the similarity these rites bore to Christianity. This presents a serious historical problem. On the surface, it would appear that Christianity borrowed much from them—initiation rites, sacred washings, sacred meals. But since the mysteries involved secrecy, information about them often dates late in the period, after they had been in existence for some time, and Christianity might even have influenced them. Clearly the two interacted, and, although scholars must concede the chronological primacy of some of the mystery religions, their relation to Christianity remains a puzzle. On the other hand, no one doubts that both offered potential initiates many of the same things, such as rebirth, personal worth, an opportunity to be one with the god. One can say securely that Christianity's offer of personal regeneration and salvation clearly met the religious needs of many people.

Although the mystery religions often met Christianity on similar ground and thus became its greatest rivals, not all popular cults were mystery religions. The Romans had the *lares et penates,* little gods of house and home, whom pious people would venerate. People could encounter the gods at sacred springs or on sacred mountains. Heroes of old could intercede for people with the gods or even help them directly. As the empire became Christian, saints replaced the heroes in the esteem of the people. Rural shrines could be found all over the empire; some saints, like Martin of Tours (d. 397), destroyed them in order to abolish idolatry. Destruction of idols had a biblical foundation (2 Kgs 23), and it continued into the Middle Ages, for example, the Anglo-Saxon missionary Boniface cut down a sacred oak of the pagan Saxons. But the pagans had more mundane needs that did not require participation in a mystery religion or even a visit to a cult site. They could seek short-term assistance from oracles, magic, and astrology.

B. Oracles

As noted earlier, besides a belief in one god versus many, nothing differentiated Christians and Jews from pagans as much as how they sought divine revelation. The biblical peoples are the peoples of the Book, that is, they look for divine revelation in written sources, but not just for doctrinal issues or major decisions. They consulted the Bible for practical advice on how to live everyday life, for example, Proverbs 17:14: "The beginning of strife is like letting out water; so stop before the quarrel breaks out." To be sure, most Christians could get through the day without consulting the Bible, but they always had it if they needed it; pagans did not.

Like the Christians and Jews, the pagans, too, needed advice, such as whether to carry out a business project or to arrange a marriage for a son or daughter. For this, they could go to an oracle, a place they believed had been made sacred by the presence of a god. The oracles could be local and modest or they could be large and famous, such as the oracle of Apollo at Delphi in Greece. The devotee would approach the priest or priestess, explain what she or he wanted, and then the priest or priestess would inform the devotee what to do. This could involve a simple bit of advice, but, more often, it included some form of divination, that is, a calling upon the god for information. Sometimes the devotee would sleep overnight at the oracle, presumably dream, and, upon rising, seek an interpretation of the dream. Sometimes the priest or priestess would interpret the flight of birds or the entrails of a sacrificial animal (haruspicy); there were also the casting of lots and even necromancy, the summoning of the spirits of the dead (known even in the Bible: Saul consulted the witch of Endor in 1 Samuel 28). Here are two examples of questions asked at oracles, the first a rather natural inquiry but the second quite problematic:

> Heracleidas asks (the gods) and inquires concerning a child, if he is to have one by Aigle, his present wife.
>
> Lysanias asks (the gods) if the child which Annyla is bearing is his.[16]

Most modern people cannot accept the validity of these approaches, but clearly ancient people did, because the oracles originated far back in pagan antiquity and survived well into the Christian period.

Furthermore, the Christians kept some of these ideas. They abandoned looking at the flights of birds and at entrails, but, in the Middle Ages, Christians routinely flocked to the burial places of saints or to famous shrines in the hope that the blessed deceased would communicate to them. Many wanted to be buried in the same place as the saint. Even in today's world many people still consult a medium to speak to the dead, and superstition remains rampant. Ancient pagans who were magically transported into the modern world would not

---

16. Texts cited in Grant, *Hellenistic Religions,* 33–34.

have to look too far or too long to find people who shared their views.

C. Magic

If oracular religion seems odd to us, magic does not; everyone has seen a magician at one time or another. What fascinates us is that the magician seems to be able to overcome the laws of nature; for example, it is naturally impossible to pull a rabbit out of an empty hat because if nothing is in the hat, how can the rabbit be there?

When one reads the Bible, somewhat similar events occur; for example, it violates the laws of nature to walk on water (Mark 6:48-50) or to turn water into wine (John 2:1-12). Yet Christians would say that these are not magic tricks but miracles, that is, God suspended the laws of nature to accomplish some beneficent work. The key phrase in that definition is "suspend the laws of nature."

When we see a magician in action, we do not believe that the laws of nature are being suspended or overcome or anything like that. The magician works as naturally as we do but uses mechanical tricks or prestidigitation (sleight of hand). There is a natural explanation to all the magician does, but we in the audience simply do not know what it is. If we had her or his skill, we could do it too. Miracles, on the other hand, actually do go beyond the laws of nature, and as such represent a divine intervention in human affairs.

This is a good example of how our world view differs from that of the ancients, who believed that magicians were not just tricksters but powerful people who routinely called upon divine power. Pagans who asked help of magicians did not believe that they were denying the gods. On the contrary, how could the magicians perform their wonders without divine help? Another important point in our different world-views is that the ancient Christians also believed that magicians had supernatural help.

In Exodus 7:8-13 Moses and Aaron tried to convince Pharaoh to let the Hebrews leave Egypt. To demonstrate the power of the Hebrew god, Aaron, following God's instruction, threw down his staff, which promptly became a snake. "Then Pharaoh summoned the wise men and sorcerers; and they also, the magicians of Egypt, did the same by their secret arts. Each one threw down his staff, and they became snakes; but Aaron's staff swallowed up theirs." The author of Exodus wished to demonstrate the power of the true God, but he also witnesses to the power of the Egyptians, who were likewise able to turn their staffs into snakes, although not snakes as powerful as Aaron's.

In other places as well, the Bible makes clear that ancient pagan magicians had genuine power, such as the witch (medium) of Endor who summoned the shade of Samuel for Saul; Isaiah (3:3) spoke disapprovingly of the presence of the "skillful magician and expert enchanter" in Israelite society. In the New Testament Acts of the Apostles (8:9-24), Luke acknowledged the power of Simon the Magician; he also spoke of a Jewish magician and false prophet that Paul encountered on Cyprus (13:4-12). Thus, although Jews and Christians disapproved of magicians, they, along with pagans, acknowledged their power.

The Christians thus understood why pagans sought out magicians for assistance, but they could never approve of the practice. The pagans distinguished between good magic, that which was used to help people, such as overcoming infertility, and evil magic, which might be used for something like revenge. But in the Christian world-view, only two forces could overcome the laws of nature, God and demons. Since good people could access God by prayer, they did not need magic, nor would God respond to that means of invoking him. Therefore any overcoming of natural forces other than by a miracle had to be the work of the devil. Interestingly, Christian emperors and governors tolerated a fair amount of the good magic, usually because a superstitious populace continued to believe in it, thus making it very difficult to eliminate. Furthermore, in some places there was no option; with no access to a physician in rural areas, where else could peasants turn, if not to the local wise woman who could cast spells? But if magic became too prominent, the Christians suppressed it.

Even among pagans magic had a disreputable side. Roman emperors worried that their enemies might employ magic against them; the common person worried that rivals might employ magic to win over a lover. Of course, the person wishing to harm the emperor would claim that he was a tyrant; the hopeful lover would claim that she or he used magic to save the loved one from an unworthy match. From their point of view, magic served a good purpose.

For professional reasons, modern magicians keep their methods secret. Ancient magicians likewise did not spread knowledge about their craft because they believed that they could actually call upon superior forces and that such knowledge held danger for the common person. Although some magical texts survive, scholars must often play the detective to deduce much about this ancient practice.

D. Astrology

Oracles and magic could deal with immediate problems in an individual way—would the god please let Heracleidas know if his wife would have a child or not? But sometimes the immediate problem reflected a much larger situation, the orientation of the individual's whole life. To look at the problem on its own missed the point; the general picture must be consulted to deal with the particular. Astrology could help.

Most modern people view astrology, like magic, more as an entertainment than a science. People usually know their "signs," the astrological sign under which they were born; these signs derive from the names of twelve of the constellations. For example, someone born between July 23 to August 22 has Leo the lion for her or his sign. Many newspapers carry astrological charts, and astrological symbols appear on jewelry or other decorative devices. But, in spite of its continued popularity, astrology is at best a pseudo-science. Few people would admit that they make major decisions on the basis of astrology.

Astrology rests on the belief that the planets and stellar constellations influence human lives from the moment of a person's birth until the moment of her or his death. Strange as it may sound to the modern ear, most ancient astronomers were astrologers. The science grew to prominence in ancient Babylon, where scholars, convinced that the stars influenced life on earth, realized that they could not determine what the heavens were telling them unless they could accurately plot the position of the planets. This search for meaning produced some remarkably accurate naked-eye astronomical observations.[17]

Astrology had a strong deterministic element in it, and its practitioners found themselves in a familiar bind for determinists, namely, trying to explain what the stars had predicted while still preserving freedom of action for humans. But in an age of totalitarian government and strict class and social lines, many people could accept a deterministic world. "If Mars appears in triangular relation to Jupiter and Saturn, this causes great happiness and (the individual requesting this information) will make great acquisitions. . . . If Jupiter, Mercury, and Venus are in conjunction, they cause glories and empire and great prosperity. . . ."[18]

---

17. See Lindberg, *Beginnings of Western Science.*
18. A prediction cited in Barrett, *New Testament Background,* 35–36.

Astrology's appeal had no social or class limits. The Roman biographer Suetonius says that the emperor Tiberius (14–37) "lacked any deep regard for the gods or other religious feelings, his belief in astrology having persuaded him that the world was wholly ruled by fate."[19] Although after the career of Augustine many Christians had a low regard for free will (which had been corrupted by original sin), in its first centuries Christianity supported free will in its battle with astrology for people's allegiance.

Ancient astrology demanded more knowledge than the well-intentioned amateur could possibly have, and thus someone wanting to know what the stars had in store for her or him would have to consult an astrologer. This could become a profitable occupation, especially if astrologers made correct predictions for important people. Moderns have no reason to believe that ancient astrologers were fakes; on the contrary, they would have taken their duties very seriously, charting their own lives according to the stars.

The Christian struggle with astrology had a deep and widespread significance that can easily be misunderstood by taking a too modern, dismissive view of that practice.

E. Philosophy

The Christian use of philosophy will be discussed in chapter five, but we must note here that some people looking for individual salvation or meaning turned to philosophy. Philosophy does not on the surface appear to be a branch of paganism, but in some ways it is. Modern philosophy deals largely with what the senses and reason can tell us and with how language interacts with knowledge, but many ancient philosophers were frankly religious or at least dealt freely with religious questions.

The two best-known ancient philosophers, Plato and Aristotle, lived during the days of the Greek city-state, a small political entity. But after Alexander's conquests and later the Roman Empire had diminished public and political life for most people, the philosophies that most attracted people during the early Christian period were individualistic ones, Epicureanism and Stoicism.

These were both extended, complex movements; here we will note their appeal to those dissatisfied with paganism.

19. Suetonius, *The Twelve Caesars,* Tiberius 69, Robert Graves, trans. (Baltimore: Penguin Books, 1969) 144.

Epicureanism takes its name from Epicurus (ca. 342–270 B.C.), a Greek who concluded that the best one could strive for in life was to be personally happy. Shallow people identified happiness with physical pleasure, and Epicureanism has always had the undeserved aura of an aggressively sensual way of life. In fact, Epicurus led a very abstemious life, and he believed that one could achieve happiness by moderation and common sense; for example, if one were satisfied with a meal, why eat gluttonously just because more food is available? The truly philosophic person would try to structure a life free from disturbance.

Epicurus believed in the gods but did not believe that they influenced human life; he did not believe in life after death, which, for him, took away the fear of death.

> For what gives [us] no trouble when it comes is only an empty pain as we look forward to it. So death, the most terrifying of evils, is nothing to us; for as long as we exist death is not present with us, and when death comes then we no longer exist.[20]

The Epicureans understood the physical world as a collection of atoms, constantly on the move, forming new configurations, and eventually dispersing; death, in one sense, was merely the dispersal of atoms.

It is easy to see how this approach could degenerate into a sensual free-for-all of "enjoy what you can while you still have time." Most people, of course, cannot follow this prescription or even Epicurus' intended prescription of moderation, because the demands of work and personal relationships make it impossible. He advised his followers against holding public office or even getting married. The true disciple should avoid pain and passion.

Epicureanism had a limited appeal, mostly to wealthy aristocrats who could afford to retire from the world. Where possible, the Epicureans lived in communities, similar in intent to those of the Jews at Qumran and to monasteries of Christian ascetics. "The friendship of Epicurean groups was the chief attraction of the school."[21]

Stoicism, on the other hand, had a wide appeal because it prescribed a mode of life that many people could follow. The word "stoic" today connotes the image of someone who will endure any-

---

20. Cited in Grant, *Hellenistic Religions,* 158.
21. Ferguson, *Backgrounds,* 354.

thing for her or his values, and this does reflect Stoicism's ethics, but its ethics grew from its great philosophical orientation.

Zeno (ca. 336–273 B.C.), founder of Stoicism, taught in a painted porch (Greek: *stoa*) in Athens. Little is known of him, and the most famous Stoics lived much later, in the second century of the Christian era: Epictetus, a lame Greek slave (ca. 70–ca. 130), and Marcus Aurelius, emperor of Rome (161–180). Scholars frequently cite these two as examples of this philosophy's extensive appeal—a slave and an emperor, the lowest and highest ranks in the empire.

Stoics held a materialist view of the universe; even God was a material being, although a very refined one. They paid external reverence to the gods, but they believed in only one god, divine reason (Greek: *logos*), which governed the world harmoniously. Daily the world moved in an orderly fashion, but, at certain unknown times, the world destroyed itself in a great conflagration, only to be reborn once more and to repeat its history. Thus Fate governed the universe, and the Stoics considered astrology important, since it could tell people how the all-governing divine reason was moving the cosmos.

They viewed the cosmos as organic; what happened in one part of the cosmos inevitably affected other parts. This belief also made the Stoics more religious, since this enabled them to accept the veracity of oracles; for example, that the flight of birds or the cutting up of an animal sacrificial victim would affect people's lives.

One could live most happily by living in harmony with the cosmos; evil consists in rejecting that harmony.

> For we are made for cooperation, like feet, like hands, like eyelids, like the rows of upper and lower teeth. To act against one another then is contrary to nature; and it is acting against one another to be vexed and to turn away.[22]

So Marcus Aurelius could explain why things went wrong in the world.

But the individual could not always live in harmony with the cosmos; sometimes the wrongful deeds of others impinged upon the efforts of the Stoic. In such cases, the Stoic could only endure evil until she or he could make things right again; if that were not possible, the Stoic should resist the evildoers or even commit suicide if the situation became irredeemable. In the words of C. K. Barrett:

22. Marcus Aurelius, *Meditations,* II.1, in *The Stoic and Epicurean Philosophers,* Whitney J. Oates, trans. (New York: Random House, 1940) 497.

> This sounds like a cold and cheerless creed, and so perhaps it was;
> yet beyond question it nerved many a [person] to face the battle of
> life with a clear head and a brave heart, and it inculcated human-
> ity and forbearance into a world in which these virtues were not
> common.[23]

Stoicism also had a universalist element, since all people, regardless
of their status in life, were caught up in the cycles of the world and
could discipline themselves to live in harmony with the cosmos.

Unlike Epicureanism, Stoicism contained elements attractive to
the Christians. Particularly important to them was the Stoics' stern
ethical code. Christian martyrs died because they possessed a strong
faith in God, and their immediate exemplars would have been biblical figures such as Daniel, who suffered under an unjust pagan
monarch; but they could not have gone uninfluenced by the examples
of Stoics, such as the Roman Stoic Marcus Porcius Cato, who killed
himself (46 B.C.) rather than live under the tyranny of Julius Caesar.
Ironically, the one extant Stoic reference to Christians comes from
Marcus Aurelius, who countenanced the persecutions and then unfa-
vorably compared the stubbornness and "theatricality" of the
Christian martyrs to the nobility of the Stoic suicides.[24]

F. The Official Cults

What then of the "official" gods of Greece and Rome, the gods
known to us from mythology and the great literary works? What role
did they play?

This question always provokes great scholarly debate because
there is no way to answer it. References to the gods abound, but
while gods whom people invoked have the same names as those of
the myths, they do not correspond to the literary exemplars. For example, the Stoics openly invoked Zeus, but they were not appealing
to the amorous adventurer of the myths. Luke recounted (Acts 19:28)
that when the Ephesian mobs tried to lynch Paul, they cried out
"Great is Artemis of the Ephesians," a multibreasted fertility goddess
who bore little resemblance to the forbidding virginal huntress of the
myths. When the Roman writer Ovid (43 B.C.–A.D. 17) wrote his
Metamorphoses, the most important collection of ancient myths, he

---

23. *New Testament Background,* 61.
24. *Meditations,* XI.3, in *Stoic and Epicurean Philosophers,* 571.

made it clear that he considered these to be charming tales but not ones to be taken as authentic accounts of the gods.

The Roman emperors usually supported the gods with public services and buildings; this was especially true of Augustus (27 B.C.–A.D. 14). Yet most scholars believe that the gods survived only to the extent that they metamorphosed to meet the new realities of the Roman world. In general, the traditional religion did not offer the average citizen the personal satisfaction or salvation supposedly supplied by the popular cults, oracles, magic, or astrology.

The old gods survived in literary masterpieces, in monumental temples, and in beautiful statuary. Even when the Romans faltered in their belief, they never lost their reverence for the gods as representatives of tradition. The tales of the gods surrounded people in myriad ways—in the theater, in the marketplace, and in education, where the classics were used to teach even basic grammar.

But culture could not substitute for genuine belief. When the emperor Julian the Apostate (361–363) tried to revive belief in the gods, he found an unwilling populace. He visited the famous shrine of Apollo at Daphne near Antioch and left an account of his visit.

> But when I entered the shrine, I found there no incense, not so much as a cake, not a single beast for sacrifice. For the moment I was amazed and thought that I was still outside the shrine. . . . But when I began to inquire what sacrifice the city intended to offer to celebrate the annual festival in honor of the god, the priest answered, "I have brought with me from my own house a goose as an offering to the god, but the city this time has made no preparations."[25]

This is a sad tale, a witness to the decline of a great tradition. In the early fifth century, at the end of the Roman period, when Augustine wrote his famous attack on official pagan religion in *City of God,* he attacked gods who existed mostly in textbooks. Local and regional gods supplanted the older gods but often did so by keeping the name or some of the attributes.

Although scholars must still investigate the interaction between Christianity and the pagan cults, there can be little doubt that these cults helped pave the way for the people's acceptance of Christianity. The Christians offered a universalist religion open to everyone, regardless

25. Cited in Stevenson, *Creeds, Councils, and Controversies,* 64–65.

of social status or ethnic background or race or gender; they offered personal salvation from the demons who attacked people and from death, which seemingly conquered all; they maintained the notion of a chosen people, a community of faith sealed by baptism. This well matched the universalism of the cults and philosophies which were open to all who could live in harmony with the cosmos; it well matched the personalism of the cults which offered self-esteem and salvation and of the philosophies that stressed individual happiness and responsibility; it well matched the "chosen people" notion of the initiates to the mysteries. Christianity did not succeed among the pagans because paganism was intellectually or spiritually bankrupt, but largely because Christianity matched or surpassed the same benefits offered by paganism.

3. Heretics and Schismatics[26]

The Greek word *hairesis* originally meant "sect," and the word "heretics" came to mean a particular group as distinct from the Church at large. Heresy means the conscious and deliberate deviation from a formally and publicly promulgated teaching of the Church; simple disagreement with what most people believe is heterodoxy. For example, the New Testament gives abundant evidence that the very earliest Christians believed that they should continue to follow the Jewish Law, until Paul changed their thinking on this point. Until Paul did, however, he was in the minority; he opposed the teaching of most others, and thus his teaching was clearly heterodox. Historians now recognize that much early Christian teaching went through several stages of formation, and the word heresy must be used carefully.

What, for example, would be heresy? By the mid-third century Christians had accepted the Gospel of Mark as a scriptural book, and in the fourth century they had accepted the New Testament as we now know it. The opening verse of that gospel says "This is the gospel of Jesus Christ, the Son of God." Since the Scripture proclaims that Jesus Christ is the Son of God, one cannot be a Christian and deny that. Teachings that were labeled heresies were usually far more subtle than this, but this illustrates the point—the Church has

26. Early Christianity witnessed many movements the majority called heresies; there were far too many even to be surveyed here. We will treat of some in chapter seven; in this chapter we will discuss heretics as "others."

formally and publicly acknowledged the Gospel of Mark to be an essential part of God's revelation. Christians could and did debate how Jesus could be the Son of God, but denying his divine sonship, however understood, would be heresy.

In the modern world we view heretics very differently from the early Christians. First, we know that many positions initially held by Christians, such as the six-day creation of the world, turned out to be wrong and the product of a dated world-view. Second, since we have seen the horrors that doctrinal intolerance can cause, such as the activities of the medieval Inquisition or Calvinist inquisitors at Geneva, we take a more sympathetic view toward heretics and a more reserved view of would-be heresy hunters. Third, we recognize that few if any doctrines emerged full-fledged from the apostolic age, and that many "heretics" were in fact pioneers, who investigated theological questions with approaches that later generations rejected; the rejection of a later age does not make someone a heretic *ex post facto*. Fourth, modern Christians approach heresy pastorally. Heresy is a wound in the Body of Christ that must be healed; just as an individual would not amputate a limb that aches, so the Church will not cut off one of its members from the Body of Christ, unless no other recourse is available. Fifth, we believe in freedom of speech, even when what is said runs counter to our beliefs.

Heresy in the ancient Church usually concerned doctrinal issues, such as the nature of the Trinity or the person of Christ. Schism, on the other hand, dealt with institutional matters, usually with identifying the true head of the Church, local or international. Schismatic Christians often found themselves in agreement on doctrinal matters, and, if the disciplinary problems could be overcome, unity was again feasible. Indeed, schism comes from a Greek verb meaning "to tear," indicating that once both groups were one, but later separated.

Attitudes among Christians toward heretics and schismatics varied considerably, although one attitude always prevailed—heretics and schismatics were the "other people." Some secularist authors considered orthodoxy (right teaching) to be the teaching of the winners, but no Christian can accept that, since it denies any intrinsic truth to Christian teaching. For example, could modern Protestants, Orthodox, and Catholics expel the Gospel of John from the Bible because they now control the Church and they feel like doing it? Yet no one can deny that the titles "heretic" and "schismatic" were hurled about indiscriminately and always malevolently.

The North African theologian and bishop, Cyprian of Carthage, (d. 258) summed up the view of many. He compared the Church to Noah's ark; if you were not on board, you drowned. *Nulla salus extra ecclesiam,* "there is no salvation outside the Church," was his view, a view widely popular in North Africa and, by the end of the Roman period, in the Church as a whole. This does not mean that Christian leaders rushed to expel heretics and schismatics; on the contrary, they first made an effort to win them to their point of view. Furthermore, confusion often reigned. For example, in the fourth century, when the struggle over Arianism raged, two and then more groups of Greek bishops raged against one another, while most Latin bishops had little idea of what was going on. But when a disputed matter had been settled, at an ecumenical council for instance, then heretics and schismatics were expected to give up their opposition and enter the larger Church. This often happened, but just as often it did not, and Christian rulers, too frequently abetted by the bishops, actually used violence to bring the outsiders back.

But when heretics and schismatics persisted, they joined the Jews and pagans in becoming "others." This made them liable to all the legal and social discrimination inflicted on pagans and Jews in the Christian empire; in fact, they often suffered more because, in the eyes of many, heretics and schismatics were traitors. Jews and pagans had never had the true faith, but these people did, and that made them worse, a frightening attitude but one quite prevalent and even quite modern and secular. In the twentieth century, the leaders of the two Communist giants, the former Soviet Union and the People's Republic of China, routinely accused the other of heretical "revisionism," that is, of not being faithful to the "true" teachings of Marx and Lenin as understood, of course, by the Soviets or the Chinese. Often their criticisms of each other surpassed in vehemence their attacks on the "capitalist" West.

Most heretical and schismatic groups eventually disappeared. The reasons varied. Sometimes they simply never won over enough members to sustain themselves and simply faded away. At other times, they invited destruction by splintering into increasingly smaller groups. Some groups became outdated, like the Jewish Christian sects that continued to oppose the Pauline way and to insist that all Christians observe Jewish regulations; they survived to the mid-fifth century but are then heard of no more. Some groups were overwhelmed by popular support of other positions; for example, radical Arian groups in the fourth century withered when the larger parties (Nicene and Homoiousion) reconciled. At times the Christian empire persecuted groups out of existence—the fate of the Priscillianists of Spain and Gaul in the late fourth and early fifth centuries. Occasionally a heretical group survived by leaving Christian territory, as did the Nestorians who migrated to Persia in the sixth century and who survive today, although in small numbers, in the Middle East, India, and the United States.

The most successful dissident groups often nationalized their movement by identifying their protest against the larger Church with the citizens' protest against an oppressive government. The two most successful movements were the Donatists and Monophysites. Both withstood persecution by Christian governments. The Donatists survived in North Africa until the Muslim conquest in the late seventh century. The Monophysites dominated Egyptian religious life and managed to spread their teachings into Syria. In both areas, they portrayed themselves as representatives of the people against the tyranny of the Byzantine emperors in Constantinople. They, too, suffered conquest by the Muslims, but, unlike the Donatists, they survived. As the Coptic Christians, they live in Egypt and also in the United States.

All communities grow and change, sometimes for the better, sometimes not, but this process of growth and change defines the group. Dissident movements forced the Christians as a whole to consider what the Church is and should be, as well as what should be the Church's basic teachings. It is sad that any Christian was cut off from her or his church, but, historically, this was inevitable. As the notion of "Christian" changed, some people had to become the "others." This still goes on today, as people cease to feel at home in a particular tradition and so change denominations or religions; Methodists become Presbyterians, Catholics become Protestants, Christians join New Age sects. Despite people's satisfaction and indeed joy with the change, such shifts can often have sad consequences, such as dividing a family or cutting persons off from a community; but at least today people can become "others" without fear of persecution.

Although committed to the salvation of the whole human race, the Christians, like any social group, often differentiated between themselves and others. The gap between them was not unbridgeable, and interaction was common; but only by the others' acceptance of the Christians' viewpoint could the gap be bridged. In fairness to the

Christians, most ancient peoples, including the "others," usually felt the same way.

Chapter Five

Intellectual and Cultural Life

The earliest Christian writers, the composers of the New Testament books, demonstrated considerable intellectual and literary skill, and thus we can dismiss the time-honored but incorrect image of an early Church of pious, poor, simple folk. On the other hand, scholars have demonstrated that the first Christians, anticipating an imminent Second Coming (Parousia) of Christ, did not develop or even set out to develop a serious, sustained intellectual and cultural life. Such a life emerged in two ways: first, the continued existence of the Church in the world guaranteed that certain problems would arise that could not be met without serious intellectual effort; second, the Christians took their movement out of its birthplace in the Near East and brought it to the corners of the Roman world (Spain, Britain) and beyond the Roman world (Persia, Ethiopia), where it encountered diverse ways of life and constant challenges to its beliefs and teachings, and to which it had to react.

Early Christianity could claim as its own some of the greatest minds in history (Origen, Augustine, Gregory Nazianzus), some of the great literary talents of the ancient world (John Chrysostom, Ephraem the Syrian), and some of the greatest artists (the unknown architects of the great Roman basilicas, the unknown mosaicists who decorated the Ravenna churches). This chapter will survey some of the basic ingredients in the vast Christian intellectual and cultural life; it must relegate many of the specifics to the footnotes.

1. Books and The Book[1]

A. Producing Bibles

Our Age of Information takes books for granted; in fact, people even wonder if books have seen their day and will soon be replaced by texts in cyberspace. Bestselling books can sell more than a million copies and be available in both hardcover and paperback format. Books are so plentiful that second-hand book sales often move titles along for pennies. But no one in the ancient world ever took books for granted.

When we refer to a book, we usually mean the content of the book, as in the phrase "that was a good book," but first and foremost a book is a physical object. We cannot know its content unless we first have a copy to hold and read. The power of mass printing has made this seem a minor point, but before the age of printing, all books were produced by hand, a laborious, tiresome, sometimes difficult process and one that virtually guaranteed errors.

When we want to read the books of the ancient Christians, we need to be sure that what we are reading is what they actually wrote, to the extent that can be determined. Here we will consider how ancient books were written and how moderns can determine what ancient authors wrote.

Pre-printing books are called manuscripts, from two Latin words, *manus* (hand) and *scribere* (to write). To produce a book, one literally had to write it by hand; to produce multiple copies of a book, one had to copy or have others copy the book as many times as necessary. Scholars call the author's original the autograph, and, ideally, this is the version they would like to use since this comes directly from the author. Although even autographs will have mistakes or gaps, such as a missing word, copies always have mistakes. Logically enough, when copies are made from copies of copies, the mistakes multiply because each copyist repeats the previous errors and makes new ones.

At first glance, all this copying does not seem like a problem. Scholars can just consult the autograph; but that presumes it has survived. In fact, few autographs survive. In the ancient world no books were copied as often as the biblical ones, yet not a single autograph survives for a biblical book, Old or New Testament. This applies as

1. For a valuable survey of books in Christianity, see Harry Gamble, *Books and Readers in the Early Church* (New Haven: Yale University Press, 1995).

well for most other ancient literature, Jewish, Christian, and pagan. If moderns want to know what the ancients wrote, they must rely on a discipline called textual criticism. Although this discipline affects all ancient literature, we will limit our discussion to the Bible.

The textual critic tries to "establish" the text, that is, to determine what text the ancients worked with. Why not try to figure out exactly what the autograph said? Earlier generations of scholars attempted that and several claimed to have succeeded; it still remains something of a goal. But modern scholars also know that different types of texts survived in different communities; scholars believe that in third-century Alexandria, three versions of the Gospel of Mark circulated. Furthermore, we know that communities interacted with the text rather than merely passed it along. Textual criticism is a living, changing discipline, especially so in an age when computer technology makes the investigation of large numbers of texts feasible. Thus it is most accurate to say that scholars try to establish a reliable text, one known to the ancients and consonant with the witness of the surviving manuscripts.

To understand a manuscript, the textual critic must be able to read the handwriting on it; the study of ancient writing is called palaeography. She or he must also be proficient in the language in which the book was written.

The textual critic must also realize how the ancient scribe (usually a man) who copied the book, worked, that is, how he prepared the writing surface and writing materials, copied the text, and bound the book. Only by understanding the process can one understand the outcome.

Ancient Christian scribes wrote on two surfaces,[2] papyrus and parchment. Papyrus, from which comes the word "paper," grew on the Nile River banks in long stems, four to five meters high. Craftsmen would cut the stems into workable pieces, lay them in strips, and then glue them together, horizontally on one side and vertically on the other. The horizontal side usually made the better writing surface, but scribes used both sides. The Egyptians shipped papyrus to all parts of the ancient world.

2. We are here discussing books. Ancient Christians wrote on other surfaces, both formally, such as on gravestone inscriptions, and informally, such as graffiti on walls. Students of ancient handwriting and languages study any remaining form of writing. The best introduction to the study of ancient writing is *Scribes and Scholars: A Guide to the Transmission of Greek and Latin Literature* by L. D. Reynolds and N. G. Wilson (Oxford: Oxford University Press, 1991).

Parchment, the other writing surface, was made from animal skins, which were stripped of all hairs, and then washed and pumiced until the skin was smooth. The flesh side, that is, the hairless side, provided the smoother surface. Although ancient scribes preferred papyrus, it was occasionally in limited supply, since it came primarily from one source; animals such as sheep and cows were available throughout the Roman world.

Books came in two forms, the roll and the codex. The roll consisted of sheets of papyrus or parchment sewn together and then rolled around a wooden rod. The reader simply unrolled the book in order to see the contents. A rolled-up book was called a *volumen* in Latin, from which comes the word "volume." The rod around which the book was rolled had a knob or "head" on the end to make it easy to pick up. The term "head" came to mean the entire roll, so if a large book required several rolls, it was said to be on several heads. The Latin word for head is *caput, capites* in the plural, from which comes the word "chapter."

Normally writing was on only one side of the roll, that with the horizontal papyrus fibers; if writing appeared on both sides, as in Revelation 5:1, the book was called an opistograph.

When writing material was in short supply, the scribe would take a manuscript with a text available on other manuscripts and use pumice to cover up the text, and then copy a new one on it; scholars call such a manuscript a palimsest. Occasionally it happened that the other manuscripts of the covered-over text did not survive, and scholars, using infrared lighting and other techniques, have discovered a valuable text under the pumice.

It is difficult for a modern person to imagine a reader easily rolling and re-rolling the book trying to find a reference, but the fact is that rolls proved very popular with Jews and Greco-Roman pagans. The first Christians would also have written their books on rolls.

But by the third century the Christians began to show a marked preference for the codex, the ancestor of the modern book. In a codex, a piece of paper is folded in the middle, creating a four-sided page. The scribe next bound the page at the fold to other pages and cut the folded tops to create more writing space. To read the text, one turned the securely bound pages to progress through the book—as you are doing now. Since the outside pages of these books could easily be damaged, scribes covered and bound them with wooden boards taken from the trunk of a tree; the Latin word for trunk, *caudex,* gave its name to this type of book. Christians found it easier to use, and, by the fourth century, 80 percent of the books used in Christian Egypt were codices.[3]

When a scribe started to write Greek or Latin in a codex, he started on the right side or *recto,* and then turned the page to the *verso;* this is because Greek and Latin are written left to right. Hebrew was written from right to left, and thus a scribe copying the Hebrew Bible would start at what we would call the back of the book.

All educated people could write, but, then as now, important people employed secretaries; for example, someone named Tertius wrote out the Epistle to the Romans for Paul (Rom 16:22). An anonymous scribe wrote out 1 Corinthians; we know this because Paul made it a point of saying that he wrote the final greeting in his own hand (1 Cor 16:21).

Ancient manuscripts present a strange appearance, even to those who read the languages they contain. For example, they rarely have breaks for sentences or even paragraphs. Because writing materials had to be laboriously produced and could be expensive, scribes tried to avoid wasting space and thus did not use breaks. Sometimes manuscripts have breaks when a particular passage, such as a parable, has finished, or if there are two columns of text. If professional scribes, rather than a member of the local church, did the work, they were more likely to use breaks because they were paid by the *stichos,* that is, a line of fifteen to sixteen syllables or approximately thirty-four to thirty-eight letters. Clearly it was not in their financial interest to write more letters than required per line, so they stopped at the appropriate *stichos* and went to the next line.

Ancient manuscripts are also characterized by a heavy use of abbreviations—a kind of shorthand—an obvious necessity in copying a book by hand. Sometimes these are simply horizontal strokes above a word to indicate that a letter is missing; for example, the word "cat" might be written "ct" with a stroke above, and the person reading the line would be able to figure out which letter was missing. The context would have to make it clear that the word was "cat" rather than "cut" or "cot"; if confusion were possible, the scribe would forgo the abbreviation. Other forms of abbreviation included specific figures used for specific words, as modern writers use the ampersand (&) to mean "and." Palaeographers long ago deciphered the ancient abbreviations, and modern scholars have little trouble

3. See C. H. Roberts and T. C. Skeat, *The Birth of the Codex* (London: Oxford University Press, 1987) for a brief discussion of early Christian book production.

reading ancient manuscripts if the handwriting is legible, a formidable problem in any age.

Textual critics collect manuscripts and try to determine which are the most reliable; they use criteria such as date, provenance (place), and the quality of the scribe. For example, a third-century copy of a second-century work will usually be more reliable than a sixth-century copy simply because the farther in time the scribe was from the original, the more likely are the chances of mistakes in copying over the centuries. If the author of the book lived in Antioch, her or his work would likely be well known among the Christians there, and this familiarity could help guarantee the reliability of a manuscript from that city. A good scribe did his job carefully, and the textual critic can see this by examining the manuscript; his opposite, a scribe who consistently made mistakes, will be equally obvious, and the critic must use his work carefully and skeptically.

But none of these criteria are foolproof. The sixth-century scribe might have had access to the now lost autograph. A scribe living in Antioch and familiar with much of the work at hand may have thought that he knew the work better than he did, and so was careless in copying. The most conscientious scribe was still dependent upon his text, and it is possible that the sloppy scribe had access to a superior manuscript.

When textual critics have worked through all these problems and have determined that, say, five manuscripts are reliable (A, B, C, D, E), they then compare the readings in these manuscripts to establish the text. "Reliable" does not mean that all manuscripts have equal value, and the textual critic often has to exercise her or his judgment with particular verses. Mistakes in the text always occur. Some mistakes are obvious: slips, such as "ont" for "not," or omissions, such as "she went to house" for "she went to the house," or spelling errors, such as "waight" for "weight," or reversals, such as "from" for "form," or homonyms, such as "their" for "there." These the scholars can correct easily. Others, such as a missing word, present far more difficulty. Maybe the scholar can determine the word from another part of the text, but this is not always the case. If multiple manuscripts of the text have survived, the scholar can usually solve such a problem.

Usually the greatest problem facing the textual critic is determining which manuscript has the correct or most likely reading. For example, suppose manuscripts A, B, and C read: "Jesus said to his disciples," and manuscripts D and E read: "Jesus said to the disciples." Which reading is correct, "his" or "the"? This may seem like a small point, and if this were the only time when the manuscripts disagreed, it would be, but this is actually the kind of problem the critic faces constantly throughout the establishment of the text.

This discussion has seemed very modern, but it is not. As early as the late second century, Irenaeus of Lyons advised his readers to get the "ancient" rather than the "new" manuscripts of the Bible; Augustine advised scholars to look for the more reliable readings. Indeed, from constant personal experience, every ancient reader knew far better than we how easily a text could be corrupted. But no problem was insuperable, and ancient readers had regular access to books.

Textual criticism as a discipline dates back to the ancient Greeks; Alexandrian scholars tried to establish a reliable text of Homer. In the third century, Origen of Alexandria was the first Christian to use this type of textual criticism, assembling manuscripts to make a critical edition of the Old Testament not only of the Hebrew text but also of several Greek versions. This monumental work appeared in a six-column version known as the Hexapla.

Another early Christian, Marcion (fl. ca. 140–160), used a different type of textual criticism. He claimed that he understood the mind of the apostle Paul, and he thus realized that several passages in Paul's writings were added by later writers that he, Marcion, would delete, an approach he also applied, but more severely, to the Gospel of Luke. This approach sounds very high-handed and open to abuse, but it does have validity. Many modern scholars claim that some parts of New Testament books were not part of the original text even though all manuscripts of the books include them. That is because they know the scriptural writer so well, or at least they think they do, that they can conclude that a particular passage is not authentic because the style or theology differs from the rest of the author's work. This can apply to an occasional verse, to a full chapter, such as Romans 16, and even to entire books; for example, virtually all scholars believe that the current text of 2 Corinthians consists of two or more individual epistles.

A final note on textual criticism: The technical process of producing a book also produced the name of the world's most widely read book. The Greek writer Herodotus (ca. 484–425 B.C.), when speaking about papyrus, referred to the plant as the *biblos*. In the next century, another Greek scholar, Theophrastus (370–285 B.C.), said that from this plant is made the *biblion,* or papyrus book, and *biblion* became a synonym for "book." The plural of this word is *ta biblia,* that is, the books, which became the phrase the Greek-speaking Christians used for the Scriptures—"the writings." When Latin speakers converted to Christianity and heard the word *biblia* used this way, they treated the word as if it were a feminine singular noun of the first declension, that is, *biblia* in Latin meant not "the books" but the collection as a whole, or, as we say, "the Bible."

B. Translations[4]

Textual criticism can tell us what the Bible said in the original; but many people, in the ancient world and today, could not read the original languages. This meant that the believing communities had to produce translations.

No one can say when translating began because no one can be certain when the biblical books took on an authoritative character. Furthermore, languages change and develop. Except for specialists, modern people cannot read texts written in their "own" language 800 years ago. No doubt the earliest traditions—about Abraham, Isaac, and Jacob—were modified as the Hebrew dialects developed.

Translations also faced the problem of the "sacred language," that is, the belief by some religious people that God stood behind the very words of the text and thus it could not be translated. But the book belongs to the community, and, as the community changed, translations became inevitable.

Yet matters are not that simple. Once people use translations, these become authoritative. In early fifth-century North Africa, a new Latin translation so outraged a congregation familiar with another version that there was almost a riot.[5] English biblical scholars tell the (probably apocryphal) story of the staunch Protestant who announced that if the King James Version was good enough for Moses, it was good enough for him! But there is more to this than meets the eye. When people have grown up believing that Jesus said "Our Father who art in heaven," the words "Our Father who dwells in

4. The best survey of Early Christian biblical translations continues to be Bruce Metzger's *The Early Versions of the New Testament* (New York: Oxford University Press, 1977).

5. See Robert O'Connell, "When Saintly Fathers Feuded," in Thought 54 (1979) 344–364.

heaven" just do not sound "authentic." Some people believe that translations themselves become inspired.

[In the United States, so popular has the King James Version become that it is common for crossword puzzles to use the clue "biblical word" for "thee" or "thy" or the like.]

In the ancient Christian world, only one translation ever had inspired status—the Septuagint. This name was given to a translation of the Hebrew Scriptures into Greek, begun probably in the Alexandrian Diaspora in the third century B.C. It gained popularity among Diasporan Jews; New Testament writers used it as well. A Jewish treatise, the *Letter of Aristeas* (2nd c. B.C.), claims that 70 (or 72) Jewish scribes made the translation under divine inspiration, since, although each of them worked separately, their translations agreed to the letter. The title "Septuagint" derives from the Greek word for 70, and scholars use LXX as an abbreviation for it. In fact, the Septuagint may never have existed as a finished text, since the translations of the various books differ in style and even in accuracy. The LXX text of Jeremiah differs from the now extant Hebrew version, and Diasporan Jews made revisions to it.

But it became the Old Testament of the Greek Christians, who cited it comfortably, and they rarely felt the need to consult the Hebrew original, although some scholars, such as Origen, did.

Since the New Testament was written in their own language, the Greek Christians did not need a translation of that, but other Christians would.

When Christianity moved West, Latin-speaking converts wanted their own versions. Jews living in the West had Latin translations of at least parts of the Old Testament, and translations of the Pauline epistles were available in Africa in the second century. As the Latin Church grew in numbers and importance, many versions of both Old and New Testaments evolved. Augustine made the wisecrack that there were as many versions as translators,[6] and he may not have been far off. Jerome began the Latin translation called the Vulgate in the late fourth century, although he did not translate all of the books himself. In the Middle Ages, the Vulgate took on the aura of an inspired translation, but this was never the case in early Christianity.

Although the Septuagint and the Latin translations served for most ancient Christians, several regional churches in the East produced translations as well.

6. *On Christian Doctrine,* xi.16; 44.

The earliest appeared in Syria in a Semitic language called Syriac. A second-century writer named Tatian (d. ca. 180) produced a harmony of the four gospels called the *Diatesseron,* literally, "through the four," and so the first Syriac scripture was not actually a scriptural book. The *Diatesseron* was enormously popular in Syria and actually preferred by many Christians to the actual gospels, a situation not remedied until the fifth century.

Alexandria and the Greek-speaking areas around the Nile delta dominated much of Egypt's cultural life, but in the rural areas people spoke Coptic, a descendant of the ancient Egyptian tongue. When Christianity penetrated those regions is unknown, although Eusebius, in his *Ecclesiastical History* (6,41), says that the persecution of Decius in 250 produced both Greek and Egyptian martyrs, that is, Alexandrians and Copts. By the end of the third century, an ascetic named Hieracas became the first Coptic native to write on biblical topics in his own language. Two more Copts, Antony (251–356) and Pachomius (ca. 290–346), led the monastic movement. Since Pachomius wanted his followers, mostly rural Egyptians, to read the Scriptures in their monasteries, at least parts of the Bible were available in Coptic by the fourth century. Led by the monks, the Coptic speakers produced a significant literature of their own, a literature inspired by the Bible.

According to Christian tradition, the apostles Bartholomew and Thaddeus evangelized in Armenia. Historians cannot say whether or not this was so, but, by the third century, Armenia had a flourishing Christian community. In 302 the Armenian king, Tiridates III, declared Christianity the official religion of his country, the first ruler of any country to do so. Armenia lost much of its independence in the fourth century, mostly to the Persians but partly to the Romans. The Armenians kept their culture alive in this difficult situation by producing a translation of the Bible, which in turn inspired other literature. Bishop Sahak (ca. 350–439) and the monk Mesrop (ca. 361–439) made the translation after first creating the Armenian alphabet; the New Testament was the first book written in that alphabet. Other Armenian literature soon followed, using the new alphabet.

Another people in the Caucasus region, the Georgians, likewise translated the Bible into their own language in the fifth century, possibly by imitating the Armenian alphabet to create their own.

The Acts of the Apostles tells of the disciple Philip's conversion of the Ethiopian eunuch (8:26-39), but the most reliable historical information places the introduction of Christianity into Ethiopia in the fourth century, when Frumentius, a captured, enslaved Christian from Palestine, converted the king and his family. Frumentius traveled up the Nile to Alexandria, where bishop Athanasius consecrated him bishop of the Ethiopians. Contacts between Ethiopia and Alexandria remained strong, and, in the fifth century, some refugee monks from a doctrinal conflict in Egypt went there and evangelized extensively. These monks, known in Ethiopia as the Nine Saints, composed liturgies and theologies in the Ethiopian vernacular, and also produced the first biblical translations there in the fifth and sixth centuries. Although Ethiopian manuscripts are rather late when compared to Greek or Latin ones (the earliest is from the tenth century, and most date to the sixteenth century or later), they often contain magnificent illustrations, proof of how the Bible interpenetrated much of Ethiopian culture.

2. The Bible and Its Interpretation

There is literally no way to overemphasize the role the Bible played in the life of the early Church. For most people, it offered a guide to moral precepts and some basic doctrinal teachings, such as one God or sin and redemption, but these depended upon how Christians understood the Bible, which in turn depended upon which books they thought belonged in the Bible.

A. The Canon[7]

Modern Christians take the Bible for granted, but for the early Christians, our Bible did not exist.

The Church never lacked Scriptures, but initially these were what Christians came to call the Old Testament. Many New Testament writers quote the Old Testament, but scholars cannot be sure what books these writers included in their Bible. Of some books there can be no doubt, for example, the books of the Torah (the first five books,

7. There is an enormous literature on the canon; any New Testament introduction will provide a guide. A good overall study is by Bruce Metzger, *The Canon of the New Testament: Its Origin, Development, and Significance* (New York: Oxford University Press, 1987).

thought to have been authored by Moses) and the great prophets such as Isaiah; but what was the Christians' complete canon, that is, the list of books believed to be inspired by God? In the gospels, Jesus refers to "the law and the prophets" (Matt 7:12) or "the law of Moses, the prophets, and the psalms" (Luke 24:44), but surely some books outside those categories, such as Job, were included. Yet another problem enters in: not all the books cited by New Testament writers were canonical; for example, the Epistle of Jude (v. 14) cites the First Book of Enoch, a Jewish apocalyptic work never accepted as biblical by Jews or later by Christians.[8]

One reason scholars are uncertain as to what books were in the earliest Christian canon is that they do not know what the canon was for the Jews. An old tradition claims that a group of rabbis met in a Jewish town called Jamnia in A.D. 90 to establish the canon, but scholars question that. So uncertain was this matter for the early Christians that it was not settled until the fifth century. Augustine included a list of the Bible books in his *On Christian Doctrine,* which largely finalized the question for Western Christians, but matters continued to be unsettled for centuries to come. In fact, the Protestant reformers rejected Augustine's Old Testament canon for a briefer one.

The canon of the New Testament represented a different challenge: was there even a New Testament? Although Christians cannot picture the Church without the New Testament, that was the case initially. Jesus died *circa* 33, and most scholars date the earliest New Testament book, Paul's First Epistle to the Thessalonians *circa* 50, so there was a brief period when there was a Church but no New Testament books. Scholars date the last book, the Second Epistle of Peter, *circa* 125; they reject Petrine authorship of the book and believe that the pseudonymous author used Peter's name to gain authority. This means that the Church existed for almost a century without a New Testament, since it could hardly have existed until all the books in it had been written.

But even when the books had been written, did it exist? To answer this, we must understand what the phrase "New Testament" means. At the very least it must mean a fixed number of books written by Christians and accepted as inspired in the same way as the books of

8. For a good discussion of the use of apocryphal books by New Testament writers, see Martin McNamara, *Palestinian Judaism and the New Testament,* Good News Studies 4 (Wilmington, Del.: Michael Glazier Books, 1983) 65–120.

the Hebrew Scriptures were. The mere existence of the books did not guarantee adoption of that view.

The story of the New Testament canon is very complex. We will just note here that Christian writers of the second century, such as Irenaeus, showed an awareness that the Christians could have written inspired books, and they began to cite New Testament books as Scripture. By the end of the second century, the Alexandrian writer Clement used the term "New Testament" to refer to a canon of books, although his list does not correspond to the currently accepted one. Just because the term had been used did not mean that it caught on; Clement's pupil, the great scholar Origen, referred to "the so-called New Testament." But in the third century, Christians gradually accepted the notion that some Christian books deserved a place in the Bible. The question for them was how to determine which books those were.

Christian scholars looked for books which were ancient and which could claim the authority of an apostle (Paul) or one of the Twelve (Matthew, John, Jude) or the disciple of an apostle (Mark, Luke) or a relative of Jesus (James). They looked for books that taught the truth, as they understood it in the second and third centuries, and thus no Gnostic scriptures could be found worthy. They also relied upon tradition, that is, they looked to see what books the various churches had used, especially the large churches with apostolic foundations, such as Rome, Ephesus, and Alexandria (believed to have been founded by the evangelist Mark). This approach was hardly foolproof, but it appealed to the Greco-Roman mind, which respected antiquity. Clearly this approach also had a polemical element. Most second- and third-century theologians and bishops loathed and feared the Gnostics, and they looked for books that would refute them, assuming throughout that their own teaching faithfully reflected that of the apostles while the Gnostics perverted it.

Modern biblical criticism has demolished much of this argumentation. For example, no one accepts that the authors of the gospels of Matthew and John were members of the Twelve or that Peter wrote either of the epistles attributed to him. Furthermore, scholars have dated the Second Epistle of Peter *circa* 125, that is, after several works not in the canon, for example, Clement of Rome's epistle to the Corinthians (dated ca. 95) and the letters of Ignatius of Antioch (no later than 117) and possibly some other works as well. Some biblical scholars would even date the Pastoral Epistles (1 and 2 Tim, Titus) as late as 140. The New Testament books can thus no longer claim to be the most ancient, nor can they claim to be apostolic works. They do not fulfill the criteria originally used to find them a place in the canon, but tradition has gained them an unassailable position in the Church.[9] Furthermore, many scholars would now argue that the inspired character of a book depends upon its acceptance by the community rather than the historical circumstances of its composition, a view that is far from being universally accepted.

But the early Christians believed that they could determine a book's apostolicity, antiquity, and orthodoxy, and their debate over "which books" continued well into the fourth century. The first time any Christian provided a list of the New Testament books that cited the twenty-seven accepted today was in 367, and the Christian who did so was Athanasius, patriarch of Alexandria. Yet even this did not settle the question. North African Christians debated the canon in the fifth century, and, as late as the seventh century, some bibles from Syria did not include the Book of Revelation.

There would have been no need to determine which books belonged in the canon if there had not been other candidates for the honor. Scholars call "apocryphal" those books that claim to be by or about biblical figures but which are not in the canon. There are both Old and New Testament Apocrypha [singular: Apocryphon], including such books as 1 Enoch, the Testament of the Twelve Patriarchs, the Third Epistle to the Corinthians, and the Gospel of Thomas, among others. For many years, scholars did not treat these books seriously because of their supposed inferiority to the Scriptural books. In a famous passage, a great editor of the New Testament Apocrypha, Montague Rhodes James, asked rhetorically why these books were not in the canon? His response: Read them.[10]

But in the decades since James wrote those words, scholars have come to view the Apocrypha in a different light. As noted above, we now know that "apostolic" authors did not write most of the canonical books, so the obvious lack of apostolic authorship for most of the Apocrypha no longer discredits them. More importantly, we know that the Apocrypha reflect the views of many early Christians; some of those books achieved great popularity. For example, the Infancy

9. During the early stages of the Reformation, Martin Luther wished to delete the Epistle of James and the Book of Revelation from the Bible, but other Protestants rejected his arguments and he himself changed his mind.

10. M. R. James, *The Apocryphal New Testament* (Oxford: Oxford University Press, 1924) xi–xii.

Gospel (Protoevangelium) of James provides the names of Mary's parents (Anna and Joachim) and includes stories about her betrothal and wedding to Joseph. It is not impossible that this gospel contains some historical information, but it has strong legendary elements, and its appeal to its contemporaries lay in its miraculous accounts of Mary's betrothal and Jesus' childhood. This will disappoint those moderns who idolize the first Church, but, for others, this gives a realistic picture of the first Christians who enjoyed tales of miracles and fantasy. Books that achieve great popularity tell us a lot about the character of the people who read them.

Many works of art are undecipherable without the Apocrypha. For example, anyone viewing Giotto's frescoes in the Scrovegni Chapel in Padua must be familiar with the Protoevangelium story to understand the paintings, proof that the Apocrypha's popularity long outlived the reservations and even condemnations of the early Church. Furthermore, we also now know that many groups used Scriptural and apocryphal books to advance their causes. For example, most scholars believe that there was a distinct Pauline party in the late first and early second centuries that edited Paul's works (and possibly added an introduction to them via the Epistle to the Ephesians), produced an account of his career in the Book of Acts, and wrote more epistles under his name (the Pastorals). Eusebius of Caesarea included in his *Ecclesiastical History* an apocryphal letter written by Jesus to King Abgar of Edessa; he did so to strengthen what he considered to be the orthodox party there. Some feminist scholars have suggested that books promoting a strong role for women were excluded from the canon for just that reason.[11] No one can doubt that forces other than orthodoxy and tradition formed the biblical canon, which continues to be one of the most important areas in early Christian studies.

B. Interpretation[12]

All ancient biblical interpretation rested on the same premise: the Bible is somehow the word of God and thus the meaning of the scrip-

11. See Elaine Pagels, *The Gnostic Gospels* (New York: Random House, 1979), especially ch. 3.

12. A vast literature exists on this. The best brief introduction is Joseph Trigg's "Introduction: Patristic Biblical Interpretation" to his volume *Biblical Interpretation,* MFC 9 (1988) 13–55; James Kugel and Rowan Greer, *Early*

tural text can never be exhausted. Jews and Christians considered the Bible a gift God gave them so that they could live and believe rightly. They had an obligation to study the text and to make it relevant to their own lives. At no point could anyone say that a particular passage had been finally interpreted; the Bible would be with the community until the end of time, speaking anew in every age. Inevitably, some did claim to find the final meaning, but Augustine skeptically asked: "Which of us can discover [God's] will with such assurance as to say confidently, 'This is what Moses meant.'"[13] [Augustine apparently never met any modern exegetes.]

Christian interpretation initially followed Jewish models.

> Rabbinic interpreters contemporary with the Fathers had developed clearly defined methods of biblical interpretation. *Midrash* (meaning "investigation") is the reinterpretation of a specific text to update it or apply it to a specific situation; primarily it deals with short passages divorced from their larger context. *Targums,* on the other hand, are Aramaic translations and interpretations of the Hebrew Scriptures and carried out in synagogues from the period when Jews could no longer understand the original Hebrew text. Within targumic interpretation, *halakah* is a division of exegesis which finds and explicates the text's moral implications while *haggadah* is an expansion of the text, filling out its story with plot or subplot and additional details, often drawn from other scriptural passages. A *pesher* is an application of biblical prophecy to the last days; it often explicates a *raz* or mystery in this way.[14]

This passage lists the aims of exegesis; the Jews made use of many methods as well, for example, oral preaching in a synagogue, a learned exposition by a scribe, or, as is found in the Dead Sea Scrolls, "[e]ntire Old Testament books, or parts thereof . . . quoted verse by verse, followed by a brief interpretation."[15] People read the Bible as it suited their wants for doctrinal or moral instruction, spiritual comfort, legal teaching; and the same principle motivated all exegesis. Then as now, scholars interpreted the Bible to meet their needs.

Biblical Interpretation, Library of Early Christianity 3 (Philadelphia: Westminster Press, 1986) introduces both Jewish and Christian interpretation; a good, accessible survey is *Biblical Interpretation in the Early Church* by Mario Simonetti (Edinburgh: T & T Clark, 1994).

13. *Confessions* XII.xxiv.33; Chadwick, 263.

14. Trigg, *Biblical Interpretation,* 16–17.

15. Simonetti, *Biblical Interpretation,* 3.

Thus, a community like that which produced the Dead Sea Scrolls and whose members believed the end of the world to be near would search the Scriptures looking for some clue about the end, while religious legal scholars would try to understand what the Torah meant in a specific situation.

Inevitably, the Christians also interpreted the Bible to meet their own needs. The New Testament presumes the Old on every page, and scholars have found the first Christian biblical interpretation there.[16] The immediacy of the exegetes' concern is apparent. The Christian movement was parting from Judaism, and yet the Church claimed to be the successor of Israel. How could this be? The answer given in the gospels, especially Matthew's, is that Jesus fulfilled the prophecies of the Old Testament,[17] and the Jews did not recognize this or, more to Matthew's point, could not bring themselves to recognize this. Thus the Church (Matthew is the only evangelist to use the word) is the *verus Israel,* the true Israel.

Scholars debate how early this approach to the text appeared. The evangelists did not hesitate to attribute it to Jesus himself. Luke 4:21 portrays him saying to a synagogue audience, "Today this scripture has been fulfilled in your hearing." Possibly this type of interpretation did go back to Jesus; certainly Paul had begun to reinterpret the Hebrew Scriptures in a Christian sense within two decades of Jesus' death. Although this could lead to friction with the Jews, the Christians actually had no choice. They believed that Jesus had fulfilled the Old Testament, and thus they had to read its books to support their belief. The danger lay, then as now, in the exclusivity of this approach and the consequent marginalization of Jewish exegesis and belief.

The career of the apostle Paul set the stage for the Christian thrust into the Greco-Roman world, and the Christians brought the Hebrew Scriptures with them. This created problems for them. Many Greeks and Romans considered the Jews a rebellious Near Eastern people, obsessed with ritual laws, strange customs, and a god who was often angry at his own people.[18] Furthermore, sophisticated converts

16. See R. Greer, "The New Testament Writers and the Hebrew Scriptures" in *Early Biblical Interpretation,* 128–136.

17. Matthew's infancy narrative occupies only one and a half chapters yet manages to fulfill five prophecies.

18. The prophets repeatedly warned the people of God's anger at such practices as idolatry.

patronized the Old Testament's mythical elements, such as a talking snake or a talking donkey, and they considered its Greek (LXX) to be barbarous. Some Christians, notably the sectarian leader Marcion (fl. ca. 140–160) suggested that the Church should simply abandon the Old Testament, since its teaching could not be reconciled to that of Jesus. Although not indifferent to such criticisms, the Church leaders of the second century replied that this was the Bible of Jesus and his disciples and their successors, and that they could not abandon so venerable a tradition. The solution to the problem lay not in abandoning the Hebrew Scriptures but in recognizing the need to understand them properly. Christians must dig more deeply into their meaning.

The Christians turned to methods of literary analysis used by Greeks to interpret the works of Homer. His two great epic poems, the *Iliad,* the story of Achilles and the Greek siege of Troy, and the *Odyssey,* the story of Odysseus' adventurous return home, were monuments of Greek culture, known and quoted by every educated person. Homer wrote probably in the eighth century B.C., and by the fifth century, his views of the gods appeared crudely anthropomorphic. Both epics present the gods engaging in unedifying and even base activities. They bicker, they steal, they abuse humans, they punish innocent people for unconscious offenses. The philosophers observed that if humans acted as the gods did, the world would be in chaos. Greek intellectuals found themselves entranced by Homer but in need of some way to interpret his gods for their new world. The way was allegory.

Allegory means that a story told on one level has its true meaning on another, higher level. The approach has biblical support. In Galatians 4:22-28, Paul says that the Genesis account of the two mothers (Sarah, Hagar) of Abraham's two sons (Isaac, Ishmael) is an allegory. Hagar, a slave, and Sarah, a free woman, represent two covenants: the present, enslaved Jerusalem, and the future, free Jerusalem, which is above. But Paul did not make this concept popular for Christians; they learned it instead from an Alexandrian Jewish scholar, Philo.

Philo (ca. 20 B.C.–ca. A.D. 50), a Jewish scholar who had a Hellenistic education, grew up in Alexandria. He believed the Torah to contain God's word, but he knew that its literal rendering could not be true, because it contained elements which were physically impossible, for example, that "Cain went away from the presence of the Lord" (who is omnipresent), and which were morally repugnant, "such things as the domestic arrangements of the Patriarchs."[19] Philo knew that the Bible was true and that God would teach neither error nor immorality, and so he concluded that the truth must be hidden under these words. More conservative Jews rejected his approach, but Philo remained a prominent figure in the Alexandrian Jewish community.

His works greatly influenced Alexandrian Christians, particularly Clement of Alexandria (fl. 180–200) and his brilliant pupil Origen (185–ca. 254).[20] The latter believed the Bible to be a sea of mysteries, and he devoted endless energy to its decipherment.

Allegory contains an obvious danger. Once the exegete decides the text does not mean what it says on the literal level and that the real meaning lies on some higher level, what constraints exist in the interpretation? Can the exegete decide the text means absolutely anything, for example, in modern terms, that angels and demons represent two groups of aliens from outer space, fighting for control of Earth? Some critics, ancient and modern, would say Yes, and that is why allegory must be discarded, but Origen and others took their work very seriously and tried to find patterns of exegesis or interpretations which complimented Christian teaching or which matched other biblical passages. Modern scholars allow for an evolution of religious understanding and thus explain some parts of the Bible as reflections of a rather primitive world-view, but such a view was foreign to the ancient mind. For example, Joshua 6 portrays the Israelites turning over "the city [Jericho] and all that is in it . . . to the LORD for destruction" (v. 17), and thus they kill the entire population, right down to newborn infants, sparing only the family of a woman who had helped their spies. The Alexandrians simply could not believe that God would demand something like that, so they said that the people of Jericho represent our sins and that God wants us to eliminate them, right down to the tiniest one. Today this would sound like a forced interpretation, but in the third century, when exegetes faced either a barbarous literal interpretation or an allegorical one that preserved the beneficent view of God, the latter method saved the Bible for the Christians.

This example leads to another problem that plagued ancient interpreters, namely, how literal was the literal level? For example, did

19. Trigg, *Biblical Interpretation,* 15.

20. There exists a vast literature on Origen; see *EEXty* and *EECh;* for Origen's exegesis, see works cited in n. 12 as well as Joseph Trigg's *Origen: The Bible and Philosophy in the Third Century* (Atlanta: John Knox Press, 1983).

Joshua actually destroy Jericho or is this just a story for our edification? Such a question divided Christian scholars, although most concluded that events did happen on the literal level but that their "true"
meaning lay on a higher plane. For example, Origen and many after
him accepted the historicity of the city of Jerusalem, but they believed
that it also had a spiritual meaning, the "city to which none of those
on earth ascends or enters,"[21] that is, Jerusalem spiritually meant
heaven. There was the inevitable example of an event that could not
have occurred on the literal level but that formed an exception. For example, Matthew says (4:8) that the devil took Jesus "to a very high
mountain and showed him all the kingdoms of the world"; but the
exegetes knew that no real mountain offered such a view.

Somewhat similar to allegory was typology, that is, the notion that
an Old Testament event prefigured ("typified") one in the New. This,
too, has biblical foundation; Matthew 12:38-41 and Luke 11:29-32
portray Jesus comparing Jonah's "three days and three nights in the
belly of the sea monster" to his own "three days and three nights . . .
in the heart of the earth." Like the story of Jonah, some Old
Testament events lent themselves to typology, such as the Hebrews'
passage through the Red Sea as a type of baptism. Other Old
Testament passages practically demanded typology. For example,
Isaac was the only son, the bearer of the promise, who carried the
wood for his own sacrifice up the hill (Gen 22); for the Christians,
Isaac *must* be a type of Christ. Indeed, this event appears very frequently in early Christian art of all types, such as catacomb frescoes,
sarcophagus carvings, and mosaics. Typology could apply not only
to Christ but to his followers. The art of the catacombs portrays biblical examples of innocent suffering, such as the three young men in
the burning, fiery furnace (Dan 3:1-30), a type of Christ but also of
those who suffered in persecutions. Occasionally, exegetes carried
this too far; Augustine found what he considered clear references to
his ecclesiastical opponents, the Donatists, in the Book of Psalms![22]

Most of these references so far have been to the Old Testament,
but exegetes dealt with the New Testament as well. The earliest commentary is a Gnostic one, Heracleon's mid-second century commentary on John's gospel. No one knows why a Gnostic commentary
came first, but the approach quickly caught on. (In fact, all that re-

21. *Commentary on John*, xxiii.16; cited in Trigg, *Biblical Interpretation*, 100.
22. *Inter alia*, Second Discourse on Psalm 21, in *On the Psalms*, I, ACW 29
(1960) 220–226.

mains of Heracleon's commentary was preserved by Origen, who sought to refute it.) By the third century Christian exegetes were attempting to decipher the gospels, epistles, and even the Apocalypse.

The study of Scripture provided the most important outlet for Christian intellectual activity. Augustine even said that all learning should be aimed for the interpretation of Scripture, and he justified the reading of pagan literature if it helped Christians to understand the Bible. He even found a biblical warrant for it. Exodus 12:35-36 tells how the Hebrews, upon leaving Egypt, plundered the goods of the Egyptians, taking some of their gold and silver. Augustine believed this to be an allegory, that the goods of the Egyptians symbolized pagan learning that Christians could legitimately appropriate to better understand God's word.[23] But Scripture did not answer every question, and the early Christians also did theology.

3. Theology[24]

Theology technically means the study of God; it derives from two Greek words: *theos,* meaning God, and *logos,* meaning knowledge. But it has always meant far more than that. The word includes virtually every scholarly discipline in the study of Christianity, for example, scholars speak of moral theology and biblical theology or of ecclesiology, the theology of the Church, or of soteriology, the theology of salvation. The medieval theologian Anselm of Canterbury provided a classic definition of theology, *fides quaerens intellectum,* faith seeking understanding. The theologian is a person of faith who wants to present that faith in a rational manner. Simultaneously, however, the theologian is one seeking; that is, the theologian realizes that she or he is dealing with the divine or with divine activity and thus with something ultimately incomprehensible.

All Christian denominations practice theology, but many debate its very nature. For some denominations, theology means what the Bible teaches and no more, and some theology can actually be done

23. His book, *On Christian Doctrine,* deals with the theme of education and Scripture; the reference to pagan literature is at xl.60; 75.

24. Except for citing examples, this section will not discuss specific theological problems, which have generated libraries. Instead it will concentrate on why the early Christians concluded that the Bible alone was insufficient for their needs and thus turned to theology. A good introduction to theology in this period is *The Making of Creeds* by Frances Young (London: SCM Press, 1991).

this way. But too often this widely popular view, presented under the guise of fidelity to the Bible, goes unexamined. Its defenders see theologians of other traditions as people who twist the simple meaning of the biblical text into something far more complicated than the scriptural authors ever intended, but these defenders do not always consider their own premises or practices. If they did, they would realize that they, too, put limits on their so-called biblical fidelity.

For example, biblical views of war present a righteous people fighting on God's side, but can there ever be such a thing as a righteous thermonuclear war, which destroys life on earth? The Bible takes slavery for granted, but would any modern Christian use that to justify slavery today?

To take this fidelity-to-Scripture principle to a ridiculous level, consider that the Book of Leviticus (13:29-37) gives advice on curing a skin disease that includes examination of the infected area by a priest. Yet how many Christians would go to a priest rather than a physician for advice about a skin infection? Sooner or later, all Christians must recognize that the Bible on its own simply cannot answer all the questions that Christians face.

Most Christians take the more open view that one should be faithful to the Bible but not be bound by it completely, for example, on questions like war and slavery. This is the challenge theology takes up—to start with biblical revelation and to try to understand it in the light of contemporary knowledge. For example, the Bible portrays God as the creator of the cosmos. How should that be understood today in view of the Big Bang theory or of the extent of the cosmos or of evolutionary theories that see the universe in constant flux? These questions do not drive God from the cosmos, but they do make us aware that the biblical view of a deity who lives in the sky, ordering a limited world by his word, needs to be reconsidered in light of modern science.

This exemplifies one element of theology that many Christians resent, its reliance on nonbiblical factors, in this case, modern astronomy. This is hardly a new question; indeed, it goes back to the second century. But to ignore extrabiblical knowledge condemns Christians intellectually to sticking their heads in the sand. Can Christians talk about sexual morality without taking into account all that biology tells about the human body, knowledge unavailable in the biblical period? Can we talk about economic justice without a solid knowledge of how a modern economy functions, knowledge that cannot be found in the Bible?

This does not mean that modern knowledge weakens belief in the Bible, but it does mean that we use what we know to understand the Bible better and to make the Bible relevant today. As we noted earlier, in considering allegory, if the choice is nonsense by reading literally, or sense by trying other methods, Christians will always choose other methods. These modern examples used economics and physical sciences, but for ancient Christians the nonbiblical discipline that dominated their theology was philosophy, which continues to play a significant role in modern theology.

A. Theology and Philosophy

Philosophy literally means the love of wisdom, from two Greek words: *philia,* meaning love, and *sophia,* meaning wisdom. It first appeared in Greece, when philosophers whom scholars call the pre-Socratics (that is, they lived before Socrates) initially began to examine their world and their modes of living almost exclusively by the use of reason rather than by religious belief or social tradition. In the ancient world, what we call science formed a branch of philosophy called natural philosophy; other branches included ethics, the study of right living, and ontology, the study of being, how things are in themselves. What later generations recognized as Greek philosophy had its greatest era during the lives of Socrates (ca. 470–399 B.C.), his pupil Plato (ca. 429–347) and Plato's pupil Aristotle (384–322).[25] This great triumvirate was followed by the Stoics, the Epicureans, and lesser-known groups, as well as those who attempted to revive the older doctrines, such as the Neo-Platonists.[26]

This formidable group of intellectuals had an awesome influence on thinking people. As the conquests of Alexander and then of his successors, the Romans, brought Greek modes of thinking to other

25. No account of this amazing chain of teacher and pupil would be complete without mention of Aristotle's most famous student, Alexander the Great (356–323).

26. Although there are many valuable histories of ancient philosophy, the student may want to look at Everett Ferguson's *Backgrounds,* 299–371, for clear discussions of the various philosophies and guides to further reading. A standard guide to the philosophy of the period is *The Cambridge History of Later Greek and Early Medieval Philosophy* by A. H. Armstrong (New York: Cambridge University Press, 1968). A solid survey of the role of philosophy in Early Christianity is *Philosophy in Christian Antiquity* by Christopher Stead (New York: Cambridge University Press, 1994).

parts of the world, intellectuals from other traditions appropriated some of this, for example, Philo.

Scholars debate how early philosophic ideas began to penetrate Christianity. In 1 Corinthians 1:17, 1:25, and 2:5, Paul explicitly contrasts the gospel message with the wisdom *(sophia)* of humans. It is not likely that philosophers had joined the Corinthians' community, but perhaps some community members had raised questions with a philosophical base. Acts 17:18 says that "some Epicurean and Stoic philosophers debated with [Paul]" and rejected his preaching on the resurrection. Colossians 2:8 warns Christians to "see to it that no one takes you captive through philosophy and empty deceit. . . ." Initial contacts between Christianity and philosophy did not promise much for the future. How then did philosophy gain a foothold in Christian thought? The answer lies in the westward expansion of Christianity and the subsequent conversion of more and more Greeks and Romans.

Few converts, to be sure, were philosophers or even knew any philosophy; but, inevitably, some did, and they asked questions, good and sincere ones, raised by believing Christians who had honest difficulties with some aspects of biblical teaching. These questions soon revealed the difficulty of sticking just to the biblical text. Mark's gospel opens (1:1) with the words, "The beginning of the good news of Jesus Christ, the Son of God." But a question arises: how is Jesus the son of God? Even in the Bible, the phrase can have many meanings. For example, all people on earth are the children of God, and Christians in a special way (Romans 8:16); is Jesus God's son the way all of us are his daughters and sons?

Genesis 6:1-4 speaks of "sons of God" who lusted after women, and the Book of Job (1:6) shows them presenting themselves before God in heaven. Is Jesus God's son in this way, an angelic member of the heavenly court?

When humans have children, there was a time when those children did not exist. Was there a time when the Son of God did not exist? And if there were a time when he did not exist, does that mean that there might be another time when he does exist, that is, can he be born, live, and die? If God had one child, can God have more?

Furthermore, children are as fully human as their parents, so if a couple has two children, there are four people in the family. Does the existence of a Son of God mean that there are two gods? Is that even possible? Is the Son a sort of lesser god, inferior to the Father? And if he is inferior to the Father, in what ways? And will he always be so? Human children are "inferior" to their parents in the sense that as dependents they do not share the parents' legal status, but that situation ends when the children grow up. Will the Son of God "grow up," so to speak?

For that matter, is Jesus actually the Son of God or is this just an image the Bible uses in the way that Psalms 17:8, 36:7, 61:4, and 91:4 picture God as a huge bird who shelters people under his wings?

These questions, which derive not from philosophy but either from the Bible or from common human experience, demonstrate how easily a biblical concept can become complicated and a point of dispute. They also demonstrate the necessity of theology to answer questions that the literal text of the Bible cannot. Finally, they demonstrate why early theologians turned to philosophy for assistance. The Bible witnesses to an article of faith, that Jesus Christ is the Son of God, but it does not answer the question of the nature of Jesus' divine sonship. Theology starts with faith, with revelation, and then goes on to investigate the matter, using whatever tools are on hand.

Jesus' divine sonship falls under the heading of christology, the theology of Christ, and a there is a vast literature on this topic.[27] We will just note here that the two classic formulations both involved philosophical terminology. The Council of Chalcedon (451) declared that the Son of God was an independent person who shared the divine nature but who also took a human nature at the incarnation, so that the Son was one person with two natures. The opponents of the Chalcedonians, the Monophysites, believed that the Son was indeed an independent person who joined a human nature to his divine one so that the two merged into one nature (in Greek *mono* means one, and *physis* means nature).

The attraction of philosophy for Christian intellectuals did not lie solely in the terminological precision it could offer them. They were also struck by what the philosophers had taught. Without the divine revelation found in Scripture, many philosophers had concluded that there was one God, that this God ordered creation, that humans should live a moral life, that a life of virtue was worth dying for (Socrates, Cato the Stoic). To many Christians this could not have

27. The standard account of the development of christology is *Christ in Christian Tradition I: From the Apostolic Age to Chalcedon* by Aloys Grillmeier (Atlanta: John Knox Press, 1975). Reliable and more accessible titles are *Jesus, Christ and Savior* by Gerard Ettlinger, MFC 2 (1987) and *The Christological Controversy* by Richard Norris (Philadelphia: Fortress Press, 1980).

just happened; they saw the hand of God behind it. Justin Martyr (d. ca. 165) argued that all truth comes from God via his Word or Logos. Therefore, anyone who spoke the truth possessed the Logos. Justin recognized that the philosophers did not possess the Logos as the Christians did, because the latter acknowledged the incarnate Logos, Jesus Christ; but Justin believed that they possessed some form of the Logos, perhaps as a seed. He went so far as to suggest that the philosophers were Christians before Christ. Indeed, the Christian was the true philosopher, the true lover of wisdom, because the Christian loved the incarnate wisdom of God.

Clement of Alexandria felt the same way. He believed that just as the Old Testament had prepared the Jews for Christ, Greek learning had prepared the Gentiles. Augustine openly acknowledged the role that the Neo-Platonist writers played in his journey toward God. Christian intellectuals found that philosophy enabled them to approach more rationally although never to solve the mysteries of their faith. To be sure, philosophical terminology could lead to serious pitfalls. In the fourth-century Arian controversies, attempts to explain the Son of God's divinity as "consubstantial" with the Father divided the Greek-speaking bishops and people, but there really was no way not to use it. Ideas and questions do not just go away. The ancient Christians had no choice but to investigate the nature of God, the relationship of the trinitarian persons, or the origins of evil, and to do so well beyond the literal meaning of the Bible. It is one of the ironies of history that books written in a Semitic environment have throughout history been interpreted in a Greek one.

B. Theology and Tradition in the Church

The definition of theology, faith seeking understanding, begins with faith. The theologian is a member of the faith community and, as such, must relate to all others in the community.

Modern scholars often reject this definition. They practice theology in an academic environment, and an atheist could teach about beliefs that she or he does not share. In fact, most modern theologians are believers who do stand in a particular denominational tradition, but they, too, accept the modern attitude that one can teach freely about something in which one does not believe.

But this would make no sense to the ancients, for whom belief and Church membership were prerequisites for doing theology. This attitude had significant ramifications. The theologian could not just say whatever entered her or his mind; the theologian had to be conscious always of the content of Scripture and how that was understood in the Church. To the modern Western mind, this impinges on the individual's freedom; to the ancient mind and the minds of many contemporary traditional peoples, membership in a community and participation in a religious tradition provided a framework and a community that, to them, the modern Western intellectual both lacks and needs.

The notion of tradition began very early, virtually as soon as Jesus began to preach, because, inevitably, his first disciples would refer back to things he had said as normative. Even that shaker of foundations, Paul the Apostle, resorted to citing traditions. When he gives his views on whether women should veil themselves, he plays his trump card: "But if anyone is disposed to be contentious—we have no such custom, nor do the churches of God" (1 Cor 11:16). The Corinthians should do what Paul says not because he is imposing his own views upon them but because he is merely telling them what the other churches have done.

In a society that changes rapidly, tradition can seem onerous, binding us to the now irrelevant customs of our parents. Tradition is fine at Thanksgiving or Christmas; otherwise we must look to the future. But in the ancient world, tradition represented both past and future, that is, people believed that they both stood in a tradition and added to it. Paul was glad to cite tradition in this instance, but he knew that what he taught about the Christians' freedom from the Law differed from what people before him had believed. Paul believed that God had called him to be an apostle (1 Cor 1:1) and that he had acted in good faith, and so he was adding to the tradition.

Tradition was organic, a living link between past and present. When Irenaeus of Lyons combated the Gnostics, he pointed to the living link between himself, through the bishop Polycarp of Smyrna, back to the first-century presbyter, John. No group developed the notion of tradition more than the bishops of Rome, who traced their lineage to the disciple Peter; by the late fourth century, Pope Siricius wrote letters not just in own name but in the name of Peter who, Siricius claimed, spoke through him.[28] Monastic writers routinely added to the rules laid down by their deceased founders, but did

28. An excellent introduction to the ancient papacy is Robert Eno's *The Rise of the Papacy* (Collegeville, Minn.: The Liturgical Press, 1990); reference to Siricius on p. 96.

so in the founders' names because they were still alive in their communities.

The most important element in tradition was the Church itself. By the second century, the Christians viewed their community as the continuation of Israel, thus taking themselves back to the days of Abraham. But the Church could go back even further. The second-century Roman writer Hermas portrayed the Church as an elderly woman who got progressively younger as his book went on. The Church had been present with God at the creation (the elderly woman) and would be with the Christians in the future (the young woman). In an era when people routinely defined themselves by their lineage, when they could trace their families back generations, when they pointed with pride to their long residency in their home cities or on their ancestral lands, the idea of a Church that lived from creation to the end had an appeal few moderns can imagine.

This attitude toward tradition appears repeatedly in Christian writings, but most of all in theology. Christian theologians labored to prove that what they taught was what the Church had always taught. Once they had established the canon of Scripture, they tried to align their teachings with that; once their individual Churches had histories, they tried to show their consistency with the teachings of their predecessors. For example, during the Donatist-Catholic schism in North Africa, both sides repeatedly stressed their fidelity to the teachings of the third-century martyr/bishop Cyprian of Carthage (d. 258), and accused the other side of betraying him. Inevitably this tack led to some serious disingenuousness, as theologians found the most remarkable things in the Bible or in their predecessors; but the point is that they wanted to align their teaching with them. The last title any ancient theologian wanted was "original."

A fifth-century Gallic writer, Vincent of Lerins, summed up the prevailing view. Christians must believe only what has been taught everywhere, always, and by everyone *(quod ubique, quod semper, quod ab omnibus creditum est).*[29]

The Vincentian Canon, as this phrase came to be called, sounded fine, but it was ultimately unrealistic because local churches developed their own traditions, and it was impossible to find anything except, perhaps, the existence of God, which was believed everywhere, always, and by everyone. For instance, no matter how powerful the Roman bishops became in Western Europe, the Africans never ac-

---

29. Cited in Stevenson, *Creeds, Councils, and Controversies,* 298–300.

cepted their authority completely, and the Greek bishops gave it an honorary status. The Africans may have been obsessed with Cyprian, yet in other parts of the Church he was seen as a good man, a martyr, but hardly someone whose teachings were normative. The Council of Nicaea (325), later venerated as the first ecumenical council, proved enormously divisive for half a century after its close. Eventually, time settled some of these differences, but never all of them, and the ancients did not always see that as a problem. On the contrary, most of them willingly acknowledged local traditions; in general, only the Roman bishops insisted on universal acceptance of their own practices.

Therefore, when Christian theologians dealt with a theological problem, such as Jesus' divine sonship, they would consider the biblical evidence (what the gospels said, how the phrase "son of God" is used elsewhere in Scripture), then they would consider what previous theologians, especially those of their own Church, had said, and only then what other interpretations, including those influenced by philosophy, were possible. They would also consider writings of those who disagreed with them; for example, in the fourth and fifth centuries, theologians from Alexandria and Antioch often disagreed on theological questions, and theologians of both schools felt constrained to defend their predecessors. That did not mean that they saw no value in what others taught or that they never criticized their predecessors, but that they worked primarily within a tradition. Tradition extended far beyond theology, for instance, into liturgy; many local churches had their own prayers and confessions of faith.

4. Music[30]

In the modern world Christian music abounds. Virtually every denomination uses some kind of music, some music publishing houses specialize in gospel music, and we have come to view the organ as virtually an official church instrument. But, like philosophy, music, too, had to win its place in early Christianity. The Bible offers many examples of music in Israelite life. Genesis 31:27 refers to sending

30. See James McKinnon, *Music in Early Christian Literature* (New York: Cambridge University Press, 1987); Everett Ferguson, "Toward a Patristic Theology of Music," in Studia Patristica 24 (1993) 266–283; Edward Foley, *Foundations of Christian Music: The Music of Pre-Constantinian Christianity* (Collegeville, Minn.: The Liturgical Press, 1996).

someone off "with mirth and songs, with tambourine and lyre," while Judges 11:34 reverses the process, referring to "timbrels" and "dancing" to welcome someone home, a notion repeated in 1 Samuel 18:6-7. Isaiah 5:12 complains of the rich, "whose feasts consist of lyre and harp, tambourine and flute and wine, but who do not regard the deeds of the LORD," an emphatically secular use of music.

Music also played a role in Israelite religious life, most prominently in the career of David, "the sweet psalmist of Israel" (2 Sam 23:1), the traditional composer of the psalms as well as a musician whose lyre playing could drive away an evil spirit (1 Sam 16:23). When Zadok the priest anointed Solomon king, the blowing of a trumpet and playing on pipes accompanied the ceremony (1 Kgs 1:39-40). The Book of Sirach (50:16) speaks of trumpets in use in the Temple itself. Significantly, the Old Testament references specify not only singing but also the use of musical instruments, such as the trumpet, harp, lyre, flute, tambourine, pipes, and, most prominently, the ram's horn. In this, the Israelites shared the customs of their Near Eastern neighbors.

For reasons scholars cannot yet explain, the Jews, after the Roman destruction of Jerusalem, abandoned musical instruments in the synagogue in favor of a purely vocal music. The rationale given by the rabbis was that mourning for the loss of the Temple precluded the use of instruments, but scholars believe that synagogue music had always been vocal in character. This practice developed a psalmody and chant that modern Jews still use.

This practice also had a tremendous effect upon Christian views of music. The New Testament makes a few references to musical instruments, most notably Paul's famous reference to "a noisy gong or a clanging cymbal" in 1 Corinthians 13:1, but the allusions to music in worship (Eph 5:19, Col 3:16) refer to singing only. The apparent restriction against musical instruments applied not only to earth but also to heaven; the Book of Revelation likewise refers only to singing (4:10, 11:16-17). Since most New Testament books were composed shortly after the destruction of Jerusalem, the practice of vocal music alone in worship seems to have been well established.

The bias against musical instruments continued for some time, and some Christians felt obliged to explain it. Theodoret of Cyrrhus (d. ca. 466) provided a historical reason. "The people of Israel spent a long time in Egypt and were introduced to the shameful customs of the inhabitants; they were taught by them to sacrifice to idols and demons, to play, to dance, and to take pleasure in musical instruments."[31] Since the Jews had subsequently abandoned idolatry and demon worship, so, too, had they given up music instruments.

Other writers made use of allegory when faced with biblical references to musical instruments. John Chrysostom combined allegory with pedagogy:

> Some also take the meaning of these instruments allegorically and say that the tympanum calls for the death of the flesh and that the psaltery looks to heaven. And indeed, this instrument is moved from above, not from below like the cithara. But I would say this: that in ancient times, they were thus led by these instruments due to the slowness of their understanding, and were gradually drawn away from idolatry. Accordingly, just as (God) allowed sacrifices, so too did he permit instruments, making concessions to their weakness.[32]

The moralists had an opinion too. The African Arnobius of Sicca (d. ca. 330) saw the use of instruments in terms of pagan lasciviousness:

> . . . under the influence of [the tibia and scabella, a wind and percussion instrument, respectively] a multitude of other lascivious souls abandon themselves to bizarre movements of the body, dancing and singing, forming rings of dancers, and ultimately raising their buttocks and hips to sway with the rippling motion of their loins.[33]

Arnobius' view echoes that of the moralists with regard to the theater, the baths, and the games, that is, a fear that pagan immorality would spread to Christians. Fear of immorality led to another restriction, this time on women. Isidore of Pelusium (d. ca. 435) reflected the view of ecclesiastical writers when he said that women singers

> . . . do not feel compunction in hearing the divine hymns, but rather misuse the sweetness of melody to arouse passion, thinking that it is no better than the songs of stage. [Note the allusion to the theater.] Thus it is necessary—if we would seek what is pleasing

31. Cited in McKinnon, 106–7.
32. Cited in ibid., 83.
33. Cited in ibid., 49–50.

> to God and do that which is of public benefit—that we stop these
> women from singing in church. . . ."[34]

Isidore's views had strong support. The Church historian Eusebius of Caesarea attributed the first women's chorus in church to the self-serving machinations of Paul of Samosata, a villain to many Greek-speaking Christians.[35] Whether Paul did half the things his enemies accused him of is debatable, but the attribution carried weight. Even though both Ambrose of Milan and Ephraem the Syrian encouraged singing by both men and women, "the opposition to women's choruses was extended to all participation in the liturgy. . . ."[36]

But with these considerable reservations aside, the early Christians had many positive beliefs about music. Edward Foley has emphasized that they lived in an aural environment and that their early prayers could have included spontaneous, communal singing.[37] Many writers recommended psalmody to their congregations. They also often contrasted the Christian practice of singing psalms with reverence to the pagan practice of uncontrolled musical passions, which even extended to self-castration in some cults. The ancient Greeks had believed in the power of music on a person, and some Christians genuinely feared that power if it were unleashed. They believed that plain, unaccompanied chant of the Christians reflected the purity of their faith, which brought peace to the believer instead of the confusion of the cults. Arnobius spoke of the relation between pagan music and obscene movements of the body. In contrast, the Christians believed, there should be a harmony between musical movements and those of the soul, a harmony that reflected the divine harmony of the creation. "Just as we make known and signify the thoughts of the soul through the words we express, so too the Lord wished the melody of the words to be a sign of the spiritual harmony of the soul," said Athanasius,[38] in words with which many of his contemporaries would have agreed.

They also practiced a degree of biblical fidelity here because, in spite of the references to instruments, the Old Testament puts far more stress on the psalms. Indeed, some patristic Christian authors wrote psalms in imitation of the great David.

34. Cited in ibid., 61.
35. Eusebius, *History of the Church* 7:30. 10; Williamson, 317.
36. Article "Music" by Everett Ferguson in *EEXty,* II. 787–790.
37. *Foundations,* ch. 4.
38. Cited in McKinnon, *Music,* 53.

Although Christian musical texts do not survive from the earliest period, scholars have concluded that worshipers in general sang either antiphonally or responsorially.

As for the most famous early Christian music, Gregorian chant, scholars can find no solid link to its supposed composer or at least its patron, Pope Gregory I the Great (590–604). What later centuries understood as Gregorian chant first appears in the early Middle Ages, and while it may derive from an old Roman chant, and while it may be contemporaneous with Gregory, "the earliest written sources were not compiled in Rome; they originated in the West and East Frankish states," that is, parts of Charlemagne's empire, which was divided after his death in 814.[39]

5. The Visual Arts[40]

In Exodus 20:4, God required Moses to establish an imageless worship of him. Since the ancient pagans who surrounded Israel often personified natural powers or represented the gods in animal or human form, the Exodus prohibition against idolatry extended itself to images of persons as well as of God. While we know what many ancient Egyptians, Greeks, and Romans looked like, we have no images of David or Solomon or other Israelite leaders. This practice survived into Jesus' day and explains why the Christians made no image of him from life. Ancient Jewish visual art consisted largely of nonrepresentational decorations.

Architecture, however, was a visual art that did not run the risk of idolatry. The Bible gives an extensive account of the beauty of Solomon's Temple (1 Kgs 6–8), while Jesus' disciples stood in awe of the Temple begun by Herod and still unfinished in their day (Mark 13:1).

When Jews and Christians had their parting of the ways, and when large numbers of Gentiles became Christians, they wanted to use visual representations. Some of these had no religious significance, such as personal portraits or images made of family members. But the love of the visual soon began to manifest itself strongly. As more and more Christians wished to create visual images of God, Jesus,

39. Gerald Abraham, *The Concise Oxford History of Music* (London: Oxford University Press, 1979) 60.

40. For a well-illustrated survey of this topic, see *Early Christian Art and Architecture* by Robert Milburn (Berkeley: University of California Press, 1988).

his family, and his disciples, Christian leaders had to face the problem of whether there could indeed be a Christian representational art. These first Christians found themselves addressing a question that would bedevil the Church throughout history.

For example, in the eighth century, the Byzantine emperors Leo I (717–741) and Constantine V (741–775), convinced that images led to idolatry, instituted iconoclasm, literally, the breaking of images, when imperial troops pulled icons down from churches and smashed them. In the twelfth century, the Cistercian monks, religious reformers, objected to what they considered the excessive decorations of Benedictine churches and constructed their own churches along Spartan lines. During the Reformation, some extremist Protestants smashed statues and stained-glass windows to rid the churches of idolatry, a practice perfected by the Puritans. Representational art has always caused controversy in Christianity.

Most scholars date Christian art after the year 200, from whence the earliest images survive. But many "Christian" images actually have a pagan foundation, for example, a young man carrying a sheep on his shoulders is known from Greek art centuries before Christ. Luke 15:6 has Jesus saying, "When he [the shepherd] has found it [the lost sheep], he lays it on his shoulders, rejoicing." A dove would be another obvious theme as a symbol of the Holy Spirit, as would an anchor, a symbol of hope. Modern scholars believe that Christians purchased or commissioned representations of doves, anchors, or good shepherds, images that resonated with Christian themes but which were not specifically Christian.[41] The first unambiguous reference to Christian art appears in the work of Clement of Alexandria circa 200. He suggested that when Christians used their signet rings to make an impression in soft wax when signing a document, they should use Christian symbols, such as the dove or a ship (for the Church) or a fish, an anagram for Christ, that is, a word made from the first letters of a phrase. [The Greek word for fish included the initial letters of the phrase "Jesus Christ, God's Son, Savior."] Clement disapproved of the use of pagan symbols.

Significantly, this earliest reference to Christian art involves iconography, which we considered earlier in the book as a source for our knowledge of the early Christians. Christians viewed art as they viewed the Bible, the one a verbal, the other a visual representation

41. See Paul C. Finney, *The Invisible God: the Earliest Christians on Art* (New York: Oxford University Press, 1994).

of reality beyond words or images. While some art offered portrayals of biblical or Christian scenes, much of it tended to point to other realities. Conveniently, this was also the way in which Christians warded off charges of idolatry, that is, no one worshiped the image, which would be idolatrous, but rather the reality to which it pointed.

Literary references after Clement do not appear immediately, but scholars do not need them because, by the mid- to late-third century, the art itself has begun to appear in the most famous ancient Christian sites, the Roman catacombs, places of burial and occasionally of worship. Many frescoes adorn the walls of the catacombs, often with funereal themes, such as the story Jonah, or with themes reflecting the tenuous situation of the Christians, such as Old Testament figures who suffered unjust persecution but triumphed in the end, thanks to divine assistance. The latter part of the third century also witnesses the earliest Christian sarcophagi. A sarcophagus is a stone tomb with a lid and often with decorations on the side. Because of the cost of such a coffin, as well as of the carving, these usually indicate a rich patron.

Architecture of this date virtually does not exist. Paul speaks of the church in the house of Prisca and Aquila (Rom 16:5, 1 Cor 16:19) and in the house of Philemon, Apphia, and Archippus (Phil 1–2), while Colossians (4:15) speaks of the church in the house of Nympha. Acts speaks of a liturgical gathering in the house of Mary, the mother of John Mark (12:12). This initial pattern of having churches meet in someone's home (including the homes of women) persisted for some time, yet only one house church has been excavated, and that a third-century one in the Syrian city of Dura Europos on the Roman/Persian frontier.[42] Yet Eusebius records that in Diocletian's persecution in 303, many churches were destroyed, indicating that some buildings recognizable as Christian places of worship had been built in the late third century.[43]

As with so many other aspects of early Christianity, the conversion of Constantine ushered in a new age for the arts, especially architecture. The emperor wanted an art that reflected Christianity's new, imperial status. Impelled by the edifice complex, he turned his attention

42. Because the Persians destroyed the city in 256, the church can date no later than that. The remains of a synagogue and a Mithraeum prove that a vital religious diversity characterized the life of this strategic place. See the article "Dura" with bibliography in *EECh,* I. 545, along with a diagram of the house church in fig. 108.

43. Eusebius, *History of the Church* 8:2.2; Williamson, 329–330.

to building churches. He particularly liked the basilica model, a large, roofed, rectangular hall with aisles on either side marked off by rows of columns. The emperor's inspiration and insistence caused the erection in Rome of Saint John Lateran and Saint Peter's in the Vatican, both basilicas built on imperial property. Other churches soon followed, and wealthy and influential Christians imitated the emperor in endowing churches. Basilicas appeared all over the empire, and the popularity of the basilican style continued right through to the sixth century, with Justinian's Church of the Hagia Sophia in Constantinople, although with increasing modifications as the Christian architects experimented with diverse possibilities.

Fourth-century Christian buildings ranged over many areas and thus involved many styles.

> We have buildings that embody different functions, for example, martyr churches, palace churches, and covered cemetery churches; buildings that were planned longitudinally, and others that have a centralized (i.e., cruciform) plan. Some Constantinian churches incorporate circular and octagonal halls; some have a single nave; others, a nave flanked by two or four aisles. Some terminate in an apse, others in a rectangular bay or a transept. Some Constantinian churches have galleries, and some have windows lighting the nave. The fabric differs also from one building to the next: some are built of large ashlars, and some of concrete faced with brick. In short, variety of design and execution is the key. . . .[44]

The diversity that applied to architecture also applied to all the art forms. Catacomb frescoes and sarcophagi continued to be produced, but to these could now be added statuary, textiles, glass, gems, metalwork, ivories, manuscript illuminations, coins, and mosaics. With the end of the persecutions and with the patronage of wealthy individuals and local churches, Christian artists found themselves very much in demand, and they rose to the occasion. The skills employed by pagan artisans to produce unforgettable images of Greek and Roman gods and humans turned to Christian themes and, important for the historian, Christian people. Portraits of famous Christians, especially members of the imperial family, become common. In some cases, the portrait may be idealized, but others, such as the mosaic of Ambrose in the church of S. Vittore in Milan, clearly are from life.[45]

44. Paul C. Finney, "Art" in *EEXty,* I. 123.

45. Ambrose died in 397, and the mosaic dates shortly after 400; see a color illustration of the mosaic in *EECh,* fig. 20.

Often churches in important political centers, such as Rome, Ravenna, and Constantinople, contained the physically larger works of art, such as sculpted baptismal fonts and mosaic floors or ceilings, and the more expensive smaller items, such as elegant liturgical vessels and illuminated Bibles. Yet individual patrons could commission works for personal ornament and devotion, such as carved gemstones or wedding caskets.

The art emerged from a church that had changed, and, not surprisingly, the themes also changed. The fourth-century theological emphasis on the Trinity caused the baptism of Jesus, the only trinitarian scene in the Bible, to become very popular. When the Council of Ephesus in 431 proclaimed Mary as the Mother of God, images of the Virgin proliferated along with portrayals of the nativity. The cult of saints became popular in the fifth and sixth centuries, accompanied soon by visual images of the saints. Since Christianity was now the religion of the imperial family, Jesus appeared more and more wearing the imperial purple, emphasizing the link between Church and State, while rulers often appeared with nimbuses to emphasize their sacred character. The triumph of Christianity also appeared in various works of art, portraying Christ as an emperor in heaven surrounded by his apostles as a sort of celestial court. Finally, since many people in that era could not read, artistic programs often had a pedagogical intent, to familiarize the illiterate with the great tales of the Bible.

The earliest Christians approached cultural life rather hesitantly, especially since so much of that life had pagan roots and connections. Because of farsighted individuals like Clement of Alexandria and Augustine of Hippo, the Christians realized that they could maintain their faith and still participate in the cultural life of the ancient world. The significance of this decision cannot be calculated. Can we really envision a Christianity without great theologians like Thomas Aquinas and Rudolf Bultmann, great composers like Giovanni da Palestrina and Johann Sebastian Bach, great artists like Michelangelo and Christopher Wren, a Christianity without the Book of Kells, the Cathedral of Chartres, Handel's "Messiah"? The early Christian decision to be open to the world rather than to withdraw from it completely impacted not only the first generations of believers but all generations of believers and nonbelievers after them.

Chapter Six

Living in the World

In recent decades, scholars have made extensive use of the social sciences to understand early Christianity, to see how the economic and class backgrounds of Christians affected their view of their world. This chapter will survey some of these social questions.[1]

Several times in this book, we have emphasized the difference in outlook between our age and that of ancient peoples. It perhaps appears most clearly in the physical world, their acceptance of a geocentric universe and of a world with vast unknown areas, but their views on social questions also varied severely from ours.

Modern people condemn racism, the practice of evaluating someone primarily on her or his race, echoing Martin Luther King's plea that we judge people by the contents of their character and not by the color of their skin. To be sure, racism survives and even flourishes in many societies, including some that claim to oppose it; but in general, people reject it because it is immoral and unfair. We like to think that we are unique, that we have achieved some level of education or skill or the like, and we resent the idea that someone would ignore our achievements and evaluate us solely on our race.

But this was not the view of the ancient world. People took it for granted that some races or even just one race (their own, naturally) had achieved more than others and could be justly considered superior. Furthermore, these people had no reluctance about saying this.

---

1. Several volumes in the Message of the Fathers of the Church series deal with social questions: vol. 13, *Women in the Early Church* by Elizabeth Clark (1983); vol. 19, *The Early Fathers on War and Military Service* by Louis Swift (1983); vol. 20, *Social Thought* by Peter Phan (1984).

The best-known example would be the Jewish notion of a Chosen People. But the Egyptians prized their antiquity, and the Greeks openly considered themselves to be the intellectual superiors of the Mediterranean world, two claims indifferent to the Romans, who believed that their military, governing, and organizational abilities made them the superior race.[2] The African writer Tertullian said that some pagans considered the Christians a *tertium genus,* a third race, different from Jews and Gentiles but worse.[3] The anonymous second-century author of the *Epistle to Diognetus* suggested that the Christians were the members of every race but superior to every race: "They live, each in his or her native land, but as though they were not really at home there. . . . They dwell on earth, but they are citizens of heaven."[4]

People were understandably offended if someone of a different race claimed that her or his race was superior, but they would not have been offended at the premise. They simply would have considered it to be incorrect.

The same was true for social classes. In modern democratic societies, we take it for granted that people can move ahead on their own abilities. Americans like to contrast two presidents: George Washington, who grew up wealthy in a mansion on a plantation, and Abraham Lincoln, who grew up poor in a log cabin and had to read books by firelight. These pictures must certainly be nuanced, but they express the American attitude that worthy people from all classes can reach the top in the United States.

The modern world has also rejected notions of royal and noble blood. Some countries still have monarchies and noble families, but their blood does not entitle them to a role in government. In fact, their constant presence in the pages of tabloid newspapers proves how lightly many people take their status. To understand the ancient attitude, we must completely reverse this picture.

Although ancient society was not completely static, for the most part people stayed where they were socially. If you came from a noble family, you would enjoy the benefits of privilege for your

2. In the great Roman epic poem the *Aeneid,* VI.1145–1154, the shade of Anchises, Aeneas' father, foretells Rome's future and says that others (the Greeks) can busy themselves with the arts and sciences, but the Romans will rule and give laws.

3. *Against the Heathen* I.8; ANF 3, 116–117.

4. *Epistle to Diognetus* 5; FC 1, 359.

whole life. Furthermore, you would accept your high economic and social status as deserved, even though you did nothing to earn it, and other members of society would accept it, too. If you were born a peasant, you would probably die a peasant, as would your children and grandchildren. If you were born a slave, you might earn manumission (freedom), but against formidable odds. Sometimes military service would enable someone to advance, since ability on the battlefield brought immense advantages to the state, and more than one Roman emperor had been a soldier who had become a general and then staged a coup d'état. But most people did not expect to change their social status.

Furthermore, bloodlines counted in the ancient world. We see it most obviously in the nobility, where someone could announce that she or he was of some distinguished *gens* (family line) and claim the honor that went with it. But bloodlines extended into many social areas. Today we try to judge people as individuals, and if we learn that someone's mother or father was a criminal, we would think it inequitable to hold that against the child who should be allowed to make her or his own way. Yet ancient people would often presume that "bad blood" passed on from parents to children, and few would think it wrong if parents refused to let one of their children marry someone whose mother or father were socially undesirable.

Explanation is not justification. We are certainly right to reject these views of the ancient world, but we will not understand how they viewed social questions unless we accept that many of their evaluative standards differed significantly from ours.

Because social questions range so widely and so deeply, we will restrict ourselves here to five of them to provide an idea of how Christians approached social issues. As usual, the pre- and post-Constantinian distinction plays a role.

1. Slavery

Probably nothing about the early Christians puzzles and embarrasses modern Christians more than their tolerance of slavery, the ownership of one human being by another. Perhaps moderns should not be so puzzled, since nominally Christian societies, including democracies like the United States, permitted legalized slavery down to the nineteenth century. But the practice—even the idea—is so odious that we cannot help but wonder how people publicly committed to the idea of loving all persons could tolerate slavery. In fact, they did more than tolerate it; some of them provided theoretical justification for it. This particular issue illustrates better than any other how the early Christians were people of their age.

Virtually every ancient people practiced slavery. The Bible tells how the Hebrews were slaves in Egypt before the Exodus, but they also practiced it themselves right from the time of Abraham (Gen 20:14) to the end of the biblical period. In Persia, all who did not belong to the royal family could be considered the king's slaves. The great Greek philosopher Aristotle believed that some people were servile by nature and thus could be legitimately exploited. In general, ancient thinkers considered slaves property of their masters and thus to be dealt with as property, although biblical teaching often emphasized the human relation of slave to master and thus limited the master's activities (Exod 21:20-26).[5]

Most ancient peoples enslaved only outsiders, usually captives from a war, although as those captives produced children, generations of slaves came into being. The Romans' many wars over some centuries brought enormous numbers of captives to their slave markets. Whereas slavery in the Near East often involved domestic slaves, working primarily in the home, slaves in the Roman world worked on huge agricultural plantations or in industries considered very dangerous, such as mining. Since the Romans considered slaves to be property, no task was too onerous or life-threatening for them. More than any people before them, the Romans incorporated slavery into the economy. Slaves could be slaves of the state, of the gods (that is, of the temple), of wealthy people, or even of people of modest income. The Roman writer Libanius (*Oration* 31.1) observed that his teachers had so little money that they could afford only two or three slaves.

Manumission occurred more in domestic and urban environments than in the fields and the mines, possibly because the masters got to know the slaves better. Furthermore, in the cities, slaves could accumulate what the Romans called a *peculium,* money or property that a master would allow his or her slave to use to purchase freedom. A freed slave, known simply as a freedwoman or freedman, could become a citizen and play an active role in society, although with some restrictions. Children of freedmen had no restrictions upon them.

---

5. Ferguson, *Backgrounds,* 56–59, has a brief account of slavery and a bibliography. See also the relevant sections of Phan's *Social Thought.*

Some freedmen rose to positions of great importance, such as Pallas (d. 62), who became the financial secretary to the emperor Claudius and helped the notorious Agrippina put her even more notorious son Nero on the throne.[6] Yet, although slaves always had the possibility of manumission, comparatively few achieved it.

This was the world into which Christianity was born, and, although the Christians and Jews had a more lenient attitude toward slavery, they, like the pagans, probably could not envision a world without it.

The Jews insisted that slaves rest on the Sabbath (Deut 5:14) and that they observe Jewish religious practices (Deut 12:12). The Christians took the same approach, opening their religion to slaves (Col 3:24) but still insisting that slaves remain in their state and be loyal to their masters (Eph 6:5-8; 1 Tim 6:1-2; Titus 2:9-10). The pseudonymous author of 1 Peter actually goes so far as to say:

> Slaves, accept the authority of your masters with all deference, not only those who are kind and gentle but also those who are harsh. For it is a credit to you if, being aware of God, you endure pain while suffering unjustly. If you endure when you are beaten for doing wrong, what credit is that? But if you endure when you do right and suffer for it, you have God's approval. For to this you have been called, because Christ also suffered for you, leaving you an example, so that you should follow in his steps (1 Pet 2:18-21).

The rationale for this appalling attitude ("you have been called" to slavery) was provided by Paul, for whom slavery was merely a present, external condition: "For whoever was called in the Lord as a slave is a freed person belonging to the Lord, just as whoever was free when called is a slave of Christ" (1 Cor 7:22). On two occasions, Paul says that all people, Jew and Greek, male and female, slave and free, are all one in Christ (1 Cor 12:13; Gal 3:28). Paul's classic statement on slavery appears in his Letter to Philemon, whose slave, Onesimus, had run away to Paul. The apostle asks Philemon to take Onesimus back, not as a slave but as a brother; indeed, the master should receive the slave as if he were Paul himself (Phlm 8–21).

Many Christian apologists for Paul try to explain his attitude as one caused by eschatology, that is, Paul's belief in the imminent end of the world. If the world were going to end soon, there was little to be gained by changing status. In 1 Corinthians, Paul followed remarks

---

6. Nero's gratitude had limits; he eventually executed Pallas to get his money.

about slavery with a similar statement about marriage: "Are you bound to a wife? Do not seek to be free. Are you free from a wife? Do not seek a wife" (7:27).[7] Other scholars suggest that Paul recognized that Christianity offered the world a religious revolution, and he did not want it confused with a political or social revolution. Finally, others sincerely believe that being a Christian could transform the slave's acceptance of his or her lot.

In chapter two we saw that modern scholarship deals, among other things, with the social and psychological situations of ancient writers, and let us do so now. We must ask if Paul would have held these views if he were a slave? Would the pseudonymous Peter?

It sounds fine to talk about a slave's lot being transformed by Christianity, but let us consider the slave's lot. The great Stoic philosopher Epictetus was a slave. When he was a boy, his master beat him so severely that he was lame for the rest of his life. The writer of Peter's letters may talk about enduring pain, but on occasions masters literally maimed slaves.

Most slave owners in a patriarchal society were men, and although male slaves like Epictetus suffered, particular burdens fell on women slaves. Since the male master owned a female slave's body, she could not refuse it to him; to phrase it less decorously, her body was available for repeated rape. One might say with 1 Peter that she should endure this, but why? And even if she could endure this herself, suppose her master had pedophiliac tendencies and wanted to rape her eight-year-old daughter as well? Was it a Christian virtue for the child to endure such treatment? Was it a Christian virtue for the mother to endure such treatment of her daughter?

It is specious to try to save Paul and the other Christians on this point. Slavery was a horrible system that went against everything Jesus preached, and the first Christian writers, almost all men, could not rise above their cultural backgrounds.[8]

Christian writers from the second century onward basically accepted the biblical view. They accepted slaves as members of the Church, and they urged masters to treat slaves well. They recommended mutual respect between master and slave, and they hoped

7. One has to be struck at how he images marriage like slavery—people are "bound" or "free."

8. In the fourth century, the Spanish Council of Elvira imposed a harsher penalty on a woman who committed adultery rather than on one who beat her female slave to death; see David Hunter, *Marriage in the Early Church* (Minneapolis: Fortress Press, 1992) 26.

that masters would try to convert their non-Christian slaves. But repeatedly Christians told slaves to honor their masters and accept their lot. Although from the fourth century onward there was a practice called *manumissio in ecclesia,* a legal act by which a master freed a slave in a church, no evidence indicates that this encouraged masters to free their slaves. In fact, its main importance lay in the recognition it gained for the Church's role in civic affairs.

Christians also recognized the rights of slaves in marriage. Pope Callistus I (217–222), an ex-slave, went beyond the prevailing Roman civil code and recognized the validity of marriages between a male slave and a free woman.

Christian thought ranged over a vast area, and inevitably it included the origins of slavery. John Chrysostom considered slavery to have arisen from sin, but Augustine provided the classic early Christian statement on the matter.

He believed that God "did not wish the rational being, made in his own image, to have dominion over any but irrational creatures, not man over man, but man over beasts." But when humans enslaved themselves to sin, they introduced slavery into the world.

> The first cause of slavery, then, is sin, whereby man was subjected to man in the condition of bondage; and this can only happen by the judgment of God, with whom there is no injustice, and who knows how to allot different punishments according to the deserts of the offenders. . . . And obviously it is better to be a slave to a human being than to a lust. . . .[9]

Augustine goes on to say that slavery is not natural to humans, but that since sin has perverted human nature, slavery exists. He also recommends lenient or at least just treatment of slaves, in keeping with early Christian tradition.

But one can easily see the harm this does. Slavery may not be natural to humans, but because sin is emphatically here to stay, so is slavery. There is thus no reason to abolish slavery, especially since human slavery is less harmful than slavery to a lust. The reader will not be surprised to learn that Augustine came from a slave-owning family and was himself free.

Occasional voices spoke against slavery, the most important being that of Gregory of Nyssa (ca. 335–394), a great theologian and bishop. He says to slave owners:

9. *City of God* XIX.15; cited in Phan, *Social Thought,* 238–239.

> Tell me, how much is your life worth? What have you found among the creatures that is as valuable as your human nature? How many cents did you pay for reason? How many pence did you think God's image is worth? . . . Now, tell me, who is the one who buys, who is the one who sells the one who is God's image, who must rule the whole earth, who has received from God the dominion that exists on earth as heritage? Such a power belongs to God alone, and may I say, not even to God.[10]

But Gregory's was a lonely voice.

Let us close this section by considering the one Christian writer who knew slavery from the inside.

While some Christian writers were temporarily enslaved as captives of barbarians in the late Roman period, only one spent considerable time as a slave.[11] That was Saint Patrick, who grew up as a Christian in Roman Britain, was kidnaped by Irish pirates, and spent six years as a slave in Ireland. He escaped and later returned to Ireland as a missionary. During his episcopate in Ireland, a British princeling named Coroticus slaughtered and kidnaped some of his converts as they were taking part in a baptismal ceremony. Patrick demanded that Coroticus return the prisoners rather than sell them into slavery. Patrick did not write any nonsense about how their Christianity would enable them to transform their lot as slaves into something virtuous, but he did write of his particular concern about the women captives, who would be allotted as prizes to the soldiers of Coroticus.[12] Regrettably, we do not know the outcome of this event; one can only hope that Patrick succeeded in getting the captives back. But it is significant that the one Christian writer who knew in tragic personal detail what a slave's life actually entailed— especially that of a female slave—saw nothing redeeming in that life.

2. Women

Because of the relation of the study of women in early Christianity to the situation of women in the Church today, as well as the enormous scholarly concern to study a topic that was literally ignored for centuries, a voluminous literature on women in early Christianity ex-

10. *Homily on Ecclesiastes* 4, cited in Phan, ibid., 128.

11. Pope Callistus I had been a slave, but he left no writings.

12. *Epistle to the Soldiers of Coroticus* 19, R.P.C. Hanson, trans., in *The Life and Writings of the Historical Saint Patrick* (New York: Seabury Press, 1983) 72.

ists. Much of it has been generated by feminist scholars but also by scholarly organizations for women's studies and graduate programs in the field.[13] This book can only sketch a vast and constantly developing field.

Anyone studying women in the ancient world must accept two facts. First, all ancient Mediterranean societies were patriarchal, that is, societies dominated by men. Since few if any ruling classes ever acknowledged their biases, they evolved a value system to justify their oppression of others, for example, that women were physically or intellectually or emotionally inferior to men—or, for that matter, all three—and this value system will manifest itself constantly in the ancient material. The great pagan philosopher Aristotle actually said that a deficiency in the conception process produced girl babies; if all had gone well, the baby would be a boy.[14] To him, a woman was a misbegotten male. Second, although some writings by early Christian women have survived,[15] almost all of the written sources emerged from the pens of men. Therefore, scholars do not have much access to what women thought of themselves, their lives, their place in the Church, and researchers must interpret material produced by men.

Although the scholars must accept these facts, they can still profitably study women in early Christianity. Acknowledging limitations does not mean being bound by them, and some of the new methods of study discussed in chapter two have helped here.

Because of the normative value of the New Testament for Christians, much scholarship has centered on that. That Jesus' attitude toward women differed considerably from that of his contemporaries has long been known, but now an even clearer picture has emerged. For example, Luke 8:1-3 tells how Jesus

> . . . went on through cities and villages, proclaiming and bringing the good news of the kingdom of God. The twelve were with him, as well as some women who had been cured of evil spirits and infirmities: Mary, called Magdalene, from whom seven demons had

---

13. A recent starting point would be "Feminist Theology: A Review of Literature," by Susan Ross and Mary Catherine Hilkert, in Theological Studies 56 (1995) 327–352.

14. *On the Generation of Animals,* IV.3.

15. For a collection of these, see Patricia Wilson-Kastner *et al., A Lost Heritage: Women Writers of the Early Church* (Washington, D.C.: University Press of America, 1981).

gone out, and Joanna, the wife of Herod's steward Chuza, and Susanna, and many others who provided for them out of their resources.

Although we do not know how many women the "others" represented, there was apparently a sizeable group.

Significantly, these women provided financial resources for the movement. In a religion that has often disparaged the material, this may not seem important, but no movement can succeed without material assistance; for example, in a modern church, someone has to pay for the upkeep of the church, the lighting, the heating or air conditioning, and the like. Thus these women were essential to the success of the movement.

But note also that they traveled with Jesus and his male disciples (the Twelve), and at least one of those women (Joanna) was married. Ancient Jewish society would have considered it scandalous for women to go about with men to whom they were not married or related, yet they were willing to risk that for Jesus, who in turn did not fear the scandal that might attach to him.

Jesus' unconcern for scandal reappears in the Gospel of John, in which he speaks to a woman whom he does not know and who is a Samaritan (John 4:7-42). Even his closest disciples "were astonished that he was speaking to a woman" (4:27). In spite of limitations on women as witnesses in a legal proceeding, the Christians acknowledged that the earliest witnesses of Christ's resurrection were women; but when they told the male disciples, the women's words "seemed to them an idle tale, and they did not believe them" (Luke 24:11).

When the early Church replaced the ministry of Jesus, the situation developed in two stages: ". . . after an initial stage of relatively public activity by women—characteristic of enthusiastic new sects throughout the ages—their roles were increasingly regulated and curtailed."[16]

The earliest Christian writings are Paul's epistles. The apostle wrote on issues facing particular communities, and he did not spell out roles for women or give accounts of women's activities unless these pertained to the specific issue. Yet he did leave enough clues to put together a limited picture.

Without doubt, women played a significant role in the Pauline churches. He referred to Phoebe, of the Church of Cenchreae, as a *di-*

16. Elizabeth Clark, "Women," *EEXty,* II. 1181–1183.

akonos (Rom 16:1), the same word for male deacons, suggesting that Phoebe played the same role as the men. Paul greeted Prisca, who worked with him and even risked her life for him (16:3); he also greets Junia, "prominent among the apostles" (16:6). In all, Paul mentioned twenty-eight people in Rom 16, nine of whom were women. When he wrote to Philemon, he sent greetings to his wife Apphia and "the church in your house" (Phlm 2); significantly, the word for "your" in Greek is in the plural, so the church met in the house of both Apphia and Philemon.

Luke's Acts of the Apostles recounts Paul's missionary career. Scholars have reservations about the historicity of the account, but its acceptance by the community proves that the early Christians could relate to its contents. This is important because of what it says about house churches. The earliest Christians did not have separate church buildings, and so they met in someone's house. Hosting the community was an important task, and Luke tells us that Mark's mother (Acts 12:12) and the purple-dye dealer Lydia (16:12-15) hosted the Christians. If, as some scholars believe, the New Testament speaks "of women as leaders of house churches,"[17] that would mean that Peter, the leader of the Twelve, and Paul, the Apostle to the Gentiles, entered churches that acknowledged women as their leaders. Even if moderns question the historicity of these accounts, the acceptance of Acts by the Church proves that first Christians saw nothing unusual about women offering their homes for liturgies.

Colossians, whose Pauline nature scholars constantly debate, refers to "Nympha and the church in her house" (4:15). If Paul did write Colossians, this supports the evidence of Acts and Philemon; if not, it demonstrates that the practice was known in non-Pauline or at least post-Pauline churches.

Acts provides a reference to another woman's role, as teacher, recounting that Prisc(ill)a joined her husband Aquila in instructing Apollos in the Way of God (18:26).

Even negative references in the New Testament demonstrate the sizeable roles that women played. John, the author of Revelation, fulminated about the Church of Thyatira: ". . . you tolerate that woman Jezebel, who calls herself a prophet and is teaching and beguiling my servants . . ." (2:20). Jezebel recalls the pagan wife of the Israelite king Ahab (1 Kgs 16:31), the sinful woman par excellence for the

17. Elisabeth Schüssler Fiorenza, *In Memory of Her* (New York: Crossroad, 1994) 177.

Jews. Regardless of what she did that enraged John, he still witnessed that a woman taught and prophesied, the former reinforcing
what Luke said about Prisca in Acts and the latter supporting Paul's
warning that a woman should not prophesy with her head unveiled
(1 Cor 11:5), a clear acknowledgment that women did prophesy.

Even this brief survey indicates that women played a significant
role in Christianity's early decades. What happened to diminish that
role?

No New Testament text actually says what happened.[18] Scholars
presume that as hopes for an early end to the world faded, and the
Christians realized that they would be on earth longer than they had
anticipated, they decided to join the mainstream of ancient life, to become more acceptable to others. This is understandable, especially in
light of Roman antagonism. Few Christians wanted to be martyrs.
Even when that threat was not present, they still did not want to be
at odds with the empire. Christian writers constantly exhorted the
faithful to be loyal to the government (Matt 21:21; 1 Pet 2:17), and
they would have been increasingly uncomfortable with practices that
set them apart. Israel would be like the nations (1 Sam 8:5).

The fall of women's status in the Church appears most clearly in
the pseudonymous[19] Pastoral Epistles. In 1 Timothy 2:8-15, using the
argument that Adam was created before Eve and that the serpent de-
ceived Eve but not him, the author declared that women cannot
teach, cannot have authority over any man, must dress with appropriate modesty, and must "learn in silence with full submission"
(2:11). The Epistle to Titus reinforced the notions of modesty and
submission but added a sacral note: older women should teach
younger women "to be self-controlled, chaste, good managers of the
household, kind, being submissive to their husbands, so that the word
of God may not be discredited" (2:5). Clearly the author was worried
about what others might think. Submissive women presented no
threat to social norms.

Once the Christians had turned this corner, there was no going
back—at least not until the twentieth century. In general, Christian
writers of the following centuries followed the Pastoral Epistles,
which they thought to be Pauline. They had no trouble reconciling
these with Galatians 3:28 that there is neither Jew nor Greek, slave
nor free, male nor female in Christ because they simply transferred

18. Clark, "Patrons, Not Priests," 253–254.
19. The author of these three letters claims to be Paul.

this to a future state with no bearing on earthly life, just as they had done with attitudes toward Jews and slaves. But in spite of this, women did have roles to play in early Christianity.

One Church office remained open to women, although primarily in the East, that is, the Greek-speaking area of the Roman Empire. In the early second century, Pliny, a Roman governor in northern Asia Minor, arrested and tortured two *ministrae*, female ministers whom scholars usually assume to have been deaconesses. In the third century, deaconesses assisted at the baptism of women because baptism was usually of adults in the nude (for the symbolism of being born again). They also ministered to women who were ill. Qualifications for the office varied; some Churches set a minimum age; all expected the candidates to be of good moral character. The office lasted into the early Middle Ages, although the rise of infant baptism rendered superfluous their previously important baptismal function.

The office of deaconess may have been the only ecclesiastical office for women, but there were two orders to which women could belong: virgins and widows. Both had their parameters, both ideological and practical, set by men, who let their view of women infiltrate their thinking on these orders. Many educated men of the ancient world feared passion, specifically sexual passion. The Stoics praised the virtue of *apatheia*, not apathy in the sense of being disinterested but rather in the mastering of the passions. Since male writers saw women as sources of temptation to male passionate behavior, they naturally tried to control women's passions as much as their own—maybe even more so. Perhaps guided by the gospel traditions that Jesus never married and that his mother gave birth to him virginally, the Christians praised consecrated virginity, that is, the willing avoidance of sexual intercourse for a religious reason. Although known in both paganism and Judaism, consecrated virginity attained far greater status in Christianity. Both men and women practiced this, sometimes in their homes, sometimes in community, although most patristic literature on the topic deals with female virgins.

Consecrated virginity caused tension within homes, since parents counted on their children to continue their family lines. In the late fourth century, when some prominent Roman Christians opted for virginity, there was concern that some noble houses would be extinguished.[20] On the other hand, consecrated virginity provided young

---

20. Ann Yarborough, "Christianization in the Fourth Century: the Example of Roman Women," in *Church History* 45 (1976) 149–165.

woman with the only permissible alternative to arranged marriages, which made the state attractive to some. When the first monks went into the desert, they practiced sexual abstinence, and monasteries became the initial homes of the order of virgins, the forerunner of later religious orders for women. Cyprian of Carthage (d. 258) first pronounced virginity a superior way of life to marriage, and most other Christian writers followed his lead.[21] Virginity was a form of asceticism, a form of physical self-denial usually involving far more than virginity—abstinence from food, from regular bathing, from contact with society. Monastic life centered on asceticism. Several prominent women, Mary, the sister of Pachomius (ca. 320–340), Melania the Elder (ca. 341–ca. 410), Melania the Younger (ca. 383–438), and Paula (347–404) founded monasteries; the wealthier women also endowed the monasteries. Several monastic accounts speak of women who abandoned lives of luxury or sin and went into the desert. One legend tells of Pelagia, a prostitute, who abandoned her notorious career, lived as a recluse, and practiced severe penances.[22]

Like virgins, widows were recognized as a distinct group in the Church.[23] In 1 Timothy 5, verses 3-16 demonstrate that widows had achieved recognition by the end of the first century. The epistle lists some requirements for Church support—the widow must be sixty years old, have been married only once, and have a good reputation. The author worried about young widows whose "sensual desires alienate them from Christ;" he defined "sensual desires" as their wish to marry again. Although a widow, especially an older one without children or a younger one with young children, often found herself in a precarious financial state and deserved compassion, the Fathers did not extend Church support without conditions, most importantly, that she decide not to marry again. If she met the criteria, she could be enrolled in the order of widows; in 253 the Church at Rome supported 1,500 widows and the Church of Antioch at the end of the fourth century supported 3,000.[24] Some Fathers thought a second marriage was permissible, but most frowned upon it.

21. See article on "Virgins," in *EEXty,* II. 1165–1167.

22. "The Life of Pelagia the Harlot" by James the Deacon in *The Desert Fathers,* Helen Waddell, ed. and trans. (London: Constable & Company, Ltd., 1960) 259–281.

23. B. B. Thurston, *The Widows—A Woman's Ministry in the Early Church* (Minneapolis: Fortress Press, 1989).

24. Article on "Widows," in *EEXty,* II.1177–1178.

Yet if the Church leaders wished to put restrictions upon the lives of widows, they also provided for them and their orphan children, no small step in an age when many were left to the tolerance of relatives or to the streets.

In addition to alleviating the stress of widowhood, the Christians also tried to raise the status of married women. An arranged marriage formed the destiny of every woman, or rather of every girl, since "[t]he earliest legal age for a formal betrothal was seven, when the parties were assumed to know what was happening and to give formal assent. The earliest age for a legal marriage was twelve, and most girls were married by sixteen. . . ."[25]

Ancient society presumed chastity on the part of the wife, but a man could have an affair with another woman as long as she was not married, that is, as long as he did not lure someone else's wife into adultery. This view persisted from paganism into Christianity.

For the most part, Christians accepted Roman marriage practices—the woman needed a dowry, she had to have been a virgin for her first marriage, she owed her husband children (preferably sons) to carry on his name—but on the matter of sex outside of marriage, the Fathers often defended the wives. John Chrysostom put it bluntly: "The sexual act is adulterous not only when the woman is bound to another man; it is also adultery for the man who is himself bound to a wife."[26]

But if the Christians advanced the status of women by demanding sexual morality of husbands, they did little to help abused wives, even those beaten by their husbands. A woman could not divorce her husband unless he engaged in criminal activity, which did not include wife-beating. A woman's only way to escape such a relationship would be to enter a monastery, not always desirable and hardly a practical step for one with children.[27] Few of the Church Fathers had any real appreciation for marriage, which explains their lack of concern for the difficulties facing married women.

Part of the problem for the Fathers was that marriages entailed sexual activity which in turn entailed lust, a consequence of original sin. Sexual activity was necessary to produce children, leading Jerome to say that the only good thing about marriage was that it

25. Gillian Clark, *Women in Late Antiquity* (New York: Oxford University Press, 1993) 13–14.

26. *Homily 5 on 1 Thessalonians 2,* in E. Clark, *Women in the Early Church,* 74.

27. See G. Clark, *Women in Late Antiquity,* 17–27.

produced virgins, but even the production of children could not reconcile Augustine to sex. Since he could not figure out any other way to produce children, he acknowledged that even if Adam and Eve had not sinned, women and men would still have to have intercourse, but they would do so with neither lust nor passion.[28]

Yet Augustine did write a book defending marriage, especially against extremists who condemned it. He recognized that marriage provided a natural bond between people, which was intrinsically good, but he could not resist saying, even in this treatise, that continence is better than marriage and that sexual intercourse between married people, unless for the procreation of children, was a venial sin.[29]

Most Church Fathers saw the temptress Eve in all women. The African Tertullian asked his female readers: "And do you not know that you are each an Eve? The sentence of God on this sex of yours lives in this age; the guilt must of necessity live too. You are the devil's gateway." Because of women "even the Son of God had to die."[30] This attitude obviated any deep sympathy for women and marriage by the Fathers. Instead they preferred to contrast Eve with Mary, who fulfilled the roles of virgin and mother, uniting the ideal traits of innocent, ascetic virginity with sexless yet nourishing motherhood.

The Fathers were willing to restrict the activities of women, but, as is usual in most societies, women with money and power formed exceptions to the rule. Such women had influence with important ecclesiastics; both Pelagius and Jerome became spiritual advisors to noble Roman women. Pope Damasus I (366–384) tried to cultivate rich women by passing along the latest gossip; his nickname in Rome was "the ladies' ear-tickler."[31] [Scholars do not know how successful this tack was.] When the emperor Theodosius II died in 450, his sister, Pulcheria, became empress and took a nobleman named Marcian as her consort. She opposed her brother's ecclesiastical policies, which had resulted in the Second Council of Ephesus in 449,

28. See Hunter, *Marriage in the Early Church,* for patristic attitudes toward marriage.

29. *On the Good of Marriage,* III.3, VI.6, and VIII.8, cited in Hunter, *Marriage,* 108–112.

30. Tertullian, *On the Apparel of Women,* I.l, ANF 4, 14.

31. See J.N.D. Kelly, *The Oxford Dictionary of Popes* (Oxford: Oxford University Press, 1986) 32–34.

and to offset this, she, along with her husband, called the Council of Chalcedon in 451.[32]

3. Church and State

This phrase refers to the relations between a primarily religious body and a primarily secular, civil one, but these are modern distinctions. In the ancient world, no one could govern successfully without placating or winning the support of the divine, and no one could foster the Christian way of life without the support of the civil authorities. There was a Church and there was a state, but their actions were always intertwined, especially after the conversion of Constantine. In the apostolic age, the imminence of the Second Coming dominated the issue. In the Synoptic Gospels, Jesus tells his disciples to "Give to the emperor the things that are the emperor's, and to God the things that are God's" (Matt 22:21; Mark 12:17; Luke 20:25). In John's gospel, Jesus tells Pontius Pilate, "My kingdom is not from this world" (18:36). The form of civil government did not matter much to people who expected that government and all earthly things would soon disappear.

Another approach to the civil government was to live in peace with it until the end. Paul tells the Roman community, "Let every person be subject to the governing authorities; for there is no authority except from God, and those authorities that exist have been instituted by God" (Rom 13:1). God stands behind the order of the world, and we can trust him.

When the end failed to come and the Christians realized that they would be in the world for an undetermined time, they had to reconcile themselves to Rome. In 1 Peter 2:17 the faithful are urged to fear God and honor the emperor. Luke said the same thing, but far more subtly.

Luke realized that the judicial executions of both the founder of Christianity and its chief apostle could hardly commend this new religion to the pagans, so he played those down. For example, in the beginning of his gospel, he portrays Jesus' parents obeying the census order of Caesar Augustus (2:1-14). But he saves his best argument for the actual sentence of death by portraying Pilate as

32. She was not the only woman to call an ecumenical council. The Byzantine empress Irene called the Second Council of Nicaea in 787.

acknowledging three times that Jesus is innocent (23:4, 14, 22) and then handing Jesus over to the mob while releasing the rebel and murderer Barabbas. Luke's point is that Pilate was a poor governor, one who condemned an innocent man, handed him over to a mob, and released a known criminal and rebel. Who could take seriously the sentence against Jesus given by such a governor?

In the Acts of the Apostles, Luke returns to the theme. Throughout the gospel, various Roman officials save Paul from being lynched by angry pagan or Jewish mobs. Paul proclaims his faith in Roman justice by asking to have his trial before Caesar (Acts 25:11); like Jesus, he, too, convinces the authorities of his innocence (26:32).

But this reconciling approach did not win over all Christians. John of Patmos, a prisoner of the Romans, portrayed Rome as the great beast (Rev 13:1-10) and the scarlet-clad whore of Babylon (17:4-5). Already suffering himself and anticipating a persecution among the Western Asian Churches to which he wrote, John spit out his resentment of Rome.

Although John definitely represented a minority view in the New Testament, his witness carried great weight. Down to the Constantinian period (and beyond in North Africa), some Christians would see Rome as apocalyptically evil, while others would try for reconciliation.

The biggest problem facing the Christians was the pagan character of Rome. Issues that would offend us, like a monarchical government, did not offend them; ancient people even became accustomed—they really had no choice—to assassinations and the occasional coup d'état. Since the average person had no voice in government, it mattered little how things changed at the top. If the emperor appointed honest and efficient governors, and if the local nobility cared for the people of the region, then no one resented the government. People acknowledged the class system, and notions of democracy or ideal states remained the province of the few.[33] But sometimes for the Christians, Rome represented idolatry, since participation in government and the military (see the next section) usually involved some obligatory veneration of those false gods. Often the Christians wished to have the arrangement that the Jews had, to pray for the emperor in their own way but otherwise to be left alone religiously.

33. Peter Green, *From Alexander to Actium* (Berkeley: University of California Press, 1993) 391–395.

Yet, unlike the Jews, Christians proselytized aggressively, and their numbers grew considerably in the second century. The pagans noticed this increase, and one pagan, a learned provincial named Celsus, wrote, *circa* 175, a learned and effective attack on Christianity, one so strong that no Christian was able to respond to it for more than half a century, when Origen wrote his great apology *Contra Celsum.*[34] Celsus warned the pagans that the Christians would subvert the traditions and beliefs of the empire if they were not soon stopped. Scholars simply do not know what effect Celsus' book had, but, by the third century, attacks on the Christians mounted.

In the mid-second century, Christian apologists tried to make the Christian case to the Romans, to convince them that the Christians did not represent a threat but were, in fact, good citizens. They apparently had little influence on Roman policy, but they do witness to the continuing efforts of some Christians to reconcile their faith with the empire.

The martyrs, however, left a far different witness.[35] In 177 a vicious persecution broke out in the Gallic city of Lyons, and several Christians suffered terribly in defiance of Rome. About the same time, Christians in a North African town called Scilli did likewise.[36] For the martyrs and their many admirers, Rome remained the apocalyptic Whore of Babylon. One strong protagonist of martyrdom, the African Tertullian, maintained the larger biblical tradition when he wrote to the pagan governor Scapula: "To the emperor, therefore, we render such reverential homage as is lawful for us and good for him. . . . We therefore sacrifice for the emperor's safety, but to our God and his, and after the manner God has enjoined, in simple prayer."[37] Yet Tertullian's fierce hostility to paganism and to an empire that persecuted the Church provided the justification for what became the

34. A translation of Celsus' work can be found in *Celsus: On the True Doctrine,* R. J. Hoffmann, trans. (New York: Oxford University Press, 1987); a translation of Origen's work can be found in *Origen: Contra Celsum,* Henry Chadwick, trans. (Cambridge: Cambridge University Press, 1953).

35. The Greek word *martyr* means "witness." The standard treatment of this topic remains *Martyrdom and Persecution in the Early Church* by William H. C. Frend (Oxford: Blackwell, 1965).

36. Significantly, both groups of martyrs included women. They may have been barred from church office, but they contributed to Christian life with their deaths.

37. *Ad Scapulam* 2, ANF 3, 105–106.

African attitude toward the state, whether pagan or Christian—always wary, often hostile.

In the third century the persecutions became worse; in 250 the emperor Decius launched the first empire-wide persecution. The Whore of Babylon tradition was riding high.

But then the unexpected—and in some eyes impossible—happened: a Roman emperor, Constantine I (306–337), converted to Christianity. In 313 Constantine and his co-emperor Licinius issued the Edict of Milan, which gave the Christians freedom of worship. By 319 Constantine had become a believer himself. When he defeated and executed Licinius in 324 and became sole ruler, a new era in Church-state relations had begun.

Obviously the apocalyptic tradition could no longer apply. The Christians now governed the empire. For that matter, the other biblical tradition, of respect and prayer for the emperor, also no longer applied. There was no need to hope for imperial neutrality or tolerance; the emperor would now be involved on the side of the Church. The pagan emperors persecuted Christians partly because they would not venerate the gods, upon whose good will the empire's well-being depended. Constantine also believed that he needed divine good will, but now of the one Christian god. As emperor, he had an obligation to see that his citizens acted in such a way as to please God, and he could not be indifferent to the affairs of the Church or to keep out of them. In the fourth century, no one would have expected him to.

But governments do not just act. They have to have some kind of legitimacy, a rationale for existing. Enter the historian Eusebius of Caesarea (ca. 260–339). He genuinely admired Constantine, and he just as genuinely believed that God's plan for Christianity included Constantine. The emperor's acceptance of his new god was not an accident. God had chosen Constantine to found the Christian empire, a successor to the pagan one. In many of his works, but especially in panegyrics and orations written specifically to the emperor, Eusebius promoted the idea of a Christian empire, legitimizing Constantine's rule and thus of his intervention in the Church.[38]

Constantine's interventions were extensive, including even the calling of the first ecumenical council at Nicaea in 325. His descendants and successors also adopted his view, which remained popular in Eastern Christianity right down to the twentieth century, when the

---

38. See his *Life of Constantine,* NPNF 1, 481–559, and *Oration in Praise of Constantine,* ibid., 581–610.

czar of Russia dominated his Church. When the emperor Theodosius I (379–395) proclaimed Christianity the official religion of the empire in 381, the link seemed permanent.

But not everyone accepted the Eusebian view, especially in the Latin West. Many Western bishops, appalled at imperial intervention on behalf of some churchmen the Westerners considered heretics, stepped back from endorsing the emperor's dominance of Church affairs. In Ambrose of Milan (373–397) these bishops found their spokesperson. Ambrose believed that the emperor was the son of the Church and, in religious matters, subject to the clergy. A brave man, the bishop of Milan put his ideas into practice, twice forcing Theodosius to do public penance. Ambrose's ideas became the standard attitude for the papacy, which throughout the Middle Ages sought to restrain the power of the secular rulers by the exercise of religious threats and interdictions.

Ambrose also played a role in very symbolic action. In 382 the Christian emperor Gratian (367–383), who had refused to accept the traditional pagan, imperial title of *pontifex maximus* (chief priest), removed the statue and altar of the goddess Victory from the senate house at Rome. Led by a thoughtful senator named Symmachus, the pagans requested the return of statues and altar, but Ambrose answered Symmachus' arguments and strengthened Gratian's resolve. The new Church-state situation was now visibly clear.[39]

At the end of the Roman period in the West, Pope Gelasius I (492–496) advanced the theory that the emperors governed for the temporal welfare of their subjects, while the popes governed for the eternal welfare of the Christian people. The emperors might be supreme in their own sphere, but since the papacy dealt in a higher sphere, the emperors had to obey them in religious matters.[40] Since religious matters intertwined constantly with temporal ones, this theory would give the papacy considerable sway in political events.

Augustine also weighed in on this question, but in a very different way. In his great work *City of God,* he argued that all people belong either to the City of God or to the terrestrial City. Although God dominates the divine city and the devil the terrestrial one, the two cities have interacted and interpenetrated each other since the begin-

39. Relevant texts in Phan, *Social Thought,* 182–184.

40. Gelasius's letter to the emperor Anastasius I on this topic can be found in *Church and State Through the Centuries,* Sidney Ehler and John Morall (London: Burns & Oates, 1954) 10–11.

ning. Only at the Last Judgment will they be finally separated. For Augustine, no political entity has an intrinsic value, but rather it must be judged by how it contributes to the building of the City of God. In this way, too, must a "Christian" emperor be judged. Emperors and empires come and go; only the City of God will persevere.[41]

Only one perfect society ever existed on earth, in the Garden of Eden before original sin. Fallen humanity cannot, contrary to the ideas of the Greek philosophers, establish a truly just society, because sin cripples our efforts. A just earthly society can keep the peace and stave off chaos, but the true Christian looks only to the City of God.

Not surprisingly, emperors did not care for the views of Ambrose, Gelasius, or Augustine. Although these writers influenced the Church's view of the state, emperors repeatedly acted like sacred personages with extensive powers within the Church. In general, the Westerners managed to keep the emperors at bay until the end of the Roman period (476), although in the Middle Ages emperors like Charlemagne (768–814) and Otto III (983–1002) dominated the Church, appointing and deposing bishops and even popes. The Eastern bishops tolerated imperial claims, although this often depended upon their view of the emperor's orthodoxy. Whereas Western bishops accepted imperial support but did so carefully, Eastern bishops welcomed that support against those they deemed heretics, only to resent it when the "heretics" used it against them. In the period after Justinian I (527–565), so dominant did the Byzantine emperors become over the Church that scholars sometimes call this phenomenon "caesaropapism," that is, the emperor acted like the pope.

4. War and Peace

A surprising number of modern Christians believe that the ancient Christians were pacifists, rejecting war as immoral and un-Christian. This may be based on Jesus' well-known injunction from the Sermon on the Mount, "But if anyone strikes you on the right cheek, turn the other also . . ." (Matt 5:39). Jesus also urged people to be at peace with one another (Mark 9:4), and he promised peace to those who believed in him (John 14:27). Yet the New Testament also offered a distinctly martial view as well.

41. *City of God* xix; texts in Phan, *Social Thought,* 233–238.

In addition, in telling his disciples to turn the other cheek, Jesus also said, "I have not come to bring peace, but a sword" (Matt 10:34). In Matthew 24 he predicted a violent end to this world in a Second Coming in which "two will be in the field; one will be taken and one will be left. Two women will be grinding meal together; one will be taken and one will be left" (vv. 40–41). This frightening picture finds reinforcement in the Book of Revelation, which tells of uncompromising warfare between the forces of good and evil, those of the Lamb and those of the beast, with no mercy shown to the enemy.

To these New Testament images, we can add a number of Old Testament episodes. In the Book of Joshua, the invading Israelites put to death everyone in the city of Jericho except for the family of Rahab, and they do so at the command of the Lord. The Lord also stands behind the wars of the Judges and the campaigns of David. Indeed, the Lord not only encourages the Israelites but actually fights for them; Deuteronomy 20:4 tells them, "for it is the LORD your God who goes with you, to fight for you against your enemies, to give you victory." Many Jews and Christians like to cite Isaiah 2:4, "they shall beat their swords into plowshares, and their spears into pruning hooks." Few ever quote Joel 3:10: "Beat your plowshares into swords, and your pruning hooks into spears." Whether moderns like it or not, the Bible, when read literally, provides wide support for the notion of a holy war.

These conflicting passages do not mean that we should envision an early Christian schizophrenia on this matter; this is rather an issue that had to be carefully nuanced.

No Christian thought that war was a good in itself, but it was necessary to defend the empire. Christians living on the Persian frontier would have expected protection from Rome's age-old enemy, while those living near the African desert or the Rhine River would have been glad to see imperial troops keeping the barbarian tribes at bay. Indeed, possibly some Christians supported a form of imperialism, believing that Roman arms extended Roman civilization to barbarian areas.

In fact, the ancient debate was usually not over whether war was good but whether Christians could serve in the military, and even that was not a great concern before the third century.

> [T]here appears to have been no pressing reason for coming to grips with the problem [of military service] at all during the first two centuries after Christ. As a group, Christians were not actually

responsible for maintaining or directing the institutions of government, and their duties to the state were fulfilled largely by obeying
the laws and living peacefully.[42]

In the third century, two great Christian intellectuals, the North
African Tertullian and the Alexandrian Origen, both made a case for
pacifism. Tertullian fretted over the twin issues of idolatry and the
shedding of blood, both of which he considered unavoidable in the
military although, apparently for purpose of argumentation, he said
that Christians could be in the military without harm to their consciences if they found some way to avoid idolatry and bloodshed. He
carefully distinguished between the Christian contemplating military
service and a soldier who converted after enlisting, but he clearly opposed military service.[43] Yet one of his works on the topic, *On the
Crown,* that is, on the military crown worn as part of a celebration,
discussed a Christian soldier who refused the crown as an act of idolatry, to the distress of his fellow Christian soldiers. Clearly, many
Christians did not share Tertullian's view on the incompatibility of
Christianity and military service.

Origen's opposition to war and military service made use of his allegorical interpretation of Scripture and even took on those biblical
passages that seemed to support war. On the popular saying of Isaiah
2:4, he wrote "[W]e have come in response to Jesus' commands to
beat into plowshares the rational swords of conflict and arrogance
and to change into pruning hooks those spears we used to fight with.
For we no longer take up the sword against any nation, nor do we
learn the art of war any more."[44]

The spears are still spears, but the swords have become those of
conflict and arrogance. But he had more allegorizing to do. "Unless
those carnal wars [that is, of the Old Testament] were a symbol of
spiritual wars, I do not think that the Jewish historical books would
ever have been passed down by the Apostles to be read by Christ's
followers in their churches."[45] In Origen's view, the wars of the
Israelites, which would become important to later writers, never actually occurred.

42. Swift, *The Early Fathers on War and Military Service,* 26.

43. For the texts, see Swift, *Military,* 38–47; also see John Helgeland *et al.,*
eds., *Christians and the Military: The Early Experience* (Philadelphia: Fortress
Press, 1985) 21–30.

44. From *Contra Celsus* 5.33; text in Swift, *Military,* 57.

45. From his *Homilies on Joshua* 15; text in Swift, ibid., 59.

Origen realized that by allegorizing away the wars of the Old Testament, he may have opened Christians to the charge of being indifferent to the empire's welfare.

> The Christian's role . . . is not to fight wars on behalf of the empire and the emperor, but to fight the much more important internal spiritual battle against the demons who cause the wars. Thus one can conclude that not only do the Christians not abandon the emperor to his foes, they are actually fighting for him in the most important way possible. For if all were to become Christians, the need for force to defend the empire would, by that fact and to the extent of the conversion, have been eliminated.[46]

In fact, Origen was wrong. When the empire converted, war did not cease, but it is clear that his pacifism would not leave the empire defenseless. Demons cause conflicts, and when we defeat them, conflicts would cease—an idealist view but, in essence, a Christian one.

The pre-Constantinian literature includes several accounts of military martyrs, that is, of Christian soldiers who at one point or another believed that their religion and the idolatry of military life conflicted. They chose the former, and paid for the choice with their lives. Obviously, they could not have been martyred if they had not been in the military in the first place, but the accounts indicate far more than the continuing disregard of the views of the Christian pacifists. For example, in the *Acts of Maximilian,* set in 295, we learn that there were Christians in the imperial bodyguard, responsible for the direct, personal safety of the emperors.[47] In the *Acts of Julius the Veteran,* who was martyred in 303, we learn that Julius had served for twenty-seven years without problem. He said at his trial, "I went on seven military campaigns, and never hid behind anyone nor was I the inferior of any man in battle."[48] Significantly, Julius fought as a soldier and yet was honored by the Church as a martyr.

With the conversion of Constantine and the establishment of a Christian empire, the question of idolatry disappeared, but the question of bloodshed did not. The question was then not whether Christian soldiers would shed blood, but how they might do so justly. Here began the much-debated question of the just war, a problem still facing modern Churches.

46. Helgeland, *Military,* 42.
47. Text in ibid., 58–59.
48. Text in ibid., 63–64.

The fourth and fifth centuries saw civil wars among the Romans. Constantine's three sons had each inherited a part of the empire. In 340 Constantine II was defeated and killed by his brother Constans, who in turn was defeated and killed, himself, in 350 by the usurping general Magnentius, who was defeated the following year by the last brother, Constantius II. In 383 the usurper Magnus Maximus defeated and murdered the emperor Gratian. Five years later Theodosius I defeated and executed Magnus. In 394 Theodosius had to defeat the rebellion of the pagan patrician Eugenius. While all the internecine fighting kept the Romans occupied, barbarian tribes began their incursions into the empire, and in 378 the emperor Valens suffered both defeat and death at Adrianople at the hands of the invading Visigoths. These barbarian invasions put an end to the Roman Empire in the West in the late fifth century and still continued into the sixth.

The abundant warfare of the later centuries and, more immediately, the wars of Christians versus Christians made it impossible for the Fathers not to think about the notion of a just war. During the revolt of Eugenius, for example, Christians could see the justness of a Christian army fighting a pagan one. But when there were Christians on both sides, ambiguity arose. Naturally, Christian leaders lamented the prospect of coreligionists battling one another, something clearly contrary to Christ's teaching and completely unenvisioned by early writers, but lamentations did not change the fact: Christians were battling Christians. How then could warfare be just?

The two great theoreticians of this topic were Westerners, Ambrose and Augustine. Significantly, both studied the Bible intensely. For Ambrose, the wars of the Israelites against the Philistines and other pagans proved that war could be just, a theory he quickly extended to the Roman Christians' wars against the barbarians and especially to the battle of Theodosius, the new David, against Eugenius, which was fought not far from Milan and which kept Ambrose and his congregation in constant prayer. But for Ambrose, the justness of the cause did not guarantee the justness of the war itself. That depended upon how the participants fought it—their true goal and their conduct to their enemies. For instance, if a Christian general fought a pagan army, he had a just cause, but if his real goal was not the defense of the Christian empire but the extension of his power, he did not fight a just war.

For Ambrose, the purpose of war is peace. One must not harm noncombatants, a strong statement in an age when defeat often resulted in the wholesale enslavement of noncombatants. One should honor agreements made with the enemy, and one should try to reconcile the opposing forces. The victor should treat the defeated mercifully and should establish a just and lasting peace; otherwise, it would only be a matter of time before new hostilities begin. If the combatants observe conditions such as these, one can fight a war justly. Best of all, of course, is no war, and certainly not between Christians who should be bound together by love.[49]

Augustine's theory of a just war derived largely from his attitude toward the fallen condition of humanity; ". . . [on the question of war and peace] it is hard to overestimate the importance of Original Sin in the bishop's thinking."[50] War formed part of the sinful human condition; as such, it was unavoidable.

Augustine had no use for utopias. As a working bishop in a declining Roman world, he had to deal on a daily basis with ambition, violence, threats of violence, and instability. Too many people had what he called the *libido dominandi,* the lust for power. The Christian had to accept and work with that as part of fallen human nature.

Like his master Ambrose, Augustine found in the battles of Israel a justification for war. He also found many New Testament supports, such as Jesus' curing of the centurion's servant (Matt 8:5-13) and the conversion of the family of Cornelius, another centurion (Acts 10), proof that soldiers could be just men. More subtly, he observes that when John the Baptist told the soldiers neither to extort nor bring false charges against anyone but rather to be satisfied with their pay, John did not reproach the soldiers for their occupation.[51] Like Ambrose, Augustine believed peace was the goal of war. The Christian soldier should repel the aggressor and be gracious to the vanquished. The soldier who fought a war for empire or ambition followed not Christ but the devil.

Following the dichotomy of his *City of God,* Augustine recognized that there are two goals in life, earthly and heavenly. True peace resides in heaven. Earth once enjoyed true peace, but Adam and Eve shattered that by original sin. Therefore, Christian rulers can fight wars to ensure earthly peace, a genuine good in its own right but always inferior to the true peace awaiting Christians in the City of God.

49. Swift, *Military,* 98–110.
50. Swift, ibid., 111.
51. These examples from his *Letter to Boniface,* cited in Helgeland, *Military,* 76–77.

5. Wealth and Poverty

Although too common, wars are not everyday experiences, nor does the average person have to make decisions involving war and peace. But the poor we have always with us (Mark 14:7), and concerns about wealth and poverty affect every Christian. It is natural for people to want material security for themselves and their family members, and even to enjoy more than the bare necessities. On the other hand, we have an obligation to give to the poor and not just from our abundance but from our substance, as did the widow in the Temple (Luke 21:1-3).

How do we reconcile the two? Is it really so sinful to buy an expensive gift for someone you love? But could you not have bought a less expensive gift and donated the surplus money to the poor so that someone else might be able to eat? But how do you know that the poor person will spend the money on food and not gamble with it? But is not a question like that just a self-justification for not donating money to the poor? These intractable questions have faced every generation of Christians, starting with the earliest.

Early Christian teaching on this question originated in the Bible, and even there we find some ambiguities. Genesis 24:35 recounts that "The LORD has greatly blessed [Abraham], and he has become wealthy," owning "flocks and herds, silver and gold, male and female slaves, camels and donkeys." In 26:12-13 we learn that the Lord also blessed Isaac and he became rich. So did his son Jacob (32:5). Later in history "King Solomon excelled all the kings of the earth in riches" (1 Kgs 10:23). The biblical writers leave no doubt that God enabled these men to achieve their wealth, and this wealth reflected the divine favor.

Yet the Old Testament also insisted that God aided the poor. The Israelites had to leave land fallow every seventh year "so that the poor of your people may eat," God told Moses in Exodus 23:11. The psalmist asked "May he [God] defend the cause of the poor of the people, give deliverance to the needy, and crush the oppressor" (Ps 72:4). The prophet Amos castigated the rich "who oppress the poor, who crush the needy" (4:2). In general, the Old Testament saw wealth as something good but warned the wealthy not to use their position to harm those with less. The rich had an obligation to alleviate the sufferings of the poor.

The New Testament shared those attitudes. The better-known passages show Jesus identifying with the poor (Luke 6:20), his lamenting the rich young man's attachment to material things (Matt 19:16-22), followed by his striking comment that "it is easier for a camel to go through the eye of a needle than for someone who is rich to enter the kingdom of God" (Mark 10:25). Luke told the parable of the rich man and Lazarus, which ends with the beggar Lazarus in heaven and the rich man in hell (Luke 16:19-31). The Epistle of James makes it clear that some Christians deferred to the wealthy (2:1-7), whom the author clearly disliked, and he finished his epistle with an attack on the wealthy for their presumed oppression of the poor (5:1-6).

Yet Jesus dined with wealthy tax collectors, and when some of his disciples suggested that the ointment that an unnamed woman poured on his head could have been sold and the money given to the poor, Jesus responded that "she has performed a good service for me" (Mark 14:4-6). Luke told (8:1-3) how rich women aided Jesus, and Paul was glad to collect money from those who have it for "the saints at Jerusalem" (Rom 15:26). These last two citations show the first manifestation of a constant problem for Christian theorists—if there were no Christians with money, how could the Church have aided the poor?

In the opening chapter of Acts, Luke recounted that the earliest disciples "had all things in common; they would sell their possessions and goods and distribute the proceeds to all, as any had need" (2:44-45). This passage would have significant influence upon Christian social thought, especially in the Middle Ages, but here we will just note that while Luke clearly said that the rich must give up what they have, the Christians were not poor, since each had what she or he needed. Luke liked this theme, repeated it in Acts 4:32-35, and coupled it with the merciless deaths of Ananias and Sapphira, who held back some of their goods (Acts 5:1-13).

Thus, the New Testament generally followed the Old. Wealth had an intrinsic neutrality and could even be good if used properly. This proper use meant helping the poor. As for the poor, they are to be pitied and assisted, but Christians should not idealize their poverty. If, as the New Testament frequently implies, their poverty saves them from the greed of the rich, it is good, but clearly the Christians would not have insisted so strongly on the need to soften the blows of poverty if they considered it intrinsically good. The Christians also recognized, no matter how reluctantly, that even the most heavenly oriented movement needs money as long as it sojourns on earth. Finally, some New Testament passages manifest a mistrust of the wealthy, who are presumed to oppress the poor.

With one exception, the Christian writers of the second and third centuries did not elaborate much on the New Testament teaching. They insisted upon the need for the rich to help the poor, and they warned of too great an attachment to wealth. Yet they appreciated the help that money could provide; for example, in the early third century, an Alexandrian named Ambrose provided considerable financial support for Origen, literally making it possible for the great scholar to write some of his books. But in general, the pre-Constantinian Christians, despised and suspect, did not number many of the wealthy among their ranks, and the theoretical approach to riches and poverty awaited the fourth and fifth century—except for Clement of Alexandria (fl. ca. 190–210).

Some wealthy members of his congregation took literally Jesus' injunction to "sell what you have and give to the poor" (Mark 10:21). Clement professed a pastoral concern for them, that is, if they believed that they had to give up their possessions for salvation and they could not give them up, the rich would "give up all hope of attaining eternal life, surrender themselves totally to the world, cling to the present life as if it were the only thing left to them, and so move farther away from the path of the life to come. . . ."[52] Clement insisted that the text should not be understood literally, since, on that level, it contained nothing new or Christian. Greek philosophers, "men like Anaxagoras, Democritus, and Crates," renounced worldly goods:

> If there is something new that . . . the Son of God reveals and teaches, then it cannot be the outward action that he is commanding; others have done that. It must be . . . something greater, more divine and more perfect. It is the stripping off of the passions from the soul itself and from its disposition. . . .[53]

Clement pointed out that Jesus ate with "Zacchaeus and Matthew, the rich tax collectors, and never told them to give up their wealth." Jesus expected his followers to assist the poor: but "if no one had anything, what opportunity would there be left for sharing one's goods?" Thus, "we must not then throw away the wealth which is also beneficial to our neighbors. These things are called 'possessions' because they are possessed and 'wealth' because they are useful

52. *Who Is the Rich Man Who Is to Be Saved?* 2, cited in Phan, *Social Thought,* 71.

53. Ibid., 11–12; p. 72.

and provided by God for the use of people. . . . If you are able to make right use of it [wealth], then it will serve justice. If it is wrongly used, then it will serve injustice." From this theoretical basis, he drew the logical conclusions about poverty. "Thus it is of no advantage to anyone to be poor in material things, while being rich in passions."[54]

This brief treatise[55] set the general pattern for the Christian approach to wealth and poverty. All earthly things will pass. We judge them by how they affect us spiritually. If we do not allow wealth to master us, and if we use it to help the less fortunate, then it has served justice. It remains neutral; how we use it is either good or evil. The same is true for poverty. While the poor must be pitied, there is nothing inherently good about poverty; how the Christian deals with it is what counts.

When the Roman Empire became largely Christianized in the fourth century, the practical situation changed drastically, and it inevitably affected the theoretical situation. With most wealthy people now Christian, the Fathers could no longer blame the pagans for the vast financial inequities in Roman society. They also found that dealing practically with wealth became more difficult. For example, if a rich Christian couple decided to give away all that they had, their decision could negatively impact a variety of markets, such as land and commodities, which in turn hurt the fortunes of other Christians, such as small landowners and farmers. The Fathers continued to use Clement's arguments, emphasizing the dangers that riches posed for the soul, the value of voluntary poverty via renunciation of goods, and the need to assist the poor. Since they could now target their remarks directly to rich congregants, the Fathers produced some of the most scathing sermons ever preached on the injustice of the system that privileged so few and impoverished so many. But they took their argument even further.

How, they asked, did wealth arise? Eve and Adam possessed nothing privately. They lived off the fruits of the trees, wore no clothing or jewels, tilled the garden without slaves, and, until seduced by the serpent to want more, were happy with their lot. Only after they had disobeyed God did this natural, communal life disappear. Furthermore, when we are next in a paradisal situation, in heaven, there will be no rich or poor or even material goods; all people will share the Lord's bounty. With this framework in mind, some Fathers

54. Ibid., 13–15; pp. 73–75.
55. For the text in its entirety, see ANF 2, 589–604.

concluded that wealth was inextricably bound with sin, and none more so than John Chrysostom.

No doubt much of John's attitude emerged from his background as a former monk who became a preacher in Antioch and bishop of Constantinople (398–404). He went from a life of complete renunciation of goods to life in an active, wealthy city to life in the imperial capital, where all the members of the court strove for power and possessions. He encountered the rich face-to-face and did not like what he found.

The Edenic image appears frequently in his writings. "God has given us but one dwelling place, this world; he distributed all created things equally; kindled one sun for all; stretched above us one roof, the sky; set one table, the earth. . . . God in the beginning made not one person rich and another poor . . . he left the earth free to all alike."[56]

"Then, whence comes the great inequality of conditions in life? From the greed and arrogance of the rich." If a contemporary rich person were to say, I did not oppress the poor, but rather inherited my wealth from my ancestors, John replied, "But can you, going back through many generations, show that the riches were justly acquired? No, you cannot. The root and origin of them must have been injustice." Since all wealth originated in injustice, rich people are living off the thefts of their ancestors and thus owe debts to the poor. In the story of Lazarus and the Rich Man (Luke 16:19-31), the rich man went to hell because he did not share his possessions; ". . . not giving a part of one's possession is already a kind of robbery."[57]

The rich are not rich in God's goods. "God gives us abundantly all things that are much more necessary than money, such as air, water, fire, sunshine, and things of this kind. And yet it cannot be said that the rich have more sunshine than the poor. . . .[But] if the necessities of life were not common, the rich, with their usual greediness would perhaps take them away from the poor."[58] Note the phrase, "their usual greediness." John was not attempting to be even-handed on this issue.

Although something of an idealist, John realized that he could not change the situation, that the rich would not abandon their riches. He

56. Citations taken from John's *Homilies on the Gospel of John* 15.3 and his *Homily on 1 Timothy* 4; texts in Phan, *Social Thought,* 146, 159.

57. First two citations from works cited in previous note; third from *On Lazarus* II.4; texts in Phan, ibid., 147, 158–159, 138.

58. *Homily to the People of Antioch* II.6; text in Phan, ibid., 139.

repeatedly warned them of their perilous spiritual situation, and he told them they must help the poor. Later generations of social thinkers, especially in the nineteenth century, would take up some of John's theories on the origin of riches.

For the Latin West, Augustine provided the basic teaching, although he generally agreed with John Chrysostom. For Augustine, the disparity between rich and poor was but one of the numberless consequences of original sin. He taught that wealth was not wrong in itself, as long as the rich person could keep it in perspective and use it for the good. When wealth threatened one's life as a Christian, one had to rise above it. He delightedly pointed out

> . . . how many men of wealth, how many rural householders, and merchants, and soldiers, how many civic leaders, and even senators, persons of both sexes, suffered for the true faith and religion [that is, became martyrs], giving up all those vain and temporal goods which they used but were not enslaved to, thus proving to unbelievers that they possessed these goods but were not possessed by them.[59]

Yet, in spite of these rich martyrs, Augustine recognized and warned about the danger of riches. Like John Chrysostom, he said that refusal to share surplus goods with the poor is a form of theft.[60] He did not consider poverty a good in itself. Characteristically, he put that view in a memorable phrase about the rich man and Lazarus. "If the poor man's merit had been his poverty, not his goodness, he surely would not have been carried by angels into the bosom of Abraham, who had been rich in this life!"[61] But in spite of this, he considered wealth a far graver threat to the soul than poverty.

Few if any persons have ever looked into the human soul as carefully and as deeply as Augustine. He did not believe in an earthly utopia. Adam and Eve had ruined the first one, and the next and last one would come when the Earthly City had passed away and the City of God was universally triumphant. He had no illusions about doing away with wealth. He recognized the temporal right to temporal goods and the right of the state to protect that right by law.[62] In a very

---

59. *The Way of the Catholic Church* I.35.77; text in Phan, ibid., 204.
60. *Sermon* 206.2; text in Phan, ibid., 226.
61. *Letter* 157.23; text in Phan, ibid., 209.
62. *On the Gospel of John* VI.25; text in Phan, ibid., 219.

imperfect world, he strove to convince the rich to use their goods to help the poor. He knew he could do no more.

How ironic that a religion which expected an early end to the world has had to live in that world for two thousand years. Christianity has interacted with its environment for all that time and will do so in the future. At times, the Christians succumbed to their environment, finding ways to legitimize and justify slavery; at other times, they have risen above it, questioning the very basis for the disparity between rich and poor. With the exception of slavery, which no Christian would defend today, the social issues discussed in this chapter continue to challenge the Church.

Chapter Seven

A Brief History of Early Christianity[1]

This survey divides Early Christian history by centuries, largely for the convenience of the student. Occasionally these chronological boundaries are approximate at best, and many movements and individual careers transcended those boundaries.

Since Early Christianity involves six centuries and, if all were to be named, hundreds of people, only very general lines can be drawn. Virtually any event mentioned below can be and has been debated by scholars, and we simply cannot follow each debate. For example, Eusebius says that Constantine saw the ChiRho in a vision, Lactantius says he saw it in a dream,[2] and scholars have questioned both accounts. For this book, what is important is that Constantine was convinced that the Christian God had aided his campaign.

1. The First Century

When Jesus died, somewhere between 30 and 33, his people, the Jews, lived in the Roman province of Judea, one of the easternmost provinces of the empire, but one in regular contact with the capital.

1. This survey of early Christian history concentrates on external events. It makes no attempt to understand the Christians' spiritual motives or inner attitudes. There are many histories of Early Christianity. A concise survey is *The Early Church* by Henry Chadwick (New York: Penguin Books, 1967); a larger study is *The Rise of Christianity* by W.H.C. Frend (Philadelphia: Fortress Press, 1984). A recent study is *The Early Church* by E. Glenn Hinson (Nashville: Abingdon Press, 1996).

2. Texts of both in Stevenson, *A New Eusebius,* 283–284.

Although the great Parthian Empire lay close by, Jesus' disciples looked not East but West. This Western orientation was more than just political; it was also cultural and economic.

Centuries before the Romans came, Alexander the Great and then his successors had made the Jews part of their empires, states which looked to the West and which used Greek as a *lingua franca.* This explains why all the books of the New Testament were written in Greek. There is simply no way to determine the true depth and extent of the cultural mix, but many Jews would have had some knowledge of Greek language and culture, and those Jews in the Greek-speaking Diaspora, such as the apostle Paul, would have known them well.

As for the economy, whenever the Romans conquered an area, they developed it financially, building roads and aqueducts and occasionally cities. They eliminated bandits and pirates so that people and goods could travel safely. [No one can conceive of what the history of Christianity would have been if bandits or pirates had murdered Paul.] A system of provincial governors guaranteed that the emperor knew of conditions throughout the empire. The letters of one governor, the younger Pliny, to the emperor Trajan illustrate how wide-ranging and detailed such communication could be.[3] The Romans wanted peace and taxes, and they provided the former to get the latter.

Thus westward expansion appeared to the earliest missionaries to be both natural and feasible.

Another factor entered in. The Acts of the Apostles portrays Paul following the route of the Jewish Diaspora in Asia Minor, Greece, and Rome. As usual, the scholar must be careful with the historicity of Acts, but this account rings true. The Diaspora provided the first missionaries with people who believed in one God, who accepted the notion of divine Scriptures, and who expected the Messiah.[4] Few Jews converted, but the missionaries logically hoped for hearers who could relate to the basics of their message.

The earliest Christian writings, the epistles of Paul, date approximately two decades after Jesus' death. They deal largely with the immediate problems of Paul's Churches and say little about the Church between Jesus and Paul. For that, one must consult the Acts of the

3. *The Letters of the Younger Pliny,* Betty Radice, trans. (Baltimore: Penguin Books, 1963).

4. It is uncertain at what point the Christians began to consider Jesus the Messiah, although they did so certainly by the end of the first century.

Apostles, which provides a highly interpreted account; but scholars have found within the gospels material reflecting the life of the first community. What follows is a cautious reconstruction of the period before Paul.[5]

Jesus apparently did not establish any kind of office in the community; Acts 1 shows his immediate disciples (the Twelve) confused and uncertain after his ascension. Luke portrays the disciples asking Jesus just before the ascension if he would then establish his kingdom (Acts 1:6), reflecting the idea that they expected his second coming immediately after his death. When that did not occur, they had to create some rudimentary organization and plan, which Luke says they did under the guidance of the Holy Spirit (Acts 2).

Their belief in the Holy Spirit's presence in the Church gave the disciples the courage to preach about Jesus and to make converts. But the disciples still expected an imminent return of their master, and they thus made few plans for an extended future, in spite of sizeable conversions (4:4). The faithful "devoted themselves to the apostles' teaching and fellowship, to the breaking of bread and the prayers" (2:42).

Luke portrays the earliest Christians as virtually a Jewish sect, worshiping in the Temple (3:1) and with no discernible interest in spreading the message to non-Jews, although Jews or Jewish proselytes from outside Palestine were included. This inclusion caused tension within the community and prompted Jesus' immediate disciples (the Twelve) to appoint others (the Seven) to minister to these outsiders (Acts 6:1-6).

After the martyrdom of Stephen, one of the Seven, "a severe persecution began against the Church in Jerusalem, and all except the apostles were scattered throughout the countryside of Judea and Samaria" (8:1). This is a difficult statement historically [why would the authorities not expel the leaders of the group?], but Luke makes it clear that when some Christians found themselves in non-Jewish territory, such as Samaria, they also found themselves faced with the question of whether the message could be for Gentiles as well as Jews.

Although Matthew's gospel portrays Jesus as commanding the disciples to "make disciples of all nations" (Matt 28:19), the first Christians did not turn to the Gentiles. Luke is probably correct that

5. The reader is urged to consult a New Testament history or a commentary on Acts for specific points, as well as for a life of Paul.

only when faced with the actual, direct question of Gentiles eager for the message did the Christians begin to think about a mission to them.

Luke personifies the earliest missionaries in Philip, whose work had to be approved by the leaders of the Jerusalem community (Acts 8:14). Luke then portrayed Peter baptizing the Roman centurion Cornelius and his family (Acts 10). But these were, so to speak, only the preliminaries, and Luke turned to the real hero of Acts, the apostle Paul, whose story occupies about 60 percent of the book.

Before turning to Paul, let us see what bits of information Luke provided about other Christians. First, the Church expanded toward the coastline, to Lydda, and then on to the Mediterranean, to Joppa and Caesarea, and then north to Antioch, where "the disciples were first called 'Christians'" (11:26), and then across the sea to Cyprus. Second, the charismatic element made an early appearance, when Agabus and other prophets came from Jerusalem to Antioch (11:27-28) to announce an imminent famine, a message the disciples took seriously. Third, although the Romans have not yet appeared, their toady, the Jewish king Herod Agrippa I, martyred James, one of the Twelve, *circa* 41 (12:1-2). Fourth, the Christians enjoyed some success in converting the wealthy, since Mary, the mother of John Mark, had a maid (12:12). Fifth, Peter ceased his work in Judea, although Luke does not say where he worked after that (12:17).

Only Jesus has attracted more scholarly attention than Paul, every aspect of whose work has fostered controversy. Scholars have grave doubts about Luke's account in Acts, since Paul does not preach on themes found in his letters. Luke does not mention that Paul ever wrote anything, and the chronology of the letters cannot be reconciled with that of Acts. We will not try to solve these problems or to give a biography of Paul, but rather to outline his career and its impact on Church history.[6]

Paul's impact fell in three areas. First, he was a great missionary, bringing his message to Asia Minor, Greece, and Italy. Second, he provided both the theoretical and practical bases for expansion into Gentile territory, justifying extending the message to Gentiles and denying the requirement to follow Jewish regulations (including circumcision) upon conversion. Third, although his epistles dealt with immediate and particular problems, they covered much theological ground, giving shape to fundamental Christian teaching on such top-

6. Murphy-O'Connor addresses these and other questions in his *Paul: A Critical Life.*

ics as Christ, the Church, and the resurrection. Without much exaggeration, one could say that Jesus founded Christianity and Paul founded the Church.

Paul became a Christian *circa* 35. After a period of reflection, he began his missionary activity. Although scholars debate the specifics of his career, throughout the 40s and 50s of the first century he founded or strengthened Churches in Asia Minor and Greece, keeping a close watch over them. He had good reason to do that, since his belief that Gentiles could be admitted without having to observe Jewish religious regulations caused some controversy. At some point (scholars are unsure as to the date), Paul met with the leaders of the Jerusalem Church and more or less settled the matter in his favor.

Paul made little reference to the organization of his communities. He listed different ministries, rather unhumbly putting apostle first, then prophet, teacher, healer, and others with gifts for "forms of assistance, forms of leadership, various kinds of tongues" (1 Cor 12:27-28). Significantly, he did not list bishops or presbyters; furthermore, as noted in previous chapters, women played a significant role in his Churches.

As his Churches grew, Paul stayed in contact with them by personal visits (1 Cor 2:1), by messengers such as Timothy (4:17), or, increasingly, by letter. He even acknowledged that some people found his letters more impressive than his person (2 Cor 10:10). Starting with 1 Thessalonians, *circa* 49, Paul created the first Christian literature and, although no one knew it at the time, the first Christian Scriptures.

At some point in his career, Paul ran afoul of the Romans. Luke blamed it on the Jews (Acts 22–26). Paul anticipated difficulty in Jerusalem (Rom 15:31), but his letters give no specifics. Scholars accept that Paul went on trial in Rome and died there *circa* 62, although later tradition made him a victim of Nero's persecution, which is also possible.

Paul left behind an enormous legacy, but before the Christians could deal with it, two other events occurred that significantly influenced the development of Christianity.

In 66, the Jews revolted against the Romans. The war lasted four years and ended with the defeat of the Jews and the destruction of Jerusalem.[7] This struggle ended the influence of the Jerusalem Church.

---

7. The famous Jewish resistance at Masada occurred in 73 and did not significantly affect the outcome of the war.

Although later Christians saw this event as divine retribution for the death of Jesus, and although Eusebius claimed that, in the face of Jewish persecution, the Jerusalem community emigrated east across the Jordan to Pella,[8] the exact situation is uncertain. But one thing is certain. This first Church, to which leading missionaries, including Paul and Barnabas, had to report, and which had been presided over by James "the Lord's brother" (Gal 1:19),[9] effectively disappeared for centuries.

The other event was Nero's persecution of the Roman community. In 64 a fire in Rome raged for almost a week and destroyed about 40 percent of the city. The populace believed that Nero had ordered the fire,[10] and, to shift the blame from himself, he accused the Christians. The Roman historian Tacitus says that the people believed the accusation because the Christians were "a class hated for their abominations" and their belief was a "dangerous superstition."[11] It is likely that the Romans looked askance at them because they were new, foreign, and had rites that could easily be misunderstood, for example, references to eating Jesus' body and drinking his blood.

The persecution affected only the Roman community, probably did not last long, and was not renewed, but it set a dangerous precedent. The Roman state had persecuted the Christians. Furthermore, the persecution took the life of Peter, the leader of the Twelve.

The Christians faced a desperate situation—Peter and Paul dead, the Jerusalem Church destroyed, Rome a persecutor—but a new generation of leaders came to the fore, led by the evangelist Mark.[12] Writing *circa* 70, he created a new literary form, the gospel, organizing a theological account of Jesus' career and teaching. No doubt he wrote partially because the generation of eyewitnesses was dying out, but also because he wanted to formulate an understanding of Jesus. By giving a permanence and a shape to traditions about Jesus, Mark aided a community in distress.

8. *Ecclesiastical History* iii.5.3; Williamson, 111.

9. Whether James was a full blood brother of Jesus is debated, since the term "brother" could mean a cousin.

10. The legend of his playing the fiddle while Rome burned is a very late one.

11. Tacitus, *Annales* xv.44.2–8; cited in Stevenson, *A New Eusebius,* 2.

12. Scholars debate whether the traditional author of the gospel is the Mark referred to in the New Testament (Acts 12:12, 25; 15:37, 39; Col 4:10, 2 Tim 4:11; Phlm 24; 1 Pet 5:13). Here we will use the traditional designation without trying to answer this question.

Luke wrote probably between 80 and 90. Like his contemporary, Matthew,[13] he had reservations about Mark's work and rewrote much of it in his own gospel, but his real importance for Church history lies in Acts. In effect, what he did there was validate the Church. For him, the Church was not a group of believers waiting for the end, because Luke was apparently the first important Christian to realize that the end was not near. He told of Jesus' ascent into heaven (Acts 1:9) and the descent of the Holy Spirit to inspire the disciples to continue their master's work. Luke emphasized this continuity by having the disciples repeat some of Jesus' miracles (compare Acts 3:6 to Luke 5:24) and by paralleling Stephen's death to that of Jesus. Looking toward a Gentile Church, Luke told the story of the universalist Paul, spreading his message to all the Roman world.

Since the Christians would be living in this Roman world, Luke portrayed Roman officials as sympathetic to Paul, and he ended Acts with Paul in Rome, discreetly leaving out his execution. By validating the Church, Luke made it possible for Christians to look toward a future on earth and to plan for it.

Not all Christians shared Luke's view. John, a prisoner on Patmos, had no use for the Romans. While Luke can be seen as the forerunner of those who wished to live in harmony with the empire, John set the tone for those who loathed it. His apocalyptic images of the Great Beast and the scarlet-clad Whore of Babylon always had an appeal for some, especially in time of persecution. John wrote *circa* 95. Another John, traditionally identified with the Beloved Disciple, *circa* 100 wrote a gospel that revealed a significant break with the Jews. Jewish influence continued to be strong into the second century, but John forecast the future pattern of misunderstanding and mistrust. The two Johns demonstrated Christian attitudes toward the outside world; the three Pastoral Epistles[14] centered on the organization of the Church. Gone are the prophets and apostles and speakers in tongues, replaced by *episkopoi,*[15] presbyters or elders, and deacons (1 Tim 3, 5). Clearly, the pseudonymous author agreed with Luke that

---

13. As with Mark, we are using the traditional names of the gospels' authors, even though Matthew the disciple (Mark 3:18) cannot be the author of the gospel, although Luke (Phlm 24, Col 4:14, 2 Tim 4:11) could be.

14. 1 and 2 Timothy and Titus; works claiming to have been written by Paul.

15. The word bishop derived from this Greek term (*episkopos* in the singular), but its original meaning would have been "overseer" or "supervisor."

the Church would be on earth for an indeterminate time, and that it required some organization. This emerging Church had little room for charismatic ministries or, as we saw earlier, for women in leadership roles.

The transition from charisma to institution was not all bad, and much of it was necessary. The Church had grown. There were more Christians, and they were more spread out. Furthermore, they still faced the Roman threat. *Circa* 95 the emperor Domitian had apparently persecuted the Christians;[16] *circa* 112 the Roman governor of northern Asia Minor, Pliny, did persecute them.[17] Some organization was required to meet this threat.

Another "threat" appeared. As more and more converts came from a Greco-Roman background rather than a Jewish one, they approached Christian teaching differently. This often produced very creative tension and brilliant explorations of doctrine, but it also demonstrated how vulnerable the Christian message could be to misunderstanding.

By the end of the first century, Docetism had appeared. Scholars give this name to the belief that Jesus did not have a body but only "seemed" (from the Greek verb *dokeo*) to have one. Sincere, Greek-educated converts could not accept the belief that the Son of God, who in Greek thought would have to have been a spiritual being, could take on flesh. Since people had seen Jesus, the Docetists explained his appearance by saying that he just seemed to have a body. This approach had some appeal, freeing the Son of God from fleshly corruption, but it effectively negated the redemption. If Jesus did not have a real body, he did not really suffer, die, or rise. Furthermore, Docetism negated the Old Testament, which presented a God who created the world of matter and proclaimed it to be good (Gen 1:31).[18] The majority of Christians rejected this theory.

While Docetism is more nuanced than this summary, the significance of it is clear. The Christians were entering a new world, a Gentile world, and they could not be sure what they would find.

---

16. The evidence for this persecution is sparse.

17. Letter x.96; *Letters of the Younger Pliny,* 293–295.

18. Some scholars believe that the prologue to John's gospel, which emphasizes that the Word became flesh (1:14), may be responding to Docetism.

2. The Second Century[19]

Although the first century was by definition the most formative for Christianity, the second played almost as great a role. Its central problem was authority.

Although it is easy to equate authority with power, there are significant differences. Power is the ability to coerce, the way a powerful nation might intimidate a weaker one. Authority is the ability to lead, to win people over, as we would say someone is an authority in international diplomacy because she or he had a career in foreign service or had written a book on the topic. Someone with authority may wield power (a legitimately elected government has a police force), but authority rests on persuasion and acceptance by the people. As the life of the Church became more and more complex, the Christians needed some authorities to which they could turn.

The community had never been without authorities. Jesus' authority was unique and no one could replicate it, but his disciples preached and taught in his name. Paul claimed authority directly from God (2 Corinthians 1:1), and he saw the Holy Spirit behind a number of charismatic ministries in his Churches. The Pastoral Epistles favored a more organizational authority. The one authority to which all Christians appealed was Scripture, that is, what they came to call the Old Testament. Very significantly, this meant Scripture as interpreted by the Christians. For example, no one doubted that many Israelite prophecies applied to Jesus; according to Matthew, Jesus' birth alone fulfilled no fewer than five prophecies (1:22-23; 2:5-6, 15, 17-18, 23).

All these authorities played a role in the second century, and new ones arose. As the century progressed, the Christians still had not settled on a widely accepted form of ecclesiastical organization despite the orderly scheme offered by the Pastoral Epistles. The *Didache,* a Syrian work that scholars have dated from 60 to 150, spoke of wandering prophets. *Circa* 95 Clement of Rome, in an epistle to the Church at Corinth, wrote not in his own name but in that of "the Church of God which dwells as a pilgrim in Rome," which suggests that Rome had a communal form of government. But the future

19. A good survey of this period is *After the Apostles: Christianity in the Second Century* by Walter Wagner (Minneapolis: Augsburg Fortress, 1994).

lay with neither of these but rather with the episcopacy as promoted in the letters of Ignatius of Antioch.[20]

Ignatius, bishop of Antioch, had been condemned to the beasts in Rome. On his journey from Syria to Italy (ca. 115), he wrote letters to six Asian Churches and to the bishop Polycarp of Smyrna. In these he stressed the role of the bishop as a stabilizing force in the community but also as the symbol of the community's unity. He depicted an Antiochene community rent by dissension by Docetists and Judaizers, that is, those who believed Christians should continue to follow Jewish legal regulations. He, as head of a sort of centrist party, had to use episcopal authority to keep matters under control. The sudden emergence of a strong, monarchical bishop is surprising and may reflect the local situation,[21] but throughout the second century, this form of ecclesiastical organization increasingly caught on. By the end of the second century, almost all Churches were governed by bishops, often known as patriarchs in the Greek East.

The Gnostic movement produced a new kind of authority, one based upon *gnosis,* the Greek word for "knowledge."

> *Gnosis* does not refer to understanding of truths about the human and natural world that can be reached through reason. It refers to a revealed knowledge available only to those who have received the secret teachings of a heavenly being. All other humans are trapped in ignorance of the true divine world and of the destiny of the Gnostic soul to return to its home there.[22]

Gnosticism entered Christianity via conversions; by the second century there was a kind of "home-grown" Gnosticism, that is, a Christian version that sometimes actively rejected Judaism or at least the Old Testament. The Gnostics claimed that they had a special knowledge which made them superior to others in the faith [today such people are called "theologians"], and this knowledge came to

20. *Didache* 11 in FC 1, 180–181; *First Epistle to the Corinthians,* in ibid., 9; this volume also contains the seven letters of Ignatius.

21. 3 John 9 refers to a Diotrephes who enjoys being in charge of the unknown Church to which the letter is written. Some scholars wonder if he might have been a monarchical bishop, but he could just as easily have been chairperson of a presbyteral council.

22. Pheme Perkins, "Gnosticism," in *EEXty,* I. 465–470. For a collection of Gnostic texts, see Bentley Layton, *The Gnostic Scriptures,* Anchor Bible Reference Library (New York: Doubleday, 1987).

them originally from some divine source, but then from disciples who passed it along. Since this knowledge offered great power, it could be given only to those who were worthy to receive it, so the first Gnostic teachers founded exclusivist sects that passed along the knowledge secretly. "[M]any Gnostic teachers spoke of Christians in general as 'psychics' (from the Greek for 'soul') who lacked the Gnostic enlightenment that would make them 'pneumatics' (Greek for 'spirit')."[23]

Modern Christians may wonder how their ancestors could take this elitism seriously, but Christianity was still taking shape in the second century. Furthermore, most Christians practiced the *disciplina arcani* or "rule of secrecy," which forbade them to admit the unbaptized to the eucharist and sometimes even to talk to them about sacramental practices. This may reflect the influence of mystery religions upon Christianity, but the Gnostics were hardly alone in emphasizing secrecy and the explanation of doctrine only to the worthy.

Gnosticism may have appeared early in Christian history. In 1 Corinthians (1:18–2:16) Paul warned about Christians who put too much trust in the wisdom of this world; in 8:1 he warned that *gnosis* puffs up but love builds up. Scholars cannot be sure if Paul's targets were Gnostics, but many of them claimed to have cosmological knowledge, which would fit Paul's description. Most likely, Paul had to deal with some Gnostic tendencies among the Corinthians; full-blown Gnosticism awaited the second century.

Many Gnostics repudiated the Jewish Scriptures and their God who created and found goodness in the material world (Gen 1), thus also repudiating Christian fidelity to the Scriptures of Jesus and Paul. They believed that Jesus brought saving knowledge, which called into question the need for a redemptive death. Their exclusivism patronized the Christian desire to offer salvation to all, regardless of their level of knowledge. Although the Gnostics forced the Church to consider the role of knowledge in redemption, and although they wrote many creative books, including the first gospel commentary on a gospel (that of Heracleon on John), the Christians as a whole could not accept their basic approach to authority, that revelation lay in the hands of teachers who passed it along only to a chosen core of disciples.

If the Gnostics looked to knowledge for salvation, others looked to the spirit. In the middle of the second century, a convert named Montanus claimed the inspiration of the Holy Spirit and began to

23. Ibid., 374.

prophesy ecstatically. He soon had two women companions, Maximilla and Priscilla. The three of them formed the New Prophecy or, as it was more commonly called, Montanism.[24]

Montanism hearkened back to the first century, or at least what Christians thought the first century to be. In an era when bishops were organizing the Church and Gnostics looked to their own exclusivist groups, the New Prophecy returned to the charismatic past. Significantly, two of its three leaders were women, another echo of the previous century. To Gnostics, the Montanists would be ignoramuses, but to the bishops, they represented a different kind of problem.

No bishop wanted to oppose the Holy Spirit, even if two of the Spirit's chief prophets were women. Furthermore, many people responded to the prophets. Montanism started in Asia Minor but soon spread south and west, even reaching North Africa and Rome. Clearly, its charisma resonated with many Christians.

But the bishops feared its uncontrolled and uncontrollable character. Dead prophets could be studied and revered, but living ones could threaten the Church's organization. More important was the overriding question of how one could know that the Holy Spirit spoke through the prophet. Might not the prophecy be a delusion or even demon-inspired? The bishops overcame their reluctance to appear anti-Spirit and attacked Montanism.

The first generation of prophets died probably before 170, but the movement survived somewhat intact into the third century. It survived, but in decline, into the fourth century. The Montanist movement marked the last time a prophetic movement would win over large numbers of Christians and even stand a chance of becoming the dominant ethos of the faith. Future prophetic movements lived on the margins.

Both Gnosticism and the New Prophecy raised the question of authority. If the Christians could not accept the knowledge of the Gnostics and charisma of the Montanists, what could they offer? The bishops claimed the mantle of successors of the apostles, but what made the bishops' teaching any more secure than that of the Gnostics? After all, episcopacy was equally new in the second cen-

---

24. There is considerable bibliography on Montanism. See now *Montanism: Gender, Authority and the New Prophecy* by Christine Trevett (New York: Cambridge University Press, 1996).

tury. Where could believers find the teaching of Jesus and the apostolic generation?

The answer lay partly in a new form of authority, the New Testament, although it was not called that in the second century. For that matter, the books of the New Testament were still being written in the second century. Most scholars date the last one, 2 Peter, *circa* 125, but some believe the Pastoral Epistles may date *circa* 140. The phrase "New Testament" may be an anachronism, but the idea was catching on. Indeed, it had been around in some form since the apostolic age.

The first great Christian theologian, Irenaeus of Lyons (ca. 115–ca. 202), brought this new authority into the center of discussion and linked it with existing authorities. Writing against the Gnostics, he realized that their supposed strength, the secret revelations, was actually their weakness. Standing their argument on its head, he argued that the main body of Christians could prove that their teachings went back to the apostles and could do so publicly. They did not have to hide behind hidden teaching that no one could validate. Irenaeus traced his teachings back to the apostles in two ways, usually termed Scripture and Tradition, although this phrase can be misleading.

Irenaeus naturally used the Old Testament, but he also relied on the Pauline epistles, the four gospels, and Acts, a book he was the first to cite. He considered the gospels and Acts as Scripture. He cites the epistles as Scripture only once, but he considered Paul authoritative. He cited some other works which would later be in the New Testament along with works which would not. Although a canon was still distant, his view was clear, and it furthered the process of canonizing a New Testament. Christian books preserve apostolic teaching, and he looked to them for that teaching.

The word "tradition," the second element in the second-century's view of authority, has had a bad press largely because some papalists of the Counter Reformation equated it with nonscriptural teachings used in the Roman Catholic Church and accepted by the papacy. But Irenaeus understood it as something organic and vibrant. The apostles taught the martyr Polycarp of Smyrna, who in turn taught him, thus connecting him to the apostolic age via a living link of orthodox bishops. Irenaeus put special emphasis on the "apostolic" sees, those bishoprics that could trace their foundation back to an apostle. When Irenaeus listed the bishops of Rome back to Peter, he was less concerned with citing episcopal authority than with proving a living link to the apostolic age. His answer to the Gnostics also answered the Montanists. If the Spirit spoke through the apostolic writings and in the continuing life of the Church, prophetic teachings would have to be consonant with the growing orthodoxy. The utterings of the "Spirit" would be subject to comparison with what Scripture and tradition taught. If the prophecy disagreed, it could not be authentic; the Spirit would not be self-contradictory. To Irenaeus goes the honor of creating the theological method that all subsequent writers would use in this era. Christian teaching relied upon apostolicity, that is, did it derive from or was it consonant with what the apostles had taught? One could discover what they taught via Scripture and tradition.[25]

The question of authority was hardly settled, and the third and fourth centuries would see new ones arise, but the second century provided reliable authorities for the Church's long, postapostolic history. The question of authority was largely an internal one.[26] The external question continued to be how to deal with Rome, and the Christians answered it in two ways: martyrdom and apologetics. Although sporadic and localized, the persecutions continued. Pliny, Roman governor of Asia Minor, moved against the Christians in 112; *circa* 136 Telesphorus, bishop of Rome, died a martyr. The Christian scholar Justin Martyr also died in Rome, *circa* 165. In 177 an especially fierce persecution broke out in Lyons; Eusebius preserves a vivid account of it. Finally, in 180, the African Church saw its first martyrs at a town called Scilli. These persecutions did not stop the growth of Christianity, and *circa* 175 a pagan named Celsus wrote a book warning all who would listen that the Christians would corrupt the empire.[27]

Although Christians were willing to die, most wanted an accommodation with the empire; some tried this via apologetics, that is, a reasoned defense of one's position. The apologists basically had three goals: to defend Christianity against false charges (cannibal-

25. Many modern scholars still use apostolicity, insisting that their theologies, no matter how innovative, explicate or derive from what the Scriptures "really" mean.

26. Another internal question in the second century was Quartodecimanism, which was explained in chapter three.

27. W.H.C. Frend, *Martyrdom and Persecution in the Early Church*; William Weinrich, *Spirit and Martyrdom* (Washington, D.C.: University Press of America, 1981).

ism, disloyalty), to attack pagan beliefs, and to present a true picture of Christian belief. Eschatological belief had largely faded; the Church had to live in the world.

This movement appeared quite early; *circa* 125 the writer Quadratus produced the first apology at the same time a pseudonymous author produced the last scriptural book (2 Peter). Several second-century apologists wrote treatises to the emperors; some wrote apologies against the Jews. In one sense, they failed; the persecutions continued. But in another, more historically important sense, they succeeded because they introduced an important new literary genre that Christians would use down to the fifth century in Augustine's *City of God*. They also raised the question of how to use pagan writings.

The most important apologist, Justin Martyr, believed that all truth came from God's Word (*logos* in Greek), and thus anyone who spoke the truth possessed the Word. For him, a pagan who believed in one God or who taught the need for an ethical life could be called Christian, in some sense, because how could she or he have known and taught the truth without the *logos*. Although the Christians possessed the Word Incarnate, they could still learn from the pagans. Not all apologists shared Justin's open-mindedness toward pagan culture. His contemporary, the Syrian Tatian (d. ca. 180), loathed it.

The apologists left two other legacies. First, they wrote the first Christian books intended primarily for non-Christians, and this forced them to sharpen their arguments for a critical audience. Second, in their replies to pagan slanders and calumnies, they provided explanations of some Christian beliefs and practices, especially liturgical ones. These accounts provide a unique, invaluable view of Christianity at a very early period.

3. The Third Century

The third century began with a persecution on the southern shore of the Mediterranean. In Alexandria it took the life of Leonides, the father of the great scholar Origen, but its more famous victims lived in Carthage. The *Passion of Saints Perpetua and Felicity* tells the story of the African martyrs, particularly of a young noblewoman named Perpetua and her slave Felicity. This exciting, well-written account provides an insight into the African Church's veneration for martyrdom as well as one of Rome's main objections to Christianity. During her trial, the judge pointed to Perpetua's anguished father and lamented how Christianity disrupted families, an echo of Celsus' charge that this new religion corrupted Roman values.[28]

But this persecution passed. There were individual executions in 206 and 211, and it was not until the 230s that larger persecutions broke out again in Rome and in Asia Minor. The previous pattern held—localized persecutions often fostered by local events. Much of the Christian world enjoyed peace for the first half of the century.

In this half-century, Christian intellectual life emerged. The gospels contain sophisticated literary motifs and theological strategies, and every generation has recognized the genius of Paul. Some second-century Gnostic teachers were brilliant, and the apologists drew upon considerable learning. The Christians were never without intellectuals. Yet the first half of the third century marked a significant turning point as the Christians produced scholars who could match the best any tradition could offer.

Alexandria had a catechetical school that attracted foreign scholars. Pantaenus, the founder, was a Sicilian Greek who taught in the Egyptian city (ca. 170–ca. 190). Little is known of him, but his successor, an Athenian named Clement (ca. 150–ca. 220), made the school famous. He taught in Alexandria until 202, when he fled the persecution. A broad-minded man, he believed that Greek learning had prepared the Greeks for Christianity just as the Old Testament had prepared the Jews. In his writings, he cited Greek pagan writers more than the Bible. Clement of Alexandria wrote with encyclopedic learning, although his books sometimes meander.

The next great Alexandrian could legitimately be called the greatest of the Greek Fathers. Born a Christian, Origen (ca. 185–ca. 253) was a child prodigy who did not burn out early but became a brilliant adult. He turned his hand to almost everything in theology. Realizing that he could not understand the Bible without a reliable edition, he practiced textual criticism, producing a six-columned edition of the Hebrew Scriptures. He wrote biblical commentaries on both Old and New Testament books as well as scholia and homilies. Perhaps his greatest contribution to scholarship was his massive introduction of allegory into biblical study. His attention to the Bible set a pattern; until the scholastic period, every great Christian scholar after him did exegesis, often allegorical.

28. The Latin text and an English translation can be found in *The Acts of the Christian Martyrs,* Herbert Musurillo, ed. (New York: Oxford University Press, 1972) 106–131.

In his book *On First Principles,* he established what came to be called systematic theology, that is, he related various aspects of theology to one another. His response to Celsus, entitled simply *Against Celsus,* was a magisterial, at times sentence-by-sentence answer to the pagan; it demonstrated Origen's considerable knowledge of secular culture. He was a pioneer, and inevitably some of his ideas, such as the possible pre-existence of souls and the redemption of the devil, went too far for his contemporaries.

Although always known as an Alexandrian, Origen left the city in 230 after a dispute with his bishop Demetrias, who objected to Origen's having been ordained while he was visiting in Palestine. When his former pupil Heraclas became bishop, Origen returned to Alexandria only to find the current bishop supporting his predecessor, so he returned to Caesarea, thus helping to spark intellectual life there. He also journeyed to Rome, Antioch, and the Roman province of Arabia. His fame caused his arrest during a persecution in 250; a year of torture could not get him to apostasize, and he was released, only to die shortly thereafter.[29]

A controversial man in his own day, he continued to be so in death, becoming the focus of controversies in the late fourth and mid-sixth centuries.[30] His prodigious output forced many Christians to focus and clarify their notions of God, Christ, revelation, Scripture, and virtually every other major topic.

Scholars do not know much about the third-century Alexandrian catechetical school after Origen, although Dionysius (fl. 233–264) served as both head of the school and later bishop of the city. He exhibited considerable skill as an exegete, demonstrating that the same author could not have written the Gospel of John and the Book of Revelation.

Carthage was a provincial city compared to Alexandria, yet it nourished the first thoroughly Latin Christianity.[31] The accounts of the Scillitan Martyrs and Perpetua and Felicity emerge from there,

29. There is a sizeable literature on Origen. A good survey is *Origen: The Bible and Philosophy in the Third Century* by Joseph Trigg; see also Henri Crouzel, *Origen* (San Francisco: Harper and Row, 1989).

30. See Elizabeth A. Clark, *The Origenist Controversy* (Princeton: Princeton University Press, 1992).

31. It is common to think of Rome as the center of Latin Christianity, but up to the mid-third century, that community's leaders, including its bishops, had mostly Greek names, e.g., Popes Soter (ca. 166–ca. 174), Eleutherius (ca. 174–189).

but with Tertullian (ca. 160–ca. 220), Latin Christian intellectual life begins.[32]

Tertullian had legal and rhetorical training; he also knew Greek. Around 195 he became a Christian. A vigorous and rigorous man, he attacked all perceived enemies, within and without the Church—pagan governors, Jews, heretics, and after his conversion to Montanism *circa* 206, his former coreligionists. He eventually abandoned Montanism and founded the Tertullianists. Like Origen, he ranged widely, especially on topics like the Trinity, but he did not construct an extensive theology. He made two major contributions to Church history, and one derived from his obsession with enemies.

Tertullian virtually founded the notion of the gathered Church, the small community beset by enemies, faithful to the truth, and eventually to be vindicated by God—a community not just cut off from society, but actually opposed to it. His famous remark, "What has Athens to do with Jerusalem? What has the Church to do with the Academy?," succinctly summarizes his attitude toward pagan culture.[33] We have the truth; they do not; we do not need them. He literally created the African ecclesiastical mentality to be manifest later in Cyprian and the Donatists, a mentality occasionally manifest in places other than Africa.

Tertullian's second great contribution to Church history was the establishment of Latin theological terminology. Every discipline must have its technical language; the earliest Christian theology used Greek terms. Tertullian created such words as *trinitas, substantia,* and *persona.* Possibly because of formal legal training, he also introduced a legal vocabulary into Church life. Many subsequent Latin writers rejected his rejection of Greco-Roman culture, and all rejected his Montanism, but they all used the vocabulary he established.

By mid-century other Latin writers had appeared. Cyprian of Carthage (ca. 205–258), who revered Tertullian, followed in his footsteps. He wrote the first ecclesiology, or theology of the Church, entitled *On the Unity of the Church.* Like his master, he favored the gathered Church, which he compared to Noah's ark, that is, those on

32. A Latin writer named Minucius Felix wrote a dialogue entitled *Octavius,* which may antedate Tertullian's work, but scholars are uncertain. They are also unsure if Minucius was a Roman or an African. No matter what, Tertullian remains the first great Latin writer.

33. By "Academy," he meant Plato's Academy, a traditional symbol of Greco-Roman learning.

board were safe but everyone else perished. Across the Mediterranean the presbyter Novatian (d. 258) became the first great Roman theologian with his book on the Trinity.

The Latin Church also became involved in theological controversy over the nature of the Trinity, questioning whether there were indeed three independent persons in the Trinity or whether the notion of a Trinity threatened the one rule of God (hence the name "Monarchianism").[34] The Monarchians explained the Trinity by suggesting, among other things, that Father, Son, and Holy Spirit were just names for divine activities. In general, the Latins rejected Monarchianism, although major trinitarian theologizing awaited the fourth century.

The latter half of the third century remains largely obscure to scholars, and we know of no successors to these first intellectuals. But they had achieved much, putting Christianity on a strong scholarly footing; they had gone down a road from which the Church would never turn back.

Practical considerations such as size, organization, and response to persecution also played a great role in the third-century Church.

By the mid-third century episcopacy was to be found everywhere, eclipsing other forms of Church governance. Priests, deacons, and deaconesses accompanied the bishops; the new order of lector (reader) appears, indicating the growing importance of scriptural reading in liturgy.[35] This growing organization proved its worth in the year 250.

The emperor Decius (249–251) believed that the Christians threatened the empire, and he decided to launch the first empire-wide persecution of Christians. Christians were required to sacrifice to the gods, upon which they received a *libellus* ("little book"), a receipt of sorts, acknowledging that they had sacrificed.[36] After almost a half century of being left alone, many Christians could not endure the persecution and apostasized. Others stood firm; the most famous victim was Fabian, bishop of Rome. The persecution enjoyed some

34. Virtually every theological controversy is a complicated one. No third-century writer had evolved a clear idea of three independent, equal trinitarian persons. The wording here is intended to indicate the positions of either side. See Rebecca Lyman, "Monarchianism." *EEXty* II.764–765.

35. Gamble, *Books and Readers,* 218–224.

36. For the texts of some *libelli,* see Stevenson, *A New Eusebius,* 214–215.

success, but it came to an abrupt end when Decius died in battle. The new emperor, Gallus (251–253), halted the persecution, but the problems did not cease for the Christians. They became internal.

What to do with those who had lapsed during the persecution and now wished to return to the Church? On the surface, the decision would have been how harshly or mercifully should the Church authorities treat them, and this was often the case. But it also provoked a dispute between official and spiritual authority.

Cyprian and other bishops worked out a system whereby the lapsed could do penance and be readmitted, but some lapsed had obtained forgiveness from the confessors, that is, those who had suffered during the persecution and who consequently had great spiritual authority—an authority that compared well with that of Cyprian, who had fled during the persecution.[37] Cyprian organized the African bishops in council and moved quickly to obviate the role of the confessors in dealing with the lapsed or at least to bring it under episcopal control. The bishops had learned the lessons of the second century; no one would exercise any spiritual authority that threatened their official one.

But what if bishops disagreed among themselves? Many Christians had joined sects that the larger, catholic Church considered heretical or schismatical. Occasionally, some wished to join the larger community. Since they had been baptized by their sect, how should they be admitted? In Rome, the bishops recognized the validity of heretical and schismatical baptism; they required prayers and the laying on of hands but no baptism. The more exclusivist African ecclesiology, summed up by Cyprian's phrase *nulla salus extra ecclesiam* ("no salvation outside the Church"), considered the sects to be no better than pagan and thus incapable of validly baptizing anyone. The Africans insisted on baptism or what the Romans called rebaptism. The Africans were content with their tradition, but Stephen I (254–257) of Rome expected them to follow the Roman way. Neither Church gave in, but Stephen's death and election of a pope, Sixtus II (257–258), who did not wish to continue the fight, ended the matter, which was not settled until the next century (in Rome's favor).

Yet this episode witnessed the first example of a dominant theme in subsequent Church history. To intimidate the Africans, Stephen

---

37. When a later persecution broke out, he stayed in Carthage and died a martyr's death in 258.

claimed that Rome was the primatial see of the West because of its foundation by Peter and Paul. No Roman bishop had made the claim before, and scholars do not know why Stephen made it then. The claim did not move the Africans, it disturbed bishops elsewhere, and Stephen's immediate successors did not repeat it. But future Roman bishops would use it again, although by citing just Peter, and they would make good their claims to head the Latin Church.

The emperor Valerian (254–260) persecuted the Christians briefly, but his son and successor Gallienus (253–268) canceled the persecution and by official decree returned Church property that had been seized, a surprisingly official recognition of the Christians' rights. The emperor Aurelian (270–275) contemplated a persecution, but an assassin took his life before he could implement his plans. In fact, the Christians felt so comfortable with the Romans that when a dispute broke out in Antioch in 272 over the legitimacy of the bishop and the ownership of Church property, they referred the matter to the emperor Aurelian, an apparent contradiction of the apostle Paul's injunction in 1 Corinthians 6:1 that Christians should not take their internal disputes to the secular courts.

This tolerance did not stem from any Roman fondness for Christianity but rather from the grave political and financial crises besetting the empire. Between 235 and 285 there were twenty-one emperors, or at least generals and politicians claiming to be emperors. Only three ruled for more than five years and fourteen for two years or less. Emperors who spent much of their short-lived reigns trying to legitimate and consolidate their power did not have the time, energy, or money to persecute Christians.

The Christians took advantage of this. Literary evidence is lacking and archaeological evidence says little more, but it appears that in the late third century the Christians made strides in the African countryside and in many parts of Asia Minor. Their numbers grew considerably. Inevitably another emperor would feel threatened.

4. The Fourth Century

In this century the Christians gained freedom of worship, and they produced a virtual golden age, at least of scholarship. The century witnessed the achievements of Athanasius, Lactantius, Eusebius of Caesarea, Basil of Caesarea, Ambrose of Milan, Gregory of Nazianzus, Gregory of Nyssa, Jerome, Antony of Egypt, Martin of

Tours, and the early career of Augustine. Significantly, the century also witnessed the achievements of Christian women; Melania the Elder, Melania the Younger, Mary of Egypt, Paula, Eustochium, Egeria, Falconia Proba, and Macrina all made the Church a force in Roman life.[38]

But before reaching this golden age, the Christians had to pass through the fire once more.

The emperor Diocletian (284–305) had reorganized the empire, shared his power with co-emperors and potential successors, and had brought peace if not prosperity. But, like so many of his predecessors, when he faced mounting problems, he looked to a non-human explanation. The gods disapproved of the emperor's tolerance of the Christians, a tolerance that had gone so far that Diocletian could actually see a Christian church from the imperial palace. In 303, the emperor decided to persecute.

Although known as the Great Persecution because of its length (two years) and the number of its victims, in fact it stood far less chance of success than earlier ones. By 303 the Christians were in all parts of the empire and had achieved considerable social status. Indeed, Diocletian had to start by purging the army and civil service of Christians. Inevitably some apostasized, leaving a terrible legacy in the postpersecution period, especially in Africa, but, as so often in the past, the majority of Christians stood firm. In spite of a well-organized and systematic effort, Diocletian, too, had to admit defeat.

The emperor tried to avoid the chaos that had characterized the third century by arranging for an orderly succession when he retired in 305, but by 307 his plan had failed. Several ambitious generals wished to be emperor, and a huge civil war broke out with, at one point, seven claimants to the throne. In the end, the victors were Constantine (306–337) and Licinius (308–324), who had banded together, the former operating in the West and the latter in the East. Constantine, however, believed that he had more help than just that of Licinius.

In a much debated event, Constantine had either a vision or a dream in which the Christian god promised to help him. He believed this promise, and, when he was victorious, he repaid the Christian god by issuing, with Licinius, the Edict of Milan (313), giving the

---

38. Articles on all of these figures can be found in the various encyclopedias and dictionaries listed in the bibliography; these articles will also have bibliographies for further study.

Christians freedom of worship. Constantine's interest in Christianity continued to grow; *circa* 319 he had become a Christian himself. In 323 he found an excuse to attack Licinius, whom he defeated and executed in 324, becoming sole ruler of Rome.

The impossible had happened; the cross joined the Roman eagle. As we saw in chapter six, Eusebius justified Constantine's reign, glorying in the new Christian empire. Except for the brief reign of Julian (361–363), all subsequent emperors would be Christian.

The Roman people did not convert en masse to gain jobs or favor with the emperor; some regions, like Italy, remained heavily pagan. But the Christians could now proselytize without fear, and they also took advantage of imperial support. Throughout the fourth century, they successfully evangelized much of the empire, making Rome Christian and, in effect, making Christianity Roman.[39] Much of the great art referred to in chapter five dates from the fourth century.

Constantine faced serious opposition, especially from the pagan nobility. Initially, he carefully avoided putting any Christian buildings in central Rome, and he kept the usual imperial titles. But this could not go on indefinitely, and so in 324 he took the decisive step of founding a new city, Constantinople (literally, "Constantine's city") on the Bosporus, now the Turkish city of Istanbul. This was to be a Christian city with no pagan monuments but many churches. To weaken the power of old Rome, the emperor established a senate for his new capital and moved much of the government there. This well-founded, strategically placed city would be a center of the Christian world for more than eleven hundred years.

The emperor reasonably assumed that his Christian subjects would show the appropriate gratitude and support his policies, but this assumption did not last long.

In 312 Constantine recognized Caecilian (d. ca. 345) as the bishop of Carthage. But some Africans protested that Caecilian had been consecrated by a *traditor,* one who had handed over[40] the Scriptures to the pagans during the persecution and therefore was not a true bishop. Constantine and bishops outside Africa supported Caecilian, but the dissidents, led by Donatus (d. 355), refused to accept the im-

39. Peter Brown's *The World of Late Antiquity, A.D. 150–750* (London: Thames and Hudson, Ltd., 1971) describes "The Conversion of Christianity" (ch. vii, pp. 82–95).

40. The Latin verb *traho* (which has several forms beginning *trad-*) means to hand over. The words "tradition" and "traitor" both come from this verb.

perial decision. Nothing could win over the Donatists, as they became known, and down to the Muslim conquest of North Africa,
Christian emperors had to deal with them.

Donatism quickly paled before a new crisis. In 318 an Egyptian
priest named Arius taught that the son of God was inferior to the
Father (a common idea in the third century), but he went on to say
that the Son was a created being who once did not exist. When
Alexander, bishop of Alexandria (313–328), condemned Arius'
teaching, the priest fled to Palestine where his views commanded
support. Soon the Eastern bishops were lining up on either side, although most supported Alexander. When Constantine had dispatched
Licinius, he turned to this problem that was dividing his empire.
Realizing that individual bishops and even episcopal conferences
could not settle the matter, the emperor had an imperial idea. He
summoned a council of the inhabited (Roman) world, the *oikumene*
in Greek, to meet at Nicaea in 325.

The first ecumenical council[41] consisted largely of Greek bishops;
few Latins even knew the terms of the debate, although the emperor's
theological advisor was a Latin, the Spaniard Hosius of Cordova. As
emperor, Constantine was responsible for the spiritual welfare of the
state, and so he took part in the council. The bishops condemned
Arius and, at the emperor's urging, declared that the Father and Son
were *homoousios,* usually translated as *consubstantialis* in Latin and
thus into English as consubstantial. This word affirmed the equality
and divinity of Father and Son, but it was open to more than one
reading, including the notion that Father and Son were identical and
that the distinctions in the Trinity were no more than names. Many
Greek bishops went home uncertain of what they had done; some
came to regret Nicaea.

But regardless of how people then or now view Constantine, his
reign may be the most significant event in Christian history after the
resurrection. The Christian empire he founded lasted in Byzantium
until the fifteenth century and in Russia until the Bolsheviks. The
empire fell in the West in the fifth century, only to be revived by
Charlemagne in the ninth and then by Otto I in the tenth. It survived
in some form or other in the West until the Hapsburgs fell from
power in World War I.

---

41. For a good discussion of all the early councils, see *The First Seven
Ecumenical Councils (325–787): Their History and Theology* by Leo Donald
Davis, S.J. (Collegeville, Minn.: The Liturgical Press, 1987).

Constantine made possible the development of Christianity in a friendly or at least non-hostile environment, thus making it the great religion of the West. The fawning Eusebius praised the emperor too much for modern taste, but he perceptively recognized that a new era had begun.

For the half century after Nicaea a debate raged, and one of Constantine's sons, the emperor Constantius II (337–361), supported the Arians, who enjoyed an ascendancy in the 340s. The Western bishops stood by Nicaea and its champion, the Alexandrian bishop Athanasius (328–373). When three Greek theologians, Basil of Caesarea (ca. 330–379), Gregory of Nazianzus (329–389), and Gregory of Nyssa (ca. 335–ca. 395)[42] entered the lists on the side of Nicaea, they forged a theology that made *homoousios* acceptable to most Greek bishops.[43] In doing that, these theologians also made firm a new source of authority, the ecumenical council. Nicaea became the touchstone of orthodoxy to which later writers regularly referred. A few other councils achieved similar status (Constantinople I in 381, Ephesus in 431, Chalcedon in 451).[44]

Thanks to imperial support, the Church now grew in influence and also in wealth. The Christian liturgy began to incorporate elements of Roman court procedure, such as the use of incense, and bishops achieved high secular status. For most Christians, the end of the persecutions brought immense relief, and many were proud of the Church's new status. But some rebelled.

From its inception, Christianity had warned believers about too great an attachment to the world (Mark 8:36, Rom 12:2), and martyrs had followed that warning completely, giving up their very lives. There were no more martyrs in the Christian empire, but the urge for total renunciation of the world persisted. Some Christians felt that they could abandon the world by denying themselves its physical pleasures and, if necessary, by leaving the society altogether.

42. Scholars call them the Cappadocians because of the region of Asia Minor that was their home.

43. For a magisterial account of this, see *The Search for the Christian Doctrine of God: The Arian Controversy 318–381 A.D.* by R.P.C. Hanson (Edinburgh: T & T Clark, 1988).

44. Many Protestant denominations do not accept the authority of any councils; others accept only the first four; the Orthodox Churches generally accept the first seven; Roman Catholics recognize twenty-one, which includes all those called by the popes.

The Christian monks did not originate the notion of withdrawal from the world; they had Greek and Jewish predecessors. But they saw themselves as the new martyrs, dying a little each day (mortification) by living lives of sometimes frightful asceticism. No one knows the identity of the first monk, but the Egyptian Antony (251–356) became the first great monk. He left society and went into the desert, first living as a hermit and then, late in his life, with some disciples. Athanasius wrote his life, detailing his asceticism, his endless struggles with the devil, and his triumphs because of his firm faith.[45] This vivid account became the equivalent of what today we would call a bestseller, and helped to establish the monks in the Church's consciousness not as a group of eccentrics but as the true Christians who had returned to a sort of parched Garden of Eden.

The ideal monk followed eremitic monasticism, that is, living as a hermit. Literally thousands of men did this, and so did some women. Roman society placed severe restrictions on women who wished to go off on their own, thus making withdrawal initially difficult for them. Monastic documents mention women hermits who disguised themselves as men.

The turning point for monasticism occurred *circa* 320 when another Egyptian, Pachomius (ca. 290–346), a former hermit, established cenobitic monasticism, that is, monks living a common life. This notion quickly caught on. Many Christians wished to withdraw from society but could not endure the isolated life of a hermit. Pachomian communities spread along the Nile. His sister Mary founded a monastery for women, a practice followed later by several aristocratic Roman women. This communal life made monasticism more socially acceptable for women. In fact, for the first time in Western history, a woman could choose a life for herself rather than enter into an arranged marriage.

To some Christians, such as Basil of Caesarea, cenobitism was superior to eremitism because Christians should live in community, not in isolation, and Basil wrote a rule for cenobitic monks. Orthodox Christians view the Basilian Rule the way Western ones view the Benedictine Rule, as a defining document for monastic life. Eremiticism persisted, but cenobitism became the dominant form of monastic life.

45. *Athanasius: The Life of Antony and the Letter to Marcellinus,* Robert C. Gregg, trans., Classics of Western Spirituality (New York: Paulist Press, 1980) 29–99.

Back in the world, the Christians were adjusting to their new status. The emperors routinely involved themselves in the life of the Church, and most people accepted this. If Christians owed obedience to pagan emperors because God established all authorities (Rom 13:1-7, 1 Pet 2:13-17), how much more did they owe to emperors of their own faith? But the emperors often acted more like emperors than Christians. Constans (337–350) used force against the Donatists to the disappointment of some Christians. Constantius II likewise used force against the supporters of Nicaea. Julian (361–363), known as the Apostate because he had defected from Christianity, tried to reestablish paganism. Many bishops expected to revere an orthodox Christian emperor, but what should they do when the emperor was a heretic? For that matter, what should they do when even an orthodox emperor pushed too far?

The question of Church and state, as we saw in chapter six, has occupied the Christians from the first century to the twentieth. Ambrose of Milan (ca. 339–397) established the basic guidelines for Christians, that the emperor is within the Church, not above it, and he did so during the reign of Theodosius I (379–395).

After Constantine's death, his sons had divided the empire. Occasionally one man ruled the entire empire, but two-emperor government had become common. Theodosius was the last single ruler of the empire, a status he achieved technically only in 394, but which he exercised for virtually all his reign.

Theodosius made Christianity the state's official religion, thus reducing the civic status of pagans and Jews. He removed all state support for paganism, and he restricted the rights of heretics. Although his conflicts with Ambrose are well known, less well known was his constant and effective intrusion into many affairs of Church life. For example, he forbade certain office holders to enter clerical life lest they avoid paying taxes. The presumption was that they entered religious life to avoid taxes, that is, the government decoded what their consciences dictated to them.

Theodosius also called the second ecumenical council, Constantinople I, in 381. The council finished off the work of Nicaea by defining the equality and divinity of the Holy Spirit in the Trinity. It also gave the bishop of Constantinople the second place of honor in the Church after the bishop of Rome, a recognition of the new capital's prominence. In 394 Theodosius extinguished a revolt of the Italian pagans, the last time pagans ever threatened the Christian state. In terms of power and prestige, his reign represented the high point of the Christian Roman empire.

The late fourth century saw several other significant developments that determined much of Christian history. In 367, Athanasius listed the books in the New Testament, the first Christian to cite the twenty-seven accepted today. His list or canon did not settle the matter immediately, and in some parts of the empire, such as Syria, it did not settle the matter for some time to come, but the corner had been turned. More and more writers accepted Athanasius' canon, and writers routinely used the New Testament in their works.

Although the great theological question of the fourth century, the Arian Controversy, involved mostly Greek authors, the Latins emerged as a significant theological and intellectual force. Hilary of Poitiers (ca. 315–367) wrote an important book on the Trinity; Ambrose wrote several important exegetical studies as well as his texts on Church and state; Jerome (ca. 342–ca. 420) produced an influential Latin translation of the Bible and wrote many scriptural commentaries; Sulpicius Severus (ca. 360–ca. 425) wrote a monastic manifesto with his enormously popular life of Saint Martin of Tours; Paulinus of Nola (ca. 353–431) wrote Latin religious poetry; the greatest Latin, Augustine, began his Christian literary career in the 380s.

In the fourth century the bishops of Rome rose to real power in the Western Church. Although they could not impose their authority in the East, they could seriously affect Eastern affairs. Papal support of Athanasius strengthened his hand against the Arians; lack of support for Basil of Caesarea dragged out a crisis in the see of Antioch and soured relations with the East. The popes zealously guarded their claims, dropping reference to the Pauline founding of Rome and concentrating on the Petrine one; Siricius (384–399) claimed that when he spoke, Saint Peter spoke through him. When he wrote to other bishops, he used the style of the imperial chancery to emphasize his status. The popes accepted the doctrinal decrees of the Council of Constantinople in 381, but they rejected the stipulation that the see of Constantinople ranked second to Rome. They accurately realized that if a bishopric's status depended on the civil status of the city, Rome might one day be second to the new capital. Except for the Africans, most Western bishops accepted papal authority.[46]

46. See Robert B. Eno, *The Rise of the Papacy*, for a brief and learned survey of the early papacy. Several Gallic bishops tried to restrain papal authority.

Finally, the fourth century saw the physical building of a Christian empire, as churches and martyrs' shrines virtually sprouted up in all parts of the empire. The Christians did not abandon the traditional Roman love of splendor but rather harnessed it to their own needs. Pope Damasus I (366–384) proudly proclaimed that Rome had become the City of Apostles and Martyrs and that the city's true twin founders were not Romulus and Remus but Peter and Paul, who had brought the true faith to the Eternal City. Artists and poets could picture the emperor as a new Moses or David or Solomon. The *verus Israel* had entered into its inheritance.

The Romans had always battled against the Germanic barbarians, with varying degrees of success. In the fourth century the overstretched empire could no longer cope with the threat. In 378 a tribe called the Visigoths defeated a Roman army and killed an emperor at the Battle of Adrianople, which opened the Danube frontier to other tribes. Although the Romans tried to limit the influx and to buy the barbarians' loyalty, the situation had passed largely out of their hands. They now had to accommodate, and, as the fifth-century Romans would learn, that was not enough.

5. The Fifth Century

Theodosius I was the last ruler of an undivided Roman Empire. His two sons, Honorius (395–423) and Arcadius (395–408), ruled in the West and East, respectively. Honorius became the first emperor to face the barbarian flood tide.

In the late fourth century, as more barbarians crossed the frontiers, the Romans employed them as federates, allies who would protect the border from other barbarians. Inevitably, some barbarian commanders rose in the ranks, and soon armies once led by generals with names like Publius Cornelius Scipio were led by Ricimer, Arbogast, and Stilicho. Some federates performed faithful service to Rome, but no one could stop the oncoming tribes that invaded Gaul, Britain, and Italy. In 410 the Visigoths sacked the city of Rome, an event that shocked the empire. The psychological damage was worse than the physical. Most barbarian tribes were wanderers who did not settle down. The Visigoths went on to invade Spain, and Rome again became a capital, but the sack had shown how weak the Western empire had become.

Throughout the century, tribes like the Burgundians, Vandals, Visigoths, Ostrogoths, Franks, Angles, and Saxons moved into Roman provinces. Some were armed nuisances; others, like the ones just named, took over complete provinces. Some later lost their territories: the Visigoths lost Spain to the Arabs, and the Vandals lost Africa to the Byzantines, who also took Italy from the Ostrogoths. Others established themselves permanently: the Franks became the French, the Angles and Saxons became the English.

Many barbarians were pagan, but some were Arian, the result of some missionary work done in the fourth century by an Arian bishop named Ulfilas (ca. 311–383). They represented a threat to the Roman order, which was now the Christian Roman order, and they presented a challenge to the Church, which now had to evangelize them, an effort that in some cases took centuries.

As the barbarians arrived in the empire, they soon realized that it was too big, complex, and populous for them to govern on their own, and they often worked with the Roman authorities. Sometimes they took Roman titles in an attempt to legitimize their rule for their new subjects and to maintain the pretense that Rome still survived. Furthermore, they often acted like the federates they had once been, working to keep out other barbarian tribes; for example, in 451 a combined Roman and Gothic force defeated the dreaded Attila and his Huns.

But, for the long term, the barbarians destroyed the Western empire, compromising its government, abusing its people, and weakening its economy. In 476, the most powerful barbarian in Italy, a Herulian named Odovacar, decided to forego the fiction of Roman rule and deposed the emperor, a child named Romulus Augustulus. He ruled on his own, until another barbarian, Theodoric the Ostrogoth, invaded Italy and murdered him. The Church history of the West unfolded against this confused and violent background.

The Eastern empire also had to deal with barbarians, but it did so successfully, either defeating them or buying them off (Theodoric came to Italy because an Eastern emperor had bribed him to do so), so that life there continued much as it had before. In the East, that meant two things: Church politics and theological disputation.

When Irenaeus of Lyons insisted upon apostolicity as a criterion for Christian belief, he elevated the status of the so-called apostolic sees, those bishoprics with apostolic foundations. Only one such bishopric, Rome, existed in the West, but several did in the East, including Alexandria, which, according to a widely-accepted local tradition, had been founded by the evangelist Mark. The Alexandrian patriarchs had combined this supposed foundation with the intellectual achievements of their see to make themselves formidable personages in the fourth century. But Constantinople, capital of the Eastern portion of the empire, threatened their supremacy. When the first ecumenical council at Constantinople rated that bishopric second behind Rome, its status received official recognition, infuriating the Alexandrians who determined to bring down the imperial see.

Experienced ecclesiastical infighters, three successive Alexandrian patriarchs managed to have their Constantinopolitan rivals deposed and exiled. Theophilus (385–412) did it to John Chrysostom (398–406), as did Cyril (412–444) to Nestorius (428–431) and Dioscorus (444–451) to Flavian (446–449). John had turned against him the all-powerful empress Eudoxia by his criticism of her behavior. When he offered protection to the Tall Brothers, Egyptian monks being hounded by Theophilus, the Alexandrian bishop joined with the empress to engineer his condemnation. The latter two cases, on the other hand, had theological connections.

By the fifth century the East had two premier theological schools, one in Alexandria and the other in Antioch. They differed largely on the question of exegesis, with the Alexandrians willing to use allegory freely to pursue the supposed depth of the text and the Antiochenes reluctant to go much beyond the literal meaning. Inevitably, such divergent approaches to Scripture resulted in different interpretations of doctrine, specifically christology, the theology of Christ.

The Christians long had difficulty reconciling the human and divine elements in Christ, largely because it was logical that the divine would simply overwhelm the human. In the fourth century, an Asian bishop named Apollinaris settled the matter neatly by claiming that the Logos, the Word of God, had replaced the rational soul in Christ, who thus became the Logos inhabiting a body. Gregory of Nazianzus replied via soteriology, the theology of salvation. He contended that Jesus had to have a soul because, as he put it, "what was not assumed could not be saved," that is, if Jesus did not take on a human soul, he could not redeem ours. In sum, Jesus had a full human nature. But, in the fourth century, the question of the Trinity had overshadowed christology.

In the fifth century, the Eastern theologians returned to the question of Christ. John Chrysostom had been an Antiochene monk. In spite of his unhappy tenure in Constantinople, the emperor

Theodosius II (408–450) chose another Antiochene monk, Nestorius, to be patriarch of the capital. A rash, aggressive man, he soon offended the piety of his subjects by saying that Jesus' mother, Mary, could be called *Christotokos,* Mother of Christ, but not *Theotokos,* Mother of God, a title in long and wide use in the East. He raised the logical point that a human woman could not give birth to God, but the question had more subtle ramifications, as Cyril of Alexandria soon pointed out.

In Alexandrian theology, the human and divine in Christ were inextricably joined, and so Nestorius' teaching on Mary seemed to separate or divide Christ. Cyril was offended theologically, but he also sensed the chance to embarrass the patriarch of the Eastern capital. Acquiring the alliance of Celestine I of Rome (422–432), Cyril convinced the emperor to settle the matter via an ecumenical council to meet at Ephesus in 431. The council combined a disgraceful mix of politics and brutality, of condemnations and counter-condemnations, but in the end Cyril triumphed, Nestorius was deposed and exiled, and Mary was proclaimed *Theotokos.* A second bishop of Alexandria had humiliated his Constantinopolitan rival. Yet this drama had two more acts to play.

The first act began in 448, when Flavian of Constantinople condemned a priest named Eutyches, who had hoped to combat residual Nestorianism by teaching that Christ had two natures, human and divine, before the incarnation, but only one after it. The Greek term for one nature was *monophysis.* Eutyches looked across the sea for help and found it. Dioscorus of Alexandria found theological support for Eutyches' position in an Apollinarian book thought to have been written by Cyril. He rushed to his supposed predecessor's defense, persuaded the emperor Theodosius to call a second ecumenical council at Ephesus in 449, and used the council, which he governed dictatorially, to rehabilitate Eutyches, depose Flavian, and proclaim Monophysitism to be orthodox. It looked to all like another Alexandrian victory. But Dioscorus made the mistake of denying a hearing to the legates of Leo I of Rome (440–461), who had brought the pope's *Tome,* a treatise on christology. The infuriated Leo sought to reverse the Second Council of Ephesus, as did Alexandria's Eastern opponents. The pope gave the council its enduring nickname, *latrocinium* or "robber council."

Leo did not have to wait long for the second act, and it began with an unusual actor—a horse. The emperor's horse stepped in a hole, throwing Theodosius, who died from the injury. His sister Pulcheria succeeded him, and she and her husband Marcian called a new council, for Chalcedon in 451.[47] At this council, Leo's views won acceptance, Dioscorus was deposed and exiled, and the basic christology became diophysite or two-natured, that is, the council proclaimed that Jesus Christ is one person as are the other two persons of the Trinity, but he possesses in his one person two natures, one divine and one human.

Chalcedon became a new Nicaea, a watershed council, while Ephesus II has no ecumenical status for the Western or Orthodox Churches.

But if the two christological councils of the fifth century had settled a theological matter, politically they left much of the Eastern empire in a shambles. Some Eastern Christians had never reconciled themselves to the first council at Ephesus in 431, but, fearful of the emperor, they withdrew beyond the eastern Roman frontier into Persia and established Nestorian churches that survived the Islamization of Persia, converted some prominent Mongols, and can be found in small numbers today under the name Assyrian Christians.

As for Dioscorus' supporters, they could not accept so humiliating a treatment for an Alexandrian patriarch, and, unlike the Nestorians, they stayed within the empire to fight. The Monophysites formed a virtual national Church in Egypt. They abused and even murdered bishops chosen by the emperor, who in turn persecuted them. Because of the importance of Egypt to the state, emperor after emperor tried to find accommodation with the Monophysites, only to find the supporters of Chalcedon refusing to budge. In the sixth century the Monophysites spread beyond Egypt into Syria and later into Mesopotamia, Armenia, and Ethiopia. Much of their territory fell to Islam, but they survive today in the Coptic Church.

The fifth-century West produced only one great theologian, but that was the remarkable Augustine of Hippo (354–430), who almost single-handedly created the Latin theology of the Trinity *(On the Trinity)*, crafted an approach to pagan literature and Christian education *(On Christian Doctrine)*, outlined biblical exegetical method (many works), wrote a remarkable spiritual autobiography *(The Confessions)*, pioneered the theology of history *(City of God)*, composed hundreds of sermons and letters, defined ecclesiology

---

47. Two women convened ecumenical councils. In addition to Pulcheria's convening of Chalcedon, the Byzantine empress Irene convened the Second Council of Nicaea in 787.

against the still powerful Donatists (whose power he weakened by advocating and justifying the use of force against them), and, against the Manichees and Pelagians, created a theology of grace, free will, original sin, predestination, election, and redemption, a genuine triumph of African theology and one destined to influence the Christian view of human nature until today.

The Manichees took their name from Manes (ca. 216–276), a Persian dualist who described a cosmic struggle between two deities, one good and one evil. In his system, there was little room for free will. Augustine had a lifelong fascination with evil, and in his youth belonged to a Manichee group. But eventually his brilliance showed him that Manichaeism offered no real solution to the problem of evil but only a cosmic myth that avoided the myriad particulars of the problem.

Virtually opposed to the Manichees were the Pelagians, who were given that name by Augustine, who in turn took it from Pelagius (ca. 350–ca. 420). He was a British monk who believed that humans could discipline their free wills so firmly that they could be saved without grace. Although Pelagius said that this was rare, Augustine felt that his teaching threatened divine grace, and, in a series of books as well as many comments in his biblical exegesis, he attacked Pelagius; but, in so doing, he ended up by arguing for divine predestination and the salvation of the elect to whom God gave grace and whom Augustine considered to be rather few. He may have produced "a frightening conception of God,"[48] but it was one that dominated much subsequent theology, especially in the Reformation. Western Christianity, as history knows it, would be inconceivable without Augustine.

An unusual development occurred in Gaul at this time. Honoratus (ca. 350–ca. 430) founded a monastery on the island of Lérins in the Mediterranean, and from this island came the leading bishops of the Gallic church in the fifth century, including Honoratus himself, who became bishop of Arles. Many Western bishops had doubts about the monks, who, after all, had renounced society and thus seemed ill-suited for episcopal office. The Gallic Church, however, trusted the monks in episcopal office and set a pattern for centuries to come; for example, both Pope Gregory I the Great (590–604) and Anselm, the archbishop of Canterbury (1093–1109), had been monks before becoming bishops. Much inspiration for Gallic monasticism came from

48. Bernhard Altaner, *Patrology* (New York: Herder and Herder, 1960) 526.

an Easterner, John Cassian (ca. 360–435) who had spent time in Egypt and then migrated west and wrote accounts of the desert monks, and guides to monastic life. Cassian eschewed the fantastic and the thaumaturgical so common to other accounts of Eastern monks, thus reassuring the conservative Western episcopate.

While Alexandria and Constantinople struggled for supremacy in the East, the papacy continued to its rise to dominance in the West. Leo I won the epithet "the Great" because of his extensive and authoritative writings, his success in getting the emperor Valentinian III (425–455) to recognize his authority over the Western Churches, and his intervention in the East with the rejection of the Second Council of Ephesus and the promotion of the Council of Chalcedon. In 452 he managed to convince Attila the Hun not to attack Rome, thus sparing the city almost certain destruction, although in 455 he failed to prevent the African Vandal king Gaiseric from looting the city.

Leo had responsibility for the city's civic welfare because Roman power was collapsing all over the West; many Western bishops had to do what Leo did—repairing city walls and aqueducts, raising armies—thus establishing the tradition of episcopal involvement in secular affairs so characteristic of the Middle Ages.

As Rome slowly fell in the West, Latin Christianity reached beyond the empire. A Briton named Ninian (fl. ca. 400) evangelized among the pagan Picts, who lived in what is now southern Scotland; little is known about him. In 431 Pope Celestine I sent a deacon named Palladius to be the first bishop of the Irish. He was soon followed by a British missionary bishop named Patricius (Patrick), who evangelized (ca. 432–ca. 461) successfully among the northern Irish pagans, thus winning for himself the epithet Apostle of Ireland.[49]

6. The Sixth Century

The sixth century opened with much of the Christian world in disarray; it closed that way too.

In the East the Monophysite schism grew larger, posing a serious threat to the Byzantine Empire, as scholars call the Eastern Roman Empire from the sixth century onward. Egypt was a large, fertile province, and Syria occupied a frontier with the Persians. The emperors could not afford to lose these provinces, and so they

49. Liam DePaor, *Saint Patrick's World* (Notre Dame, Ind.: University of Notre Dame Press, 1993).

worked constantly to bring back the Monphysites, repeatedly trying to come up with christological formulas that would pacify both them and the Chalcedonians. In 482 the emperor Zeno (474–475, 476–491) and the Constantinopolitan patriarch Acacius (471–489) prepared a document called the *Henoticon,* which condemned Nestorius and Eutyches while praising Cyril of Alexandria. The Egyptians gave it a tentative acceptance, but the Romans believed that it compromised Chalcedon and precipitated what the Romans call the Acacian schism (482–519) between the two sees.

Most Byzantines could live with such a schism, but when a Latin-speaking soldier named Justin I became emperor (518–527), he wanted union with Rome and abandoned the *Henoticon.* Justin's nephew and heir, Justinian (527–565), had considerable interest in the West and considerable tolerance for the Monophysites, since his wife, the empress Theodora (527–547), was one herself.

Justinian sent his armies west under the general Belisarius. They quickly conquered Vandal Africa, took the Balearic islands, and turned next to Italy, then ruled by the Ostrogoths. Belisarius and his successor Narses waged fifteen years of war against the Goths, destroying much of Italy in the process, but they were victorious.

Justinian now extended his personal rule of the Church to the papacy, deposing Silverius (536–537) for the more pliant Vigilius (537–555). Since the emperor wished to weaken the status of Rome, which the Byzantines considered a frontier city in barbarian territory, he centered his Italian government in Ravenna, which was on the Adriatic Sea and accessible to Byzantium. In the 540s the Byzantines built magnificent churches in Ravenna, with some of the most famous mosaics in the Christian world. This was in keeping with the emperor's architectural interests; he was also responsible for the construction of the Hagia Sophia in Constantinople.

Justinian considered himself a theologian, and not an amateur one. Personifying what many scholars call caesaropapism, he took an active and decisive role in Church government and doctrine, although Theodora was always careful to watch out for her own. When Egyptian contacts made it known *circa* 540 that a mission to Nubia (modern southern Egypt and Sudan) was feasible, both emperor and empress outfitted expeditions. Theodora's arrived first and won the Nubians to Monophysitism.

Because she had given her husband the strength to maintain his throne during riots by the Constantinopolitan mob, Theodora had her husband's complete confidence. Although he was a Chalcedonian, he did not prevent her from sheltering Monophysite bishops in the capital or in helping the heroic missionary Jacob Baradaeus (ca. 500–578) to organize effectively the Monophysite Churches.

Justinian had other interests besides the Monophysites. For generations Eastern scholars had debated the value of Origen's works, since many thought he was a dangerous heretic. One great debate had occurred *circa* 400, and another one had broken out in Palestine in the 530s. Justinian did not trust Origen and condemned Origenism in 543, although he thought that an ecumenical council would be more effective than his own condemnation.

Soon, however, his thoughts returned to Monophysitism, and he realized that he could use the authority of a council not only to condemn Origenism but also to reconcile the Monophysites. As always, the problem was how to do so without alienating the Chalcedonians. The emperor took a unique approach.

The Monophysites believed that their theology emanated from Cyril of Alexandria, and they loathed the many Antiochene theologians who had attacked him. Justinian decided to condemn passages (chapters) from the works of three such theologians: Ibas of Edessa (d. 457), Theodore of Mopsuestia (ca. 350–428), and Theodoret of Cyrrhus (ca. 393–ca. 468). All were conveniently dead, and, thus, Justinian hoped, no one would care about the condemnation of what came to be called the Three Chapters. But just as pagan emperors had underestimated the resistance of the Christians to persecutions, so did this Christian emperor misunderstand their dedication to their faith.

To many people, it was a serious affront to condemn the views of three men who had died in the peace of the Church in the previous century. More importantly, many Chalcedonians suspected the emperor of hedging on doctrinal points in order to win back the politically important Monophysites, who, in their eyes, were just heretics. Justinian, however, had a trump card; he would get the bishop of Rome to support his cause. The confident emperor called the fifth ecumenical council, Constantinople II, to meet in 553 under his presidency.

To the emperor's surprise, many bishops were hesitant, including his supposed puppet, Pope Vigilius. Justinian quickly resorted to force, compelling bishops to attend and brutalizing Vigilius to sign the decrees. Justinian got what he wanted; the Three Chapters were condemned along with Origenism. But the Monophysites did not return, thus foiling the council's main goal. Its lesser goal succeeded too well. Many of Origen's works in their original Greek were destroyed, although some of these survived in translations from other languages.

Several Western bishops, especially in Africa and northern Italy, reviled Vigilius for acquiescing, even under force, and a schism began in the West. As for the victorious emperor, Justinian spent his last years pursuing theological minutiae, and the Monophysites only ceased to be a problem when the Muslims conquered them and rendered moot the Byzantine concern for them. Byzantine emperors continued to play a role in Italy, although after Constantinople II, the papacy and other Italian bishops usually mistrusted and resented their efforts.

Whereas Monophysitism rent the East, barbarian occupations rent the West. The Vandals ruled in North Africa, the Visigoths in Spain, the Angles and Saxons in Britain, the Franks in Gaul, and the Ostrogoths in Italy. The Vandals, Visigoths, and Ostrogoths were Arians; the Angles and Saxons were pagans. The Franks converted to Christianity in 496 when their king, Clovis, accepted baptism, and the anonymous successors of Patrick in Ireland made progress in Christianizing that island. But many Romanized Christians had difficulty reconciling themselves to their new masters, no matter what their faith.

Scholarly knowledge of these societies varies, depending on the sources. Few barbarians wrote until they converted to Christianity, and not much survives from the Arianized barbarians. Consequently, the historical records often become reliable only after the conversion of a people or a king.

Little is known about Ireland before the last quarter of the century, from which several monastic writings survive. Later sources provide information about the sixth century, but these must be used carefully.

The main source for Britain is Gildas (ca. 500–ca. 570), a Romano-British monk who recorded a catalogue of disasters that he blamed on the sins of the British clergy and rulers. Scholars struggle with so biased a source. The English monk and historian Bede (673–735) provides some other information, although he provides far more for the seventh century.

Much of what scholars know about Spain comes from sources of the late sixth and early seventh centuries. Thanks to the Byzantine conquest of the Vandals in 533, knowledge of Africa is fuller, especially the African involvement in the Three Chapters controversy; also surviving are the works of the biblical exegete Primasius of Hadrumetum (d. ca. 555).

The Franks had their historian, yet he was not a Frank but rather a Gallo-Roman. Gregory of Tours (538–594) came from an old and distinguished Christian family; he numbered saints and bishops among his ancestors. It is difficult to conceive of someone who could differ more from the modern historian. Gregory blithely interweaves the divine and demonic into his narrative, the *History of the Franks;* consultation of an index to the history shows that the long-dead saint Martin of Tours (d. 397) appears as frequently as any sixth-century figure. For Gregory, saints and devils constantly influenced the Franks slow, often retrograde climb from paganism to Christianity and from barbarism to civilization. Gregory tells lurid and fascinating stories, and he fills them with unforgettable heroes and villains, albeit more of the latter. Heroic and brutal, the Frankish kings furthered the conversion of their people and seriously weakened the influence of the pagan and Arian barbarians.

For Italy the sources are very full, and the historian is grateful because four great Italians determined much of the history of the Christian Middle Ages. Their writings, along with the account of the Byzantine conquest of Italy by the Byzantine historian Procopius (fl. 530–560), provide a valuable picture of the end of the ancient world at the heart of the old empire.

Theodoric the Ostrogoth ruled Italy (493–526) but depended upon Roman aristocrats to assist him. One of these was Boethius (ca. 480–524), who rose to an important position in the Gothic kingdom. He realized that the ancient culture was dying, and he tried to preserve it by translating some Greek philosophical works into Latin, as well as writing several of his own. But enemies accused him of working with the Byzantines to overthrow the Goths; Theodoric believed the charges and had Boethius imprisoned and executed. While in prison, he wrote *The Consolation of Philosophy,* a meditation on evil and justice, which, along with his translations, greatly influenced medieval thought.

Cassiodorus (ca. 485–ca. 580) was another Roman aristocrat who served Theodoric and other Gothic rulers. *Circa* 540 he retired to his family estate of Vivarium in Calabria. He founded a monastery, wrote some scriptural commentaries, and composed a guide to secular and ecclesiastical literature. Most importantly, he encouraged his monks to copy books, including the pagan classics, thus helping to preserve many of the ancient works. He taught his monks that "every stroke of the pen is a wound in the side of the devil." Like Boethius, he significantly influenced medieval culture.

Benedict of Nursia (ca. 480–ca. 550) is known only from a life written by Gregory the Great (590–604), and scholars debate whether Gregory is actually the author. This life says that Benedict came from a noble family, was repulsed by secular Rome, became a hermit, attracted disciples, was abbot for a monastery at Subiaco, and finally, in the face of local opposition, withdrew to Monte Cassino in south-central Italy, where he spent the rest of his life. Over the decades as an abbot, he composed his rule for monks, known later as the Benedictine Rule. Although of limited influence during its composer's life, the rule became increasingly popular because of its blend of spirituality, judgment, moderation, and common sense. By the eighth century it had replaced almost all other monastic rules and became one of the formative documents of the Middle Ages. Even today most Western monks follow the Benedictine Rule.

The fourth great Italian was Gregory the Great, whose world differed from that of Benedict. He was born *circa* 540 and grew up in an Italy dominated by the Byzantines and by Arian Lombards, who invaded and conquered much of the peninsula in 568. These barbarians swept away much but not all of Byzantine rule, and, in spite of negotiations and treaties, they plagued the papacy.

Gregory was a Roman aristocrat who gave up his wealth to become a monk, but Pope Pelagius II (579–590) sent him as legate to Constantinople. Gregory learned at first hand the intricacies of dealing with the Byzantines, especially in trying to get their help against the Lombards. He returned to Rome in 586 and became pope, by popular demand, in 590.

Gregory spent his fourteen-year episcopate negotiating with the Byzantines, trying to get their assistance for an impoverished, wartorn Italy, while simultaneously trying to preserve the independence of the papacy from imperial intervention. But the Byzantine presence in Italy was destined to fade. Whether Gregory recognized this or not, he definitively turned the papacy's eyes toward the West.

Gregory strove tirelessly to keep the Lombards at peace and then to convert them. He rooted out pagan remnants in Sardinia and rural Italy. He tried and failed to end the schism produced by Vigilius' conduct at Constantinople II. He constantly asserted Roman primacy among the Western Churches.

He worked with the Spanish bishops and especially his old friend Leander of Seville (ca. 549–601) to convert the Visigoths. Their king, Recared, had officially converted in 589, but Leander and the pope wanted the conversion to affect the people. Gregory implored the

African bishops to check the strength of Donatism, on the rise again, and he tried to reform elements of the Frankish episcopacy.

Perhaps his best-known achievement was the sending of the Italian monk Augustine to evangelize the pagan Angles and Saxons in 597. Augustine established his base at Canterbury, thus guaranteeing the primacy of that see, and Gregory always kept in close contact with the English mission.

As the first monk to be pope, Gregory promoted monasticism, especially the Benedictine version, and his biblical exegesis, heavily allegorical and moralizing, became more popular than that of Augustine and Jerome in the early Middle Ages.

By the end of the sixth century, Christianity was entering the Middle Ages. Although the Byzantines seemed secure in their preservation of the Roman name and empire, the rise of Islam was only decades away. The Muslims took over Egypt, Palestine, and North Africa, reducing the empire to Greece, the Balkans, Asia Minor, part of Syria, and a few Italian possessions, the shape it would take until the eleventh century, when the Seljuk Turks took Syria and Asia Minor. Eventually this Muslim enemy, who shaped so much of Byzantine life in the Middle Ages, would eliminate the empire.

In the West, Rome had become no longer a name for an empire but for a bishopric. Popes, not emperors, would make medieval Rome a force to be reckoned with. Although pagan and heretical barbarians continued to menace the Church, in the seventh century most of them converted; by the eighth century the conversion was complete, and the Christians turned to those peoples outside the boundaries of the old empire.

In the seventh and eighth centuries, the Irish and Anglo-Saxons enjoyed cultural revivals, but now the culture was Christian; the monks Columbanus (ca. 540–615) and Bede led their peoples to new cultural heights.

The Frankish state and Church both declined in the seventh century, but entered a period of renaissance when the Carolingian Dynasty came to power in the eighth. In Italy, the papacy enjoyed independence and even prosperity in the seventh century, balancing both Byzantine and Lombard power in the peninsula until Carolingian intervention in the eighth century set the pattern for much medieval papal history.

The North African Church, so independent for so long, survived until 698, when the Muslims captured Carthage. Christianity in that part of the world disappeared. Spain had a brilliant century in store, marked by the careers of Ildephonsus of Toledo (ca. 607–667), Braulio of Saragossa (bishop from 631–651), and the encyclopedist Isidore of Seville (ca. 560–636). But this came to an end when the Muslims crossed from North Africa to conquer much of the Iberian peninsula in 711.

The Islamic domination of what had been the southern half of the Latin Christianity meant that much of the future of the Western Church lay with the converted barbarians—Angles, Saxons, Irish, Franks, Lombards, and eventually Germans and Slavs. How these new peoples absorbed and reworked the antique heritage determined the Church history of the Middle Ages.[50]

---

50. Some basic texts on Christianity in this period are *Education and Culture in the Barbarian West from the Sixth through the Eighth Century* by Pierre Riche (Columbia, S.C.: University of South Carolina Press, 1978); *The Formation of Christendom* by Judith Herren (Princeton: Princeton University Press, 1987); *The Germanization of Early Medieval Christianity* by James C. Russell (New York: Oxford University Press, 1994).

Bibliography

Translations in Series

Ancient Christian Writers, the Works of the Fathers in Translation. Founded in 1946, currently published by Paulist Press, Mahwah, New Jersey. Continuing series.

Ante-Nicene Fathers. Originally published in 1885; reprinted in 1994 by Hendrickson Publishers, Inc., Peabody, Massachusetts. Ten volumes.

Fathers of the Church, A New Translation. Washington, D.C.: The Catholic University of America Press, 1946– . Continuing series.

Message of the Fathers of the Church. Collegeville, Minnesota: The Liturgical Press/Michael Glazier Books, 1983– . Twenty-two volumes.

The Nicene and Post-Nicene Fathers. Originally published in 1887; reprinted in 1994 by Hendrickson Publishers, Inc., Peabody, Massachusetts, 1994. First series: fourteen volumes; second series: fourteen volumes.

Individual Translations

Athanasius. *The Life of Saint Antony and the Letter to Marcellus.* Translated by Robert Gregg. Classics of Western Spirituality. New York: Paulist Press, 1980.

Augustine. *The Confessions.* Translated by Henry Chadwick. Oxford: Oxford Paperbacks, 1992.

_____. *De Doctrina Christiana.* Translated by R.P.H. Green. New York: Oxford University Press, 1995.

Celsus. *On the True Doctrine.* Translated by R. J. Hoffmann. New York: Oxford University Press, 1987.

Eusebius. *Ecclesiastical History.* Translated G. A. Williamson. Minneapolis: Augsburg Publishing House, 1975.

Josephus. *The Works of Josephus.* Translated by William Whiston. Lynn, Massachusetts: Hendrickson Publishers, 1980.

Origen. *Contra Celsum.* Translated by Henry Chadwick. Cambridge: Cambridge University Press, 1953.

Patrick. *The Life and Writings of the Historical Saint Patrick.* Translated by R.P.C. Hanson. New York: Seabury Press, 1983

Pliny the Younger. *The Letters of the Younger Pliny.* Translated by Betty Radice. Baltimore: Penguin Books, 1963.

Plotinus. *The Essential Plotinus.* Translated by Elmer O'Brien. New York: New American Library, 1964.

The Stoic and Epicurean Philosophers. Edited and translated by Whitney Oates. New York: Random House, 1940.

Suetonius. *The Twelve Caesars.* Translated by Robert Graves. Baltimore: Penguin Books, 1969.

Collections of Documents

Barrett, C. K., editor. *The New Testament Background.* New York: Harper & Row, 1961.

Councils and Ecclesiastical Documents Relating to Great Britain and Ireland, I.i. Edited by A. W. Haddan and W. Stubbs. Oxford: Clarendon Press, 1869; repr. 1964.

DePaor, Liam, editor. *Saint Patrick's World.* Notre Dame, Ind.: University of Notre Dame Press, 1993.

Ehler, Sidney, and John Morrall, editors. *Church and State Through the Centuries.* London: Burns & Oates, 1954.

Ferguson, Everett. *Backgrounds of Early Christianity,* 2nd. edition. Grand Rapids: Wm. B. Eerdmans Publishing Co., 1993.

Grant, Frederick C., editor. *Ancient Roman Religion.* Indianapolis: Bobbs-Merrill, 1957.

_____. *Hellenistic Religions.* Indianapolis: Bobbs-Merrill, 1953.

Helgeland, John, et al., editors. *Christians and the Military: The Early Experience.* Philadelphia: Fortress Press, 1985.

Hennecke, Edgar, and Wilhelm Schneemelcher, editors. *The New Testament Apocrypha,* two volumes. Philadelphia: Fortress Press, 1963, 1966.

James, Montague Rhodes, editor. *The Apocryphal New Testament.* Oxford: Oxford University Press, 1924.

Kugel, James, and Rowan Greer, editors. *Early Biblical Interpretation.* Philadelphia: Westminster Press, 1986.

Layton, Bentley, editor. *The Gnostic Scriptures.* Anchor Bible Reference Library. New York: Doubleday, 1987.

Martin, Luther, editor. *Hellenistic Religions: An Introduction.* Oxford: Oxford University Press, 1987.

Musurillo, Herbert, editor. *The Acts of the Christian Martyrs.* New York: Oxford University Press, 1972.

Norris, Richard, editor. *The Christological Controversy.* Philadelphia: Fortress Press, 1980.

Stevenson, James, editor. *A New Eusebius: Documents Illustrating the History of the Church to A.D. 337.* New edition, revised by W.H.C. Frend. London: SPCK, 1987.

_____. *Creeds, Councils and Controversies: Documents Illustrative of the History of the Church A.D. 337–461.* London: SPCK, 1978.

Waddell, Helen, editor. *The Desert Fathers.* London: Constable & Company, Ltd., 1960.

Wilson-Kastner, Patricia, et al., editors. *A Lost Heritage: Women Writers of the Early Church.* Washington, D.C.: University Press of America, 1981.

Reference Works

Encyclopedia of Early Christianity. Second edition. Two volumes. Edited by Everett Ferguson, Michael McHugh, and Frederick Norris. New York: Garland Publishing, Inc., 1997.

Encyclopedia of the Early Church. Edited by Angelo Di Berardino with bibliographic amendments by W.H.C. Frend. New York: Oxford University Press, 1992.

Kelly, J.N.D., editor. *The Oxford Dictionary of Popes.* Oxford: Oxford University Press, 1986.

Kelly, Joseph F. *The Concise Dictionary of Early Christianity.* Collegeville, Minn.: The Liturgical Press/A Michael Glazier Book, 1992.

The Oxford Dictionary of the Christian Church. Third edition, revised. Edited by F. L. Cross and E. A. Livingstone. New York: Oxford University Press, 1997.

Works Cited in the Text

(Several volumes in the Message of the Fathers of the Church series (MFC) are cited here and not just under translations because they have extensive comments by the editors, which were cited in the text)

Abraham, Gerald. *The Concise Oxford History of Music.* Oxford: Oxford University Press, 1979.

Altaner, Bernhard. *Patrology.* New York: Herder and Herder, 1960.

Armstrong, A. H., editor. *The Cambridge History of Later Greek and Early Medieval Philosophy.* New York: Cambridge University Press, 1968.

Baker, Derek, editor. *Schism, Heresy and Religious Protest.* Cambridge: Cambridge University Press, 1972.

Bernstein, Alan. *The Formation of Hell.* Ithaca, N.Y.: Cornell University Press, 1993.

Brown, Peter. *Augustine of Hippo.* Los Angeles: University of California Press, 1967.

_____. *The Cult of the Saints.* Chicago: University of Chicago Press, 1980.

_____. *The World of Late Antiquity, A.D. 150–750.* London: Thames and Hudson, 1971.

Cary, Max, and E. H. Warmington. *The Ancient Explorers.* Baltimore: Penguin Books, 1963.

Chadwick, Henry. *The Early Church.* Baltimore: Penguin Books, 1967.

Clark, Elizabeth. *The Origenist Controversy.* Princeton: Princeton University Press, 1992.

_____. "Patrons, Not Priests: Gender and Power in Late Ancient Christianity." Gender and History 2 (1990), 253–273.

_____. *Women in the Early Church.* MFC 13. Collegeville, Minn.: The Liturgical Press/Michael Glazier Books, 1983.

Clark, Gillian. *Women in Late Antiquity.* New York: Oxford University Press, 1993.

Conzelmann, Hans. *The Theology of Saint Luke.* Translated by Geoffrey Buswell. London: Faber & Faber, 1960.

Crouzel, Henri. *Origen.* San Francisco: Harper and Row, 1989.

Davis, Leo Donald. *The First Seven Ecumenical Councils (325–787): Their History and Theology.* Collegeville, Minn.: The Liturgical Press, 1987.

Dodds, E. R. *Pagan and Christian in an Age of Anxiety.* Cambridge: Cambridge University Press, 1965.

Dunn, James D. G., editor. *Jew and Christians: the Parting of the Ways.* Tübingen: Mohr, 1992.

Eliade, Mircea. *The Myth of the Eternal Return.* Princeton: Princeton University Press, 1971.

_____. *The Sacred and the Profane.* New York: Harper & Row, 1961.

Elliott, John. *A Home for the Homeless: A Sociological Exegesis of 1 Peter, Its Situation and Strategy.* Philadelphia: Fortress Press, 1981.

Eno, Robert. *The Rise of the Papacy.* Collegeville, Minn.: The Liturgical Press, 1990.

Ettlinger, Gerard. *Jesus, Christ and Savior.* MCF 2. Collegeville, Minn.: The Liturgical Press/Michael Glazier Books, 1987.

Evans, G. R. *The Thought of Gregory the Great.* Cambridge: Cambridge University Press, 1986.

Ferguson, Everett. *The Demonology of the Early Christian World.* Lewiston, N.Y.: Edwin Mellen Press, 1984.

_____. "Toward a Patristic Theology of Music." Studia Patristica 24 (1993) 266–283.

Finney, Paul. *The Invisible God: The Earliest Christians on Art.* New York: Oxford University Press, 1994.

Fiorenza, Elisabeth. *In Memory of Her.* New York: Crossroad Books, 1994.

Foley, Edward. *Foundations of Christian Music: the Music of Pre-Constantinian Christianity.* Collegeville, Minn.: The Liturgical Press, 1996.

Frend, W.H.C. *The Archaeology of Early Christianity: A Survey.* Minneapolis: Augsburg Fortress Press, 1996.

_____. *The Donatist Church: A Movement of Protest in North Africa.* Oxford: Oxford University Press, 1952.

_____. *Martyrdom and Persecution in the Early Church.* Oxford: Basil Blackwell, 1965.

_____. *The Rise of Christianity.* Philadelphia: Fortress Press, 1984.

Gamble, Harry Y. *Books and Readers in the Early Church.* New Haven: Yale University Press, 1995.

Grant, Robert M. *Augustus to Constantine: The Emergence of Christianity into the Roman World.* New York: Harper & Row, 1970.

Green, Peter. *From Alexander to Actium.* Berkeley: University of California Press, 1993.

Grillmeier, Aloys. *Christ in Christian Tradition, I: From the Apostolic Age to Chalcedon.* Atlanta: John Knox Press, 1975.

Hanson, R.P.C. *The Search for the Christian Doctrine of God: The Arian Controversy A.D. 318–381.* Edinburgh: T & T Clark, 1988.

Herren, Judith. *The Formation of Christendom.* Princeton: Princeton University Press, 1987.

Hinson, E. Glenn. *The Early Church.* Nashville: Abingdon Press, 1996.

Hunter, David. *Marriage in the Early Church.* Minneapolis: Augsburg Fortress Press, 1992.

Jones, A.H.M. "Were the Ancient Heresies National or Social Movements in Disguise?" Journal of Theological Studies, n.s. 10 (1959) 280–298.

Jungmann, Joseph. *Pastoral Liturgy.* New York: Herder and Herder, 1962.

_____. *The Place of Christ in Liturgical Prayer.* Staten Island, N.Y.: Alba Publishing House, 1965.

Lane Fox, Robin. *Pagans and Christians.* New York: Knopf, 1987.

Lieu, Judith, editor. *The Jews among Pagans and Christians in the Roman Empire.* London: Routledge, 1992.

Lindberg, David. *The Beginnings of Western Science.* Chicago: University of Chicago Press, 1992.

Lot, Ferdinand. *The End of the Ancient World and the Beginning of the Middle Ages.* New York: Knopf, 1931.

MacKendrick, Paul. *The North African Stones Speak.* Chapel Hill: University of North Carolina Press, 1980.

McKinnon, James. *Music in Early Christian Literature.* Cambridge: Cambridge University Press, 1987.

McNally, Robert E., S.J. "Gregory the Great on His Declining World." *Archivum Pontificiae Historiae* 16 (1978) 7–26.

McNamara, Martin. *Palestinian Judaism and the New Testament.* Wilmington, Delaware: Michael Glazier Books, 1983.

Meeks, Wayne. *The First Urban Christians.* New Haven: Yale University Press, 1983.

Mennel, Susan. "Augustine's 'I': The 'Knowing Subject' and the Self." Journal of Early Christian Studies 2 (1994) 291–324.

Metzger, Bruce. *The Canon of the New Testament: Its Origins, Development, and Significance.* New York: Oxford University Press, 1987.

_____. *The Early Versions of the New Testament.* New York: Oxford University Press, 1977.

Milburn, Robert. *Early Christian Art and Architecture.* Berkeley: University of California Press, 1988.

Miller, Patricia Cox. *Dreams in Late Antiquity.* Princeton: Princeton University Press, 1994.

Murphy-O'Connor, Jerome. *Paul: A Critical Life.* New York: Oxford University Press, 1996.

Neusner, Jacob. *Judaism and Christianity in the Age of Constantine.* Chicago: University of Chicago Press, 1987.

Norris, Frederick W. "Black Marks on the Communities' Manuscripts." Journal of Early Christian Studies 2 (1994) 443–466.

O'Connell, Robert. "When Saintly Fathers Feuded." Thought 54 (1979) 344–364.

Pagels, Elaine. *The Gnostic Gospels.* New York: Random House, 1979.

Reynolds, L. D., and N. G. Wilson. *Scribes and Scholars: A Guide to the Transmission of Greek and Latin Literature.* Oxford: Oxford University Press, 1991.

Riche, Pierre. *Education and Culture in the Barbarian West from the Sixth Through the Eighth Century.* Columbia, S.C.: University of South Carolina Press, 1978.

Roberts, C. H., and T. C. Skeat. *The Birth of the Codex.* Oxford: Oxford University Press, 1987.

Roll, Susan K. *Toward the Origins of Christmas.* Grand Rapids: Wm. B. Eerdmans Publishing Co., 1996.

Ross, Susan, and M. C. Hilkert. "Feminist Theology." Theological Studies 56 (1995) 327–352.

Russell, James C. *The Germanization of Early Medieval Christianity.* New York: Oxford University Press, 1994.

Russell, Jeffrey Burton. *Satan: The Early Christian Tradition.* Ithaca, N.Y.: Cornell University Press, 1981.

Sanders, E. P., editor. *Jewish and Christian Self-Definition,* 1, 2. Philadelphia: Fortress Press, 1980, 1981.

Segal, Alan. *Rebecca's Children: Judaism and Christianity in the Roman World.* Cambridge: Harvard University Press, 1986.

Seltzer, Robert, editor. *Religions of Antiquity.* New York: Macmillan, 1989.

Simon, Marcel. *Verus Israel.* Oxford: Oxford University Press, 1986, translated from French original of 1948.

Simonetti, Mario. *Biblical Interpretation in the Early Church.* Edinburgh: T & T Clark, 1994.

Stead, Christopher. *Philosophy in Christian Antiquity.* New York: Cambridge University Press, 1994.

Swift, Louis. *The Early Fathers on War and Military Service.* MFC 19. Collegeville, Minn.: The Liturgical Press/Michael Glazier Books, 1983.

Thurston, B. B. *Widows: A Women's Ministry in the Early Church.* Minneapolis: Augsburg Fortress Press, 1989.

Trevett, Christine. *Montanism: Gender, Authority and the New Prophecy.* New York: Cambridge University Press, 1996.

Trigg, Joseph. *Biblical Interpretation.* MFC 9. Collegeville, Minn.: The Liturgical Press/Michael Glazier Books, 1988.

_____. *Origen: The Bible and Philosophy in the Third Century.* Atlanta: John Knox Press, 1983.

Vesey, Mark. "Conference and Confession: Literary Pragmatics in Augustine's *Apologia contra Hieronymum.*" Journal of Early Christian Studies 1 (1993) 175–213.

Wagner, Walter. *After the Apostles: Christianity in the Second Century.* Minneapolis: Augsburg Fortress Press, 1994.

Weinrich, William. *Spirit and Martyrdom.* Washington, D.C.: University Press of America, 1981.

Wilken, Robert. *The Christians as the Pagans Saw Them.* New Haven: Yale University Press, 1987.

Wilson, Stephen. *Related Strangers: Jews and Christians, 70–170 C.E.* Minneapolis: Augsburg Fortress Press, 1996.

Witherington, Ben, editor. *History, Literature and Society in the Book of Acts.* New York: Cambridge University Press, 1996.

Yarborough, Ann. "Christianization in the Fourth Century: the Example of Roman Women." Church History 45 (1976) 149–165.

Young, Frances. *The Making of Creeds.* London: SCM Press, 1991.

Young, Steve. "Being a Man: the Pursuit of Happiness in *The Shepherd of Hermas.*" Journal of Early Christian Studies 2 (1994) 237–255.

Index